CONGRESS AND THE CIVIL WAR

BOOKS BY EDWARD BOYKIN

The Autobiography of George Washington
The Wisdom of Thomas Jefferson
Living Letters from American History

CONGRESS

and the

CIVIL WAR

by Edward Boykin

THE McBRIDE COMPANY

New York

973.5
B69c

To
NANCY
Of Inspiring Memory

36190
March 1958

CONTENTS

FOREWORD

In this book I have tried to re-create a comprehensive series of momentous scenes in the cavalcade of the national legislature between 1819 and 1868; to summon back, if only for a brief while, colorful and towering personalities, who through these eventful years played leading, and sometimes lesser, roles on the largest and most exciting of American stages, the Congress of the United States.

These were tremendous years, 1819 to 1868, fraught with parliamentary turbulence and fiery debate which rocked the halls of Congress and of the nation. Few Americans realize that the Civil War actually began on Capitol Hill long before the first Confederate shell crackled blood-red over Fort Sumter in 1861.

This epoch of our history witnessed great events and undreamed of transitions. It began with the demise of the Federalists, who in 1820 nominated no candidate for the presidency, and the supposed arrival of a partyless political Utopia. It saw the impending break-up of Jefferson's Republican party, as the American body politic went spinning off into a galaxy of parties. It saw the ominous lightnings which lit up the bitter, forty-year debate on the slavery issue. It watched the onset of Jacksonian Democracy and the march of the nation to the Pacific. It heard the first threats of secession, the unending tariff battles and the rising furor of sectional hostility. It saw the compromise with slavocracy and its final, bloody overthrow. It witnessed the first flowering of America's inventive genius which was to revolutionize the world and build an American industrial empire. It brought ever-deepening interest in America's destiny in the western world.

The cold war between the North and South actually opened on the floor of Congress with the bitter disputes over the Missouri Compromise in 1819. From then on, for forty years, every act and gesture of Congress reflected the mounting tension and antagonism between these sections. It was

6

the destruction of the Missouri Compromise by Congress and the Supreme Court which touched off the explosion and clash of arms of the Sixties.

South Carolina's threat to secede in 1830 and Jackson's counterthreat "Our Federal Union: It must be preserved," were but maneuvers in this long-drawn-out cold war. The acrimonious tariff battles, with North and South arrayed against each other, were feeling-out fights for the real conflict that was to come.

I have drawn liberally on the almost inexhaustible treasure-house of the annals of Congress. I have tried to keep the reader abreast of the burning drama and mighty issues facing the growing, yet slowly dividing, nation, by interpolating brief chapters of contemporary historical events.

Powerful, commanding political actors play roles on these pages: Daniel Webster whose debate with Hayne on the nature of the Union was actually a cold war attack on the doctrine of States Rights; John C. Calhoun, militant leader of the Southern assault on what it believed was Northern aggression; Henry Clay, who sought to compromise the super-heated issues; little-known James Tallmadge, who lit the slavery pyre in the House of Representatives; youthful Robert Young Hayne, the Achilles of the South; aristocratic, eloquent Jefferson Davis to whom the dying Calhoun handed the Southern torch; silver-tongued Ned Baker whose valiant appeals in support of President Lincoln's war measures rank with the best; vengeful Thaddeus Stevens, who fired the Parthian shot of the Civil War—the impeachment of President Andrew Johnson.

I have included much sidelight drama in this book: the first-time-told story of the beautiful Italian enchantress, America Vespucci, who appeared from overseas and asked for, and almost got, Congress to give her a generous slice of land out of the vast territory named for her ancestor; the epic duel between John Randolph of Roanoke and Henry Clay; the story of Rose O'Neal Greenhow, Confederate spy, plying her dangerous trade under the very dome of the

Capitol; the Gold-Spoon Speech that blasted Martin Van Buren out of the White House; and others. The book closes with the most dramatic spectacle ever staged by Congress, the impeachment and trial of President Andrew Johnson.

I have incurred many obligations during the writing of this book, but none deeper than that to the Alderman Library of the University of Virginia, where a study was generously provided for me by Mr. Jack Dalton, Librarian of that fine repository and where I was given, also, easy access to its splendid collections. To the Misses Roy Land, Katherine Beville, Frances Smith and all others of the Alderman Library Staff who have helped me so unstintingly, I offer my sincere thanks and appreciation.

Without assistance from the Prints Division of the Library of Congress I could not have tracked down many of the illustrations to be found in this book. I am specially indebted to Messrs. Stang and Kaplan of the Prints Division Staff. To Miss Josephine Cobb, of the Still Pictures Division of the Archives Department at Washington, I am most grateful for generous cooperation.

To the Speaker of the House of Representatives, the Honorable Sam Rayburn of Texas, with whom I first discussed this work, I am greatly indebted for suggestions in respect to it. I feel a like obligation to the former Speaker, the Honorable Joseph Martin of Massachusetts, for his enthusiastic endorsement. To my kinsman and friend, the Honorable Frank W. Boykin, Representative from the First District of Alabama, I render thanks for never-failing interest and co-operation.

To my wife, Nancy Gunter Boykin, who virtually closed her life with words which encouraged me in this work, I send gratitude and love which reach across the veil.

Edward Boykin

Charlottesville, Virginia
August, 1955

1

LIKE A FIREBELL IN THE NIGHT

Eloquent and ardent, Representative Thomas Cobb of Georgia took the floor. Fixing his bitter gaze on Representative James Tallmadge of New York, Cobb shouted:

"If you persist, the Union will be dissolved! You have kindled a fire which all the waters of the ocean cannot put out, which seas of blood only can extinguish!"

But James Tallmadge stood his ground and hurled back the challenge:

"Sir, if a dissolution of the Union must take place, let it be so! If civil war, which gentlemen so much threaten must come, I can only say, let it come! My hold on life is probably as frail as that of any man who now hears me; but, while that hold lasts, it shall be devoted to the service of my country—to the freedom of man!"

Strong, hot words, those, that fell on the 186 members of the House of Representatives like live coals on a pile of gunpowder. Members were all but jerked from their seats by the sudden wrench of emotion. Angry passions, long hidden just below the surface, surged through and burst into flame. Instantly, the House was tense, excited, and embattled. The Speaker's gavel rapped repeatedly for order as defiant Southerners shot burning replies to the Northern taunt that the South was seeking to "declare the whole country west of the Mississippi a market overt for human flesh." The words "disunion," "civil war," and "secession" hurtled across the House chamber as Southern flamethrowers rose one after the other to denounce the Tallmadge Amendment to the bill admitting the newly organized State of Missouri to the union.

This Tallmadge Amendment, so little known to most Americans, was one of the most explosive packages in our political history. Ominous and fateful, it landed on the floor of the House on the afternoon of February 13th, 1819. It was a political time-bomb which sputtered for forty-two years before exploding with a violence which rocked the nation.

Yet, already, four days later, on February 17th, it gave off first warnings of its deadly import to the country. Opening shot of the Civil War, it struck at the very roots of the slavery system on which the economy of the South depended. Its echoes were destined to roll across the nation until re-echoed one tragic April morning in 1861 by cannon levelled at Fort Sumter.

Tallmadge had, unconsciously perhaps, loaded his bomb with the dynamite of disunion in these 54 words:

"And provided, That the further introduction of slavery, or involuntary servitude, be prohibited, except for the punishment of crimes, whereof the party has been duly convicted; and that all children of slaves born within the said State, after admission thereof into the Union, shall be declared free at the age of 25 years."

Overlord of the House was the suave, powerful, handsome political master, Speaker Henry Clay who, a slave owner himself, calmly sucked a stick of peppermint candy as he watched the sudden tempest sweeping the floor below him. The debate grew fiercer. Presently, taking from his pocket a handsome silver snuffbox presented to him by admirers in Kentucky, Clay took a pinch of fragrant Maccaboy. Most polished and adept snuff-user in the House, Clay knew that at the right moment he would plunge into the fray. That moment called for a clear head. He sneezed several times with much exhilaration and again rapped his gavel as the Southerners clamored excitedly against the amendment which would restrict slavery in the would-be new State of Missouri.

James Tallmadge stuck to his guns:

"Mr. Speaker, the violence to which gentlemen have resorted on this subject will not move me from my purpose, nor drive me from my place. I have the fortune and honor to stand here as the Representative of free men, who possess the intelligence to know their rights, who possess the spirit to maintain them.

"I know the will of my constituents, and regardless of consequences, I will avow it; as their Representative, I will proclaim their hatred to slavery in every shape; as their Representative, here will I hold my stand, until this floor, with the Constitution of my country which supports it, shall sink beneath me. If I am doomed to fall, I shall at least have the painful consolation to believe that I fall, as a fragment, in the ruins of my country."

That wintry afternoon—and for many to come—the walls of the Old Brick Capitol rocked with bitter, raging debate as the black spectre of the Slavery Issue spread its dark mantle over Congress. Again and again Speaker Clay called for order, but the fight was on. Two great sections of the nation were openly pitted against each other. Drawn by the violence of the debates, crowds thronged the corridors and small balcony of the House chamber. The Missouri Question fairly leaped into the arena of national politics and the eyes of a startled nation suddenly became fixed on Capitol Hill.

But the hot fight over Missouri's entrance into the Union was not the only crisis which confronted the nation in 1819. Depression lay heavy on the land. Panic and bank failures stripped thousands of their hard-earned gains. Hard times knocked at the doors of other thousands. The auctioneer's hammer resounded through the nation. There was no price for property or produce. Farm products rotted where they grew.

In February of 1819 the city of Washington had been the capital of the nation for nearly two decades. The ravages wrought by the British in 1814 were almost obliterated. In the rebuilt White House sat President James Monroe, last of the Virginia Dynasty. It was a time in our history to which a Boston newspaper gave the happy appellation, The Era of Good Feelings. Party strife was at a low ebb. The restoration of the burned-out Capitol was nearing completion.

The Fifteenth Congress, now suddenly ripped apart by strife, was meeting in the Old Brick Capitol, which occupied the site of the present Supreme Court Building. This emergency home of the Congress was a gift to the government. Citizens and merchants of Washington, fearful that Congress might move to another city rather than rebuild on the ruins left by the British, raised the money and hastily provided Congress with a temporary Capitol, a modest structure which, after housing the government, would become in turn a boarding house and later a Civil War political prison.

America had known slavery since 1619, when a Dutch man-of-war sold the first cargo of Negroes to the tobacco planters at Jamestown. The South had used slaves to work its tobacco, cotton, and rice fields. New England had grown rich supplying rum for the infamous Triangular Trade in which the slave was a medium of exchange.

Slavery had flourished in America. In a passage stricken from his first draft of the Declaration of Independence, Thomas Jefferson had indicted King George III for encouraging "this execrable commerce" in slaves, but the Constitution had permitted the importation of slaves for twenty years after its ratification, that is, until 1808.

With the invention of the cotton gin, the economic advantage of slavery to the South increased manyfold. In 1819 this advantage was greater than ever and still growing. Yet, up to then, there was no open break between the slave-holders and those who frowned on the institution.

1787 the Ordinance for the Northwest Territory, enacted by the Continental Congress, had prohibited slavery in all new states carved from the territory north of the Ohio River. Thus, the Mason and Dixon Line and the Ohio River line established a barrier between the slave and free states. Indiana, Ohio, and Illinois joined the Union as free states. If Missouri were admitted without restriction as to slavery, it would break this barrier and obstruct the path westward of new free states.

Missouri was part of the Louisiana Territory purchased from France in 1803 by President Jefferson. The terms of the Louisiana Treaty guaranteed the inhabitants of the Territory the rights of person and property enjoyed at the time of its transfer to the United States. This included the right to own slaves. The vast territory had, in fact, come to the United States as a slave area, and Louisiana had entered the Union in 1812 as a slave state. As part of the old Louisiana Territory, Missouri felt it had the right to permit slavery and its proposed state constitution legalized the institution.

When Missouri applied for statehood in 1819 there were twenty-two states in the Union, eleven free and eleven slave. The rich Missouri farmlands had been settled by Southerners who brought their slaves with them. To the Northerners in Congress, unless slavery were headed off or gradually eliminated by the Tallmadge Amendment, the admission of Missouri meant another slave state. To the Southerners restriction of slavery meant eventual abolition. Not only would settlers be robbed of their slaves, but the state would be fenced off to slave-holding Southerners who wished to emigrate there.

Moreover, it would be a violation of another clause of the Louisiana Treaty, which provided for the creation of states on an equal footing with the original Thirteen, and this would not be true were Missouri deprived of the privilege of owning slaves.

But there was still another disturbing factor. Admission of Missouri, slave or free, meant upsetting the balance in Congress where, in the House of Representatives, the North was already predominant, one hundred and five to eighty-one. In the Senate, where the South still held control, the House could be neutralized when needed.

On February 17th, 1819, after tumultuous debate, the House passed the Missouri Bill, with the Tallmadge Amendment, eighty-seven to seventy-six, and sent it on to the Senate. Before the Senate could act, mass meetings in the North were demanding that Missouri be shorn of slavery before admission to the Union. Speaker Clay's desk was flooded with petitions from Northern communities. Traveling orators spread the flame and fed the fire; the Northern press burned with inflammatory editorials.

On March 2nd, the Senate returned the Missouri Bill to the House after striking out the Tallmadge Amendment. The House refused to concur and the Fifteenth Congress adjourned with the Missouri Question still deadlocked. James Tallmadge finished his one hectic term in Congress and passed from the scene, leaving his firebrand still burning.

This first clash on the statehood of Missouri cut through the Union like a red-hot sword. The warning to the North by the voteless Representative John Scott of the Missouri Territory to "beware of the fate of Caesar and Rome" fell on ears which did not hear. From his hilltop home, Monticello, the aged Jefferson wrote: "This momentous Missouri Question, like a firebell in the night, awakened and filled me with terror. I considered it at once as the knell of the Union."

In December of 1819 the Sixteenth Congress assembled for the first time since the War of 1812 in the rebuilt Capitol. Storm signals were flying as Speaker Henry Clay called the lawgivers to order in Latrobe's beautiful Hall of Representatives, fashioned after an ancient Greek temple, with a richly decorated, domed ceiling overhead. Extending around the Hall was a colonnade of twenty-six columns of polished Potomac marble. Rich crimson curtains suspended between the pillars muffled the echoes. Over the main entrance was Franzoni's celebrated Car-of-History clock which still keeps time in this chamber, now Statuary Hall. From the ceiling hung Latrobe's much-admired hundred-candle chandelier. The fine mahogany desks and comfortable chairs of the Representatives were arranged in concentric semicircles. Over this scene Speaker Clay presided at a desk ornamented with candelabras to his right and left. On each desk were goose quills, inkwells, and sandpots for blotting. Huge silver snuff urns, filled with fragrant Maccaboy and Old Scotch, stood to the right and left of the Speaker's rostrum. Snuff was a perquisite of both the Senate and House of Representatives in those tumultuous days. Not infrequently a gentleman would pause in his eloquence, stride to the snuff urn, take a pinch, sneeze two or three times, give his nose a swipe with a silk bandanna handkerchief, and resume his oratory.

In the House, the representatives still sat with their hats on, a custom handed down from the Continental Congress. It was a great honor for the House to uncover for anything or anybody. It was the Speaker's custom to doff his hat when he rose to make a special announcement.

Missouri was still a blazing issue and her application for statehood was renewed at once. Knocking at the door of Congress, asking admission to the Union, was now another would-be state, Maine, long a part of Massachusetts.

The House promptly passed the bill admitting Maine and sent it on to the Senate, where a rider was attached admitting Missouri without restriction as to slavery. Missouri was to be lugged into the Union piggy-back by Maine. Just who suggested this happy stroke is not known; it is believed to have originated with Henry Clay when the Maine Bill was before the House. Southern senators openly admitted that their object was to compel Northern senators, who wished to admit Maine as a free state, to vote for the entrance of Missouri unrestricted as to slavery. To make the fire hotter, Senator Roberts of Pennsylvania moved a further amendment forbidding the further importation of slaves into Missouri.

The Senate fight waxed hot and heavy, attracting the largest audience since the battle for the Jay Treaty. President of the Senate was a gallant old beau, Vice-President Daniel D. Tompkins of New York, whose penchant for the fair sex admitted them in the Senate Chamber and appropriated to them those charming and commodious seats which belonged to foreign ministers and strangers of distinction, but their numbers were so great for some days that they not only filled these and all other seats, but at last literally encroached upon the floor, "to the no small inconvenience and displeasure of many gentlemen."

Spearheading the fight for the South was elegant Senator William Pinkney of Maryland, a gifted orator, whose fiery impassioned rhetoric, flowing like liquid silk, cast its charm over all who heard it.

Pinkney was the Beau Brummell of the Senate, dressed always in the height of elegance. His ruffled sleeves and tinted gloves drew many "ohs" and "ahs" from the audiences which flocked to hear tropes and metaphors. It was his custom as he rose to address the Senate slowly to take off his gloves and fold them with fastidious care on his desk. He was the eloquent knight-errant of the South, depicting in matchless words the chivalry and love of liberty of the slaveholding class.

Pinkney's chief opponent was aged Senator Rufus King of New York, who replied with calm, forcible, yet fervid arguments. King was the Old Roman of the Senate, the last Signer of the Constitution to honor that body. In 1819, he still clung to the habiliments of the eighteenth century: satin coat and waistcoat, knee-breeches, silk hose and low, silver-buckled shoes.

On February 11th King made the greatest speech of his life. In the gallery sat Secretary of State John Quincy Adams, who that night inscribed in his diary: "The great slave-holders of the House gnawed their lips and clutched their fists as they heard him." King closed his three-hour appeal in these words:

"Mr. President, I have yet to learn that one man can make a slave of another; if one man cannot do so no number of individuals can have any better right to do it, and I hold that all laws and compacts imposing any such condition upon any human being are absolutely void, because contrary to the law of nature, which is the law of God, by which He makes His way known to man, and is paramount to all human control."

Pinkney replied brilliantly. "Everyone was in raptures," said an onlooker. For four hours he held the Senate spellbound. In vivid oratory he drew a vision of an unequal Union into which Missouri would enter as a lesser state, a mere servant of the majority, were slave restrictions placed on her statehood:

"If Missouri comes in shorn of its beams—crippled and disparaged beyond the original States, it is not into the original Union that it comes. For it is a different sort of Union. The first was a Union *inter pares:* This is a Union between disparates, between giants and a dwarf, between power and feebleness, between full-proportioned sovereignties and a miserable image of power—a thing which that very Union has shrunk and shriveled from its just size, instead of preserving it in its true dimensions."

Senator Freeman Walker of Georgia flashed into the scene with words darkly prophetic of Sherman's blazing march across his state forty-four years later:

"Mr. President, if Congress persist in the determination to impose the restriction contemplated on Missouri, I fear consequences fatal to the peace and harmony of this Union will be the inevitable result. I behold the father armed against the son, and the son against the father. I perceive a brother's sword crimsoned with a brother's blood. I perceive our houses wrapt in flames, and our wives and infant children driven from their homes, forced to submit to the pelting of the pitiless storm, with no other shelter but the canopy of heaven; with nothing to sustain them but the cold charity of an unfeeling world. I trust in God that this creature of the imagination may never be realized."

On went the Senate fight, demolishing friendships and widening the breach.

"Mr. President!" It was Senator Jesse Thomas of Illinois who spoke. "I rise to offer a suggestion, or rather an amendment, that may help still the troubled waters on which we are tossed."

The Senate held its breath and its fire. Another amendment! More fuel for the flames of controversy! Illinois was a free state, but her senior Senator believed in slavery and had steadfastly opposed the restrictions on Missouri's admission.

"I propose a further amendment to the Maine Bill as it now stands before the Senate. Maine would be admitted as a free state. Missouri, already virtually a slave state, would come in as such. But this amendment which I offer would forever forbid slavery in the remainder of the Louisiana Territory north of parallel thirty-six thirty north latitude."

It was the epochal Missouri Compromise! Oil on the heaving sea of the Senate! More oceans of hot words swept in, but on February 17th, 1820 the Senate passed this monumental legislation and hurried it over to the House. This Thomas Amendment was really the death warrant of slavery in America. By forbidding the extension of slavery into the vast empire north of the historic line, it made certain that this boundless area would be settled and carved into free, not slave states. A year and four days had passed since James Tallmadge lit this still-burning pyre!

Over the House wing of the Capitol lightning continued to flash as the "Misery Debates," for so they were dubbed, raged on. It was unceasing. Day after day, night after night under the massive, flickering chandelier the battle went on. The narrow galleries overflowed. Ladies who had flocked to the Senate now thronged the House.

To a friend at this time a future President, Representative John Tyler of Virginia, wrote: "Missouri is the only word ever repeated here by the politicians. You have no possible idea of the excitement that prevails. Men talk of a dissolution of the Union with perfect nonchalance and indifference."

Came a day when the shrill, flute-like voice of John Randolph interrupted the proceedings. Pointing his finger at the ladies in the gallery, he angrily demanded: "Mr. Speaker! What are all these women doing here, so much out of place in this arena? Sir, they had much better be at home attending to their knitting."

The ladies gasped, but stayed.

On February 8th Speaker Clay took the floor to plead for "poor, unheard Missouri." Maine, he said, had Massachusetts members to plead her cause, but Missouri had no one. Clay spoke for four hours. Under his eloquence spectators sat as if entranced:

"A State in the quarter of the country from which I come, asks to be admitted to the Union. What say the gentlemen who ask the admission of Maine? Why, they will not admit Missouri without a condition which strips her of an essential attribute of her sovereignty. What, then, do I say to them? That justice is due to all parts of the Union; your State shall be admitted free of condition, but if you refuse to admit Missouri also free of condition, we see no reason why you shall take to yourselves privileges which you deny to her, and until you grant them also to her we will not admit you. This notion of an equivalent is not a new one; it is one upon which commonwealths and States have acted from time immemorial."

Clay paused, stepped to a snuff urn, and took a pinch. His audience watched every move he made, drank in every word. His sweeping gestures, the graceful flourishes of his silk handkerchief, the rapid changes of his expression, everything about him held the spectators as in a vise:

"I am opposed to slavery. If I were a citizen of Missouri I would strenuously oppose any further introduction of slaves into my State; I would try to make some provision to emancipate those already there. But I am not a citizen of Missouri and I have no right to force her to adopt my opinions, especially since she is not represented here."

But Clay, however distressed at the prospect of the breakup of the Union, did not flaunt the words "disunion" and "civil war," which he said were "uttered almost without emotion" by gentlemen on the floor. Although he believed he could win a reasonable number of Northerners to his viewpoint, he was mistaken.

Listening that day as the Kentuckian's matchless oratory soared over the Hall of Representatives was Senator Thomas of Illinois, whose compromise plan was still before the upper House. Twilight had fallen and the great chandelier blazed high above the dramatic scene. Clay finished his speech, exhausted by his brilliant effort. As he made his way through a throng of handshakers to the Speaker's office, Senator Thomas followed him. To Clay Thomas explained he had come to ask his espousal of the compromise the Senate was now debating. Hesitant at first, Clay agreed to think it over, although apparently he had already thought it over. He knew Thomas had found the way out of the crisis, provided enough Northerners in the House would accept the compromise for the sake of the Union. Thomas left and presently Clay drew on his greatcoat to go to his lodgings.

As he stepped into the shadowy corridor outside the Speaker's office a tall, lean-shanked figure sidled up to him.

It was erratic, half-mad, yet brilliant John Randolph, whose face looked like that of a boy grown prematurely old.

"Ah, Mr. Speaker," said Randolph, "I wish you would leave Congress and go to Kentucky. I will follow you there or anywhere else."

"This is a very serious proposition, Mr. Randolph," said Clay. "I am too tired to discuss it now, but if you will come to the Speaker's office tomorrow morning before the House assembles we will consider it together."

Punctually next morning Randolph arrived. Clay told him frankly that compromise was the wisest way out of the dilemma. Randolph refused to yield an iota: the slave states were right, there must be no compromise.

Clay took the occasion to remind Randolph that he was often provoked by Randolph's reckless jabs at the Speaker.

"Well, Mr. Speaker, I think you sometimes neglect me; you won't listen when I am addressing the chair; but turn your head away and ask for a pinch of snuff."

"You are mistaken. I am listening when I may seem not to be. I can repeat as much of any one of your late speeches as you yourself can."

"Well," said Randolph, "perhaps I am mistaken. Suppose we shake hands and be good friends hereafter."

"Agreed," said Clay.

Did Randolph suggest secession? Who knows? Of this meeting and of Randolph's violent, intemperate words during the Missouri debates Clay was later to say: "His acts came near shaking this Union to the centre and desolating this fair land."

As fast as the legislative wheels could race, the Missouri Compromise came from the Senate to the Hall of Representatives. Clay was now its sponsor; in brief words he commended it to the House. Hardly had he resumed his seat before the tall, familiar figure with raven black hair and piercing voice rose. John Randolph again!

"Mr. Speaker!"

Randolph's voice shot through the Hall. Clay pretended not to hear. It was a studied affront.

"Mr. Speaker!" Randolph pointed his long, elfish index finger at the Speaker. "I have but one word to say. One word, sir, and that is to state a fact. The measure to which the gentleman has just alluded originated in a dirty trick."

No man could have loathed the compromise more than Randolph. Day after day, in three- and four-hour diatribes, he hurled his verbal vitriol wildly. His chief target was Henry Clay who bore Randolph's barbs with a patience at which men marveled. It was Randolph's constant repetition of the words "Mason and Dixon's Line" in his vicious stabs at the compromise which gave them their later vogue.

Clay, however, wasted no time. He brought all the arts of his persuasive tongue and magnetic personality to bear in support of the compromise. The House was evincing signs of exhaustion; members fainted on the floor. Ignoring Randolph and his group of extremists, Clay knew he could count on most of the Southerners on the floor. He calculated that he needed at least six Northern votes to pass the compromise. With winning words and sound logic he persuaded three New York members to refrain from voting when the measure came up and three others to join up with the South.

On March 2nd, 1820, the compromise came to a vote. Excitement still flared, like puffs of smoke and jets of flame from a house on fire within. As the tally clerk called the roll, Clay watched with keen eyes; for him the Union was at stake on this vote. The clerk handed him a slip of paper. The compromise had won, ninety to eighty-seven! Although violently opposed to the very thought of it, Randolph voted for the compromise, as did fourteen Northerners with mild Southern leanings. On these renegades Randolph immediately plastered the contemptuous label "Doughfaces" because "they are plastic in the hands of demagogues."

Messengers dashed out of the hall. At the long hitching post at the foot of Capitol Hill a dozen express riders leaped into their saddles to speed the news to Missouri and points South and West.

The House was in an instant ferment. Clay's gavel hammered insistently. The bitter-enders from the North staggered under the impact of the vote.

Next morning John Randolph rose again. The House had just assembled.

"Mr. Speaker, I move that the vote on the Compromise Bill be reconsidered!"

Henry Clay had to think and act fast. Already the anti-slavery members were pressing their fourteen colleagues who had indorsed the compromise to change their votes. Invoking a seldom-used rule, Clay changed the course of American history:

"The motion to reconsider will not be in order until the routine business of the House is finished."

It was a trick. Randolph later said he knew it was a trick, but he was apparently satisfied for the moment. Clay busied himself with minor bills and petitions. The Compromise Bill lay on the desk in front of him. Taking up a goose quill he quietly signed it, called the Clerk of the House, and dispatched it to the Senate. Routine over, Randolph moved again for reconsideration.

"The motion is out of order," replied the Speaker. There was a bit of fire in his blue eyes. "The bill is no longer in the Speaker's possession. It has been sent to the Senate."

Passions subsided for the while, but this was not the end of the bitter Missouri dispute, which was to blaze up again when Missouri's electoral vote was counted a year later. On this occasion, however, Henry Clay was the Great Compromiser. He would salve away the bitterness of the second fire as he had the first, while the compromise itself went into history, and Missouri and Maine became the twenty-third and twenty-fourth states.

To Thomas Jefferson the Missouri Compromise was "only a reprieve, not a final sentence." John Quincy Adams went again to his diary: "I take it for granted that the present question is a mere preamble—a title page to a great, tragic volume."

Such it proved to be. James Tallmadge had unconsciously fired the first shot of the American Civil War, but he was forgotten, as was Senator Thomas who conceived the compromise. Henry Clay's fame rose to a new high; he was the toast of the nation. Still, one man burned with deadly hatred of the statesman who had steered the compromise through the reefs of the turbulent House of Representatives. That man was John Randolph of Roanoke.

2

THE MAGNIFICENT MONROES HOLD COURT IN THE NATION'S DUELING CAPITAL

At dawn of March 22nd, 1820, Commodore Stephen Decatur, favorite of the nation, quietly opened the door of his elegant, newly built mansion on Lafayette Square, Washington, and stepped out into the crisp morning. Throwing his naval cloak about his shoulders, he hurried off to keep a rendezvous with Commodore James Barron on the dueling grounds near Bladensburg, Maryland.

Slender, graceful, handsome, Decatur was one of the lofty, romantic figures of American naval history. In 1806 he had electrified the nation by his valor in hand-to-hand combat with the pirates of Tripoli. He had captured the British *Macedonian* in the War of 1812. In 1815 he had reduced the Algerian corsairs to abject surrender in three months. Prize money and praise were given him. With the money, he built from plans by Benjamin Latrobe the mansion that still stands at Jackson Place and H Street. Here he and his wife, "beloved Susan," lived a rich, enviable life. His was the most distinguished home in the capital; next to his friend, President Monroe, he was its most distinguished resident.

Decatur had charged Barron with cowardice when, in 1807, the American *Chesapeake,* commanded by Barron, struck her colors to the British *Leopard* without firing a shot. The Decatur-Barron feud had smouldered for years.

Now it was to be settled by shots at ten paces in the quiet vale at Bladensburg.

Hours later they brought Decatur home, dying, with a bullet in his spleen. All day grieving citizens stood in the street outside his home. That night, after hours of agony, Decatur died. Next morning the *National Intelligencer* voiced the country's sorrow: "Mourn, Columbia! For one of thy brightest stars is set. A son without fear and without reproach has in the fullness of his fame descended to the tomb."

Not since gifted Alexander Hamilton died at the hand of Aaron Burr had the nation been so stunned, so saddened. When John Randolph of Roanoke moved that the entire House adjourn, attend the funeral of Decatur, and that the members "in respect to the deceased wear crepe on the left arm for the remainder of the session," Representative John Taylor of New York objected because Decatur had "died in violation of the laws of God and his country. I cannot consent, however deeply his loss is deplored by this House, in common with the nation, to vote the distinguished and unusual honors proposed by this resolution."

The House refused the motion, and went no further. This inspired John Quincy Adams to note sourly in his journal: "This feeble and negative censure upon the practice of dueling is all that can be obtained from Congress."

In the 1820's a brace of long-barreled dueling pistols was the standard, indispensable accessory of the up-to-date statesman on Capitol Hill. Heated parliamentary debates not settled in the halls of Congress were frequently resolved with pistols at ten paces on the "field of honor," a beautiful secluded glade near—of all places!—Bladensburg, just beyond the District line, scene of the American retreat before the oncoming British in 1814. Acceptance of a challenge was virtually obligatory unless the man who was challenged wished to be branded a coward. Hardly a week passed without a rumor that Senator or Representative So-and-So had "called out" Senator or Representative Somebody-Else for hot words uttered in debate.

The code—that is, the inviolate etiquette observed by principals and seconds in this polite and formal method of assassinating someone you did not like or who had "insulted" you—was hard and fast. The most popular book of dueling rules was written by a South Carolina governor. Covering all the fine points (protocol) of committing gentlemanly homicide, it was to dueling what Hoyle's book is to poker. The whole procedure was enameled with a cold-blooded glaze of finesse, courtesy, and absurdity, yet it all added up to one thing, murder in deliberate, refined form.

Duelling was deadly, but popular. Victims of the code were legion. The best people fought duels. It was frowned on, to be sure, and legislated against, but American statesmen found it indispensable. Washington had its Bladensburg; St. Louis, its Bloody Island; Natchez, its Dueling Island; New Orleans, its Dueling Oaks. Because Washington duels so often involved gentlemen of national prominence, Bladensburg enjoyed countrywide notoriety as the "dueling capital of the nation." Technically, it was illegal to fight a duel in Washington, also in Maryland, but political "honor" must be served and avenged. Dueling was the accepted mode of settling these private grudges. Congressional etiquette for a while prohibited formal announcement of the death of a member in a duel, but this restriction vanished in the wave of anger at the cold-blooded slaying of Congressman Cilley of Maine in 1838 by Congressman Graves of Kentucky to whom Cilley had actually given no offense.

Political dueling began way back. Rarest signature on the Declaration of Independence is that of a gentleman from Georgia, Button Gwinnett. Dueling made his signature the rarity it is. After signing America's birth certificate, he went home and was promptly slain in a duel.

When Vice-President Burr appeared in the chair of the

Senate after killing Alexander Hamilton, prominent statesmen voiced hardly a word of censure; indeed, at the expira-
tion of his term they voted him the franking privilege for
the rest of his life!

Leading American exponent of the art of polite man-
slaughter was a lean, tempestuous firebrand from Tennessee,
General Andrew Jackson, who in 1820 was angling to succeed Monroe in the presidency. Jackson was veteran of five
first-class duels, to say nothing of various shooting brawls.

In the colorful cortege that bore the illustrious Decatur
to his temporary resting place rode the Magnificent Monroes, who had moved into the rebuilt White House in 1817
just in time for a stupendous New Year's party. Democratically, they invited everybody—and everybody came to
gape at the splendors. The crowd inspired a newspaper
scribe to say: "All came with their wives and gawky offspring; some in shoes, most in boots, and many in spurs;
some snuffing, some chewing, and some with powdered
heads; others with heads frizzled and soiled, some whose
heads a comb had never touched, half-hid by dirty collars,
and reaching far above their ears, as stiff as pasteboard."

So much for the democratic side of the Monroes. Their
weekly receptions were for the hoi polloi, but their dinners
only for the select, fashionable, aristocratic "court circle."
The Monroes had lived abroad constantly, associating with
royalty, dukes and court ladies. Their dinners were stately
affairs, featuring gold lace and stiff formality, many fine
wines, food prepared by French chefs and served on gold
plates, regiments of servants, gentlemen in glittering uniforms and ladies in elaborate frocks, who indulged in gold
snuff boxes and delicate sneezes—all tossed together in an
amazing kaleidoscope reminiscent of French royalty at its
best. All this was set to soft music by the scarlet-coated
marine band.

Such was the Parisian glitter the Monroes brought to
the White House. Jefferson's pellmell system was inundated

in an orgy of high-toned formality. At her first reception Elizabeth Cortright Monroe sat on a raised platform while ladies outdid themselves curtsying to her. Elegance of dress was required. President Monroe once actually refused admittance to a relative whose clothes he thought were not elegant enough to appear at dinner. Tradition avers that the Monroes popularized eating with a fork, a quaint custom (as Mrs. Monroe explained it) which her husband had picked up in Paris from decadent French monarchists. Polite society promptly began using forks. It was handier than the homespun American way of eating food off the blade of a knife, less dangerous, too, though such political giants as Webster and Clay might be seen shoveling in food with their knives long after the fork vogue arrived.

For their social entertainment the Monroes had the most elegant setting in America, the restored White House which emerged dripping with beauty from its original builder, James Hoban. It had four state parlors, a state dining room, a grand staircase, and crystal chandeliers which gleamed like showers of stars.

In 1820 there was a Western bloc in Congress, with sixteen votes in the Senate out of forty-four. The lure of the West, the promise of cheap land, and the panic of 1819 had launched a second wave of migration across the Mississippi. The Cumberland road, eighty feet wide and paved with gravel, was pushing towards the Ohio River. The Santa Fe Trail was reaching into the southwest. A new means of transportation, a steam railroad, was being tried out. On the New York curb market shares in new enterprises were skyrocketing. New York State was digging, on its own, "Clinton's Ditch," the Erie Canal, to connect the Great Lakes with the Atlantic. Florida was purchased from Spain (at the point of Andrew Jackson's pistol) for five million dollars. Steamboats were puffing along the big rivers.

James Monroe, the Last Cocked Hat as well as the last Revolutionary veteran to head the government, still bore the scar of a bullet that almost took his life at Trenton, Christmas night, 1776. But the old order was passing. With him the Virginia dynasty would expire. In 1820 he was re-elected unanimously except for one vote. The Era of Good Feelings still ran smoothly. For the moment, at least, the two most threatening issues were stilled—secession and slavery—thanks to the failure of the Hartford Convention and the Missouri Compromise.

Dominant personality in the nation was not the President but the Speaker of the House of Representatives, Henry Clay of Kentucky, who sounded the watchword of the Western world, "We look too much abroad. Let us break these commercial and political fetters; let us no longer watch the nod of any European politician; let us become real and true Americans, and place ourselves at the head of the American system."

In 1822 President Monroe proclaimed recognition of the South American Republics which had broken Spanish shackles and risen to assume their rightful places in the free world. But the prospect of a New World association of republics was suddenly threatened by a group of European powers whose rulers, led by the Czar of Russia, formed a Holy Alliance which would make the world "safe for autocracy" and, in time, seek to restore Spain's lost South American empire.

On December 2nd, 1823, President Monroe gave to the world his pronouncement against further European encroachment on the soil of the Americas—the Monroe Doctrine on which his fame so largely rests. Aimed at protecting the Latin Americas from reconquest, this cornerstone of American foreign policy in the Western world was actually conceived by British Prime Minister Canning, adroitly plagiarized by farsighted Secretary of State, John Quincy Adams, who felt that America should not "come in as a cock-boat in the wake of the British man-of-war," and promulgated by President Monroe whose name it bears.

In 1825 Monroe handed the reins of government to John Quincy Adams, who was actually defeated by popular vote at the polls, but elected by the House of Representatives. Determined to implement Monroe's Western Hemisphere policy, President Adams decided in 1826 to send a mission to a congress of the Western Republics at Panama—and thereby hangs the tale of the most fantastic Congressional duel in the history of Capitol Hill.

3

PISTOLS ON THE POTOMAC

There was a knock on the door of Senator Randolph's lodgings on Pennsylvania Avenue beyond the White House. Disentangling his long, bony legs, the senator from Virginia rose and went to the door. Outside stood General Thomas Jesup.

"Senator Randolph, I believe." General Jesup bowed respectfully. The great John Randolph of Roanoke was at the zenith of his career.

"I am your servant, sir," said Randolph courteously. "Won't you come in?"

"I am here, sir, at the request of the Secretary of State," said Jesup. "He wishes to know if you consider yourself personally liable for your attack on him two days ago in the Senate."

Randolph's dark eyes flashed. "I am not accountable to the Secretary of State or to anyone else for what I said in the Senate."

"Of that I am aware, sir. But you are reported to have stated you would hold yourself responsible for all that was said. That is, unless Mr. Clay has been wrongly informed."

"So I did." For all his biting words in debate, John Randolph was no coward. "If Mr. Clay so desires, I waive my senatorial privilege. I have no intention of hiding behind the subterfuge of constitutional immunity."

"In that event, sir," said General Jesup, "let me give you this note from Mr. Clay."

The senator's piercing eyes flicked back and forth across

the paper. Not a muscle of his boyish face twitched as he
read:

"Washington 31 March 1826

"The Honorable John Randolph

"Your unprovoked attack on my character in the Senate of the
U. States, on yesterday, allows me no other alternative than that of
demanding personal satisfaction. The necessity of any preliminary
discussions or explanations being suspended by the notoriety and the
indisputable evidence of the injury to which I refer, my friend, General
Jesup, who will present you this note, is fully authorized by me
forthwith to agree to the arrangements suited to the interview proposed.

"I Am Your Obedient Servant
"H. Clay."

The "injury" to which Henry Clay's challenge referred
and for which he demanded what the subtleties of the time
called an "interview," was inflicted by Randolph in the
Senate the day before when he rose and addressed himself
to the chair:

"Mr. Speaker! I mean Mr. President of the Senate and
would-be President of the United States, which God in his
infinite mercy prevent!"

Vice-President John C. Calhoun was impassive. If he
thought of calling Randolph to order, he gave no sign of
it by word or gesture. Perfectly poised, he took no notice
of the senator's indecorum, or the startled expressions of the
gentlemen of the Senate, but the packed galleries tittered as
John Randolph began the Philippic which brought him unending notoriety and led nine days later to pistols at ten
paces on the Potomac.

The show was on. Several senators groaned; others strode
into the vestibule. Vice-President Calhoun settled back in
his chair. Often, by the time Randolph finished one of his
harangues, hardly a quorum was left on the floor. He might
continue unabated for hours before meandering to his peroration. No one ever knew and, least of all, the senator himself.

The Senate writhed under his tirades. Maddening as were Randolph's rantings to his colleagues in the Senate, they were entrancing to the spectators. John Randolph was a showman. He put on an exhibition in which both the public and he himself reveled. Rambling, incoherent, flashing with brilliance, his rhetoric possessed a witchery which often moved the gallery to applaud. His was the wickedest tongue ever heard in Congress. From it dripped floods of vicious satire, deliberate malice, and matchless wit.

This "genius-madman" was one of the most amazing personalities in American history. There was something macabre, yet fascinating, about his tall, cadaverous figure perched on pipestem legs, booted and spurred and surmounted by the beardless, cross-wrinkled face of a boy of sixteen. His striking habiliments harmonized with the oddities of his character. A high rolling collar, rising beside his cheeks, almost concealed his small round head. His long, coarse black hair was parted in the middle and hung down the sides of his face to meet his collar. His swarthy complexion proclaimed his boasted descent from the Indian Princess Pocahontas. He often wore gloves and silver spurs on the Senate floor. He looked, said a friend, "more like a disembodied spirit than a man adequately clothed in flesh and blood."

In debate his thin voice rang out through the Senate "like the shrill scream of an angry vixen." Often, in speaking before the Senate, Randolph would consume beaker after beaker of stout, calling out every little while to the assistant doorkeeper, "Tims, more porter!"

Now, rising to his feet, Randolph peeled off two overcoats and tossed them in a heap on the floor; "undressed himself" observed a senatorial colleague. Then, removing his heavy gloves, he bowed again to the imperturbable Vice-President.

Under debate at this moment was President John Quincy Adams' proposal to send delegates to a congress of the South

American republics on the Isthmus of Panama in the summer of 1826. Moving spirit of this conclave was Simón Bolívar, liberator of Venezuela, who had invited the United States to participate: Bolívar had in mind the creation of a loose confederation of the Americas to put teeth into Monroe's recently announced hands-off policy. It would be a sort of "United Nations" of the Western world.

Unwisely, perhaps, President Adams had accepted, without consulting the Senate. This "usurpation of power" brought a storm of opposition. Cries of "no entangling alliances" echoed across the floor. Randolph was particularly enraged.

To Secretary of State Henry Clay, the Panama Congress was the realization of a long dream. Bolívar's invitation fired his imagination. First to champion the independence of these South American neighbors, Clay had rejoiced as one by one they broke the Spanish shackles which had bound them for centuries. In 1818, in the House of Representatives, Clay had eloquently focused the nation's gaze on South America: "We behold there a spectacle still more interesting and sublime, the glorious spectacle of eighteen millions of people struggling to burst their chains and be free!"

But something else rankled in Randolph's mind this March day of 1826. This was the election of 1824, the four-way contest which had brought John Quincy Adams to the Presidency. Jefferson's Republican party was falling to pieces. The wing led by Adams and Clay was soon to become the National Republican Party, precursors of the Whigs. Andrew Jackson had come out of the West and moved into the political limelight. The "Jackson Men" were soon to take the name of Democrats.

In the 1824 contest Jackson was the popular choice. When the electoral votes were counted Jackson had ninety-nine, Adams eighty-four, William Crawford forty-one, and Henry Clay thirty-seven. The lack of a majority threw the result into the House of Representatives. As low man, Clay was out of the race, but as Speaker he controlled the House as well as the votes which had been cast for him. Clay could not be President himself, but he could be President-maker by throwing his support to one of his choice.

Holding the balance of power, Clay had decided to support John Quincy Adams as the lesser of two evils. A brash military man like Jackson was unthinkable as a President! But the "Jackson Men" insisted that, since Old Hickory had won a majority of the popular votes the House was morally obliged to select him for the Presidency. Henry Clay felt otherwise. With Clay pressing furiously for the man of his choice, Adams was elected by the House on February 9th, 1825. The day after election, Adams offered the portfolio of State to Clay, who promptly accepted it. Soon ugly rumors appeared. Focal center of these rumors was Henry Clay, whom the "Jackson Men" charged openly with a "corrupt bargain." Clay, they said, had agreed to swing his support to Adams provided the New England candidate would reward him with the office of Secretary of State. The charge sounded plausible enough. Jackson himself soon joined the hue and cry: "The Judas of the West has closed the contract and will receive the thirty pieces of silver."

On March 27th, 1826, two days before Randolph rose in the Senate to make his extraordinary attack on Adams and Clay, a Jackson paper in Washington had printed an editorial openingly accusing the President and Secretary of State of "Bargain and Intrigue."

As for Randolph, his lurid mind brooded over what he could not prevent. He despised John Quincy Adams even more than he had his father. He resented Clay's support of Adams and frothed at the "bargain." Of deeper significance was a burning hatred of Clay which had seared his very soul since the fight over the Missouri Compromise six years before.

Plagued by these things, Randolph rose on March 29th,

1826, to say what he thought of the Panama mission and the two men who sponsored it. He was in rare form. His fanatical eyes flashed as the vehement outburst rolled from his reckless tongue.

"Let Judas have his thirty pieces of silver!" he cried out at the alleged coalition between Clay and Adams. They might be used, he shrieked, "to buy a Potter's field in which to inter this miserable Constitution of ours, crucified between two gentlemen, suffering for conscience sake under the burthen of the first two offices of the government!"

Denouncing the Clay-Adams partnership, he termed it "an alliance between Old Massachusetts and Kentucky—between the frost of January and the young, blythe, buxom and blooming May—the eldest daughter of Virginia—young Kentucky—not so young, however, as not to make a prudent match and sell her charms for their full value."

A senator broke in to remind Randolph that ladies were present in the gallery, but the high-flying Virginian paid no heed.

Next, he charged Clay with forging the invitation to the Panama congress: "I then say, sir, there is strong reason to believe that these South American communications, which have been laid before us, were manufactured here at Washington, if not by the pens, under the eye of our own Ministers. I will show that this Panama Mission is a Kentucky cuckoo's egg laid in a Spanish American nest."

Randolph now proceeded to utter the words which led Clay to demand the "interview":

"I was defeated, horse, foot and dragoons—cut up, and clean broke down by the coalition of Blifil and Black George —by the combination, unheard of till then, of the Puritan and the blackleg. I shall not say which is Blifil and which is Black George. I do not draw my pictures in such a way as to render it necessary to write under them 'this is a man, this is a horse.'"

Blifil and Puritan meant, of course, President Adams.

Blifil was an unsavory character in Fielding's novel, *Tom Jones;* Black George a scoundrel in the same story. Blackleg was the current term for a crooked gambler. It struck at Clay's well-known addiction to the hazards of the card table where he played for high stakes. Randolph named no names, but his daggered words were pointed enough.

The story goes, though Senate records do not confirm it, that Randolph's insane, fertile imagination hurled even more offensive words at Clay's mother, denouncing her for bringing into the world "this being so brilliant yet so corrupt, which, like a rotten mackerel by moonlight, shines and stinks."

Clay had smarted under the charges of corruption. Seated in his office in the State Department at 15th Street and Pennsylvania Avenue, he writhed helplessly as the Senate tore the Panama mission to pieces.

That same evening a friend reported Randolph's speech to Clay at his Ninth Street home. Clay was incensed, although he had long seen it coming. This latest provocation was too much to bear with equanimity. Clay determined to seek redress for such personal defamation on the field of honor. In the morning he wrote his peremptory note summoning Randolph to an "interview" and despatched it by his friend, and later his second, General Jesup, to the Virginia senator's lodgings.

Clay was neither a novice nor an expert at dueling. In his rugged, struggling days back in Kentucky he had twice faced the muzzles of pistols at ten paces. He had no scruples against the practice of the code duello.

Dueling was in high fashion in the nation's capital in 1826. Statesmen, aggrieved by hot words spoken in debate, turned instinctively to the code of honor. Disputes too violent to be settled by words were often concluded with pistols on the dueling grounds at Bladensburg, Maryland or in the woods of the Virginia shore across the Potomac. In 1826 Bladensburg enjoyed a bloody notoriety. Duels were technically forbidden in the District of Columbia, yet in a secluded vale at Bladensburg lawmakers could blaze away at each other with comparative safety from justice. Just beyond the District line, it was near enough for escape back to the District should the Maryland constable interfere, which he seldom did lest he disturb the good business which dueling brought to the local taverns, liverymen, and undertakers. The most famous victim served up on the Bladensburg griddle was the illustrious Stephen Decatur, fatally wounded there in his affair with Commodore Barron.

The code was nothing if not courteous and was filled with nice points of honor and a rigid etiquette which gentlemen must observe in preparing to shoot each other down. They could not just rush out to a hideaway and exchange shots. They must go through a harrowing procedure which kept nerves on edge up to the very moment of firing.

After reading Clay's challenge, Randolph went to his desk and wrote an acceptance—brief, terse, and super-decorous. It was April Fool's Day. The Senate was not in session, so Randolph hurried to Brown's Hotel to enlist his close friend, Senator Thomas Hart Benton, as his second. Unfortunately, Benton was Mrs. Clay's distant cousin. Such was the punctilio of the code that, for this reason, Benton forfeited the dubious honor of seconding Randolph, who turned to another friend, Colonel Tatnall of Georgia. While Tatnall hurried off to Clay with Randolph's acceptance, the latter confided to Benton his secret resolve: "I do not intend to fire at Mr. Clay."

Complete secrecy shrouded these preliminaries. A duel between two such distinguished figures would be a choice morsel for the public palate. What a commotion would ensue were it known that the Secretary of State had challenged the great John Randolph of Roanoke to a meeting in the field!

Seconds were soon chosen. For Clay: General Jesup, a soldier of some renown, and Senator Josiah Johnson of

Louisiana. For Randolph: General James Hamilton and Colonel Tatnall, who bore Randolph's acceptance to Clay at his office at the State Department.

In accepting Clay's challenge, Randolph was shrewd. Protesting Clay's right to call him out, he charged that Clay had violated the privileges of the Senate, the independence of debate, and the sanctity of the Constitution. Randolph made a distinction between the man and the senator. As senator, he had constitutional immunity which he would not surrender or compromise; as a man, he would give satisfaction for what Clay deemed an injury. This was a delicate point. He would receive Clay's fire, but not return it. To do so would admit Clay's right to call him out for an "interview." "This is a very fine distinction, and one which few could appreciate," wrote Senator Benton, who was himself a duelist of no mean ability. He and Andrew Jackson had once settled scores at pistol's point. Old Hickory still carried a Benton bullet in his shoulder. To Benton we are indebted for a gossipy, amusing account, one of the best in our political annals, of this duel.

In the meantime the challenger and challenged proceeded with their respective duties. In the Senate Randolph spoke for three hours on April 3rd against a resolution limiting the Presidency to two terms. On the day before the duel he spoke again for hours against a change in the judicial system.

At the State Department Clay busied himself with further arrangements for the Panama mission, which he fully expected the Senate to confirm, but he gave no sign of anything unusual unless it was a feeling of relief that he could at last strike back at the most violent of his detractors.

For four days the seconds wrangled politely in an effort to avert the "affair." It was charged that Clay's friends had given him false reports of what Randolph had actually said in the Senate. To give Randolph an opportunity to offer an explanation which might salve Clay's wounded honor,

General Jesup despatched a note to Colonel Tatnall stating that the injury which Clay hotly resented was Randolph's charge that Clay had forged or "manufactured" the invitation to the Panama congress and had called Clay a blackleg. If Randolph would disavow these charges, either publicly or privately, the affair might be avoided.

Randolph was adamant. He refused to retract and would not authorize a word beyond what he had written in his acceptance. This, of course, dashed all hope of an "accommodation," and the seconds met in a room at Brown's Hotel to make the final grim arrangements. Mutual friend Benton looked on, a sort of umpire to see that the scales were held even.

The "meeting" (the euphemisms of the code were delightful) would take place on the Virginia side of the Potomac, across from Georgetown, near the end of the old Chain Bridge at Little Falls. Senator Randolph had requested this location. If he fell as a Virginia senator refusing to compromise his views as such, he would fall in defense of his rights and Virginia soil would receive his blood. Virginia law proscribed dueling, but as Randolph meant only to receive Clay's fire, without returning it, it would not be dueling, merely target practice for Clay—or so Randolph reasoned. This also was a subtle distinction.

The time was set: Saturday afternoon, April 8th, 1826, at four-thirty. Weapons would be pistols at ten paces. Two seconds would attend each principal; a surgeon would be on hand for the bloody aftermath. Senator Benton, as friend to both parties, could look on if he chose. The gentlemen would be allowed no "practice fires." After taking their stances a second, chosen by toss-up, would utter the words, "Fire—One, Two, Three, Stop!" in quick succession. By lessening the time allowed for firing, the seconds hoped to lessen the chances of fatality.

On the night before the duel Senator Benton called at the Clay home on Ninth Street. Politics had recently estranged Clay and Benton, who called to reassure Clay that, notwithstanding their late political differences, his personal esteem was unaltered. Actually, Benton still hoped at this late moment to find a way out of the deadly impasse which faced his two friends.

In the parlor Benton found Clay and his wife, Lucretia, who had no apparent knowledge of the impending duel. Clay had spared his wife, still desolate over the recent loss of a daughter. Little John Clay was sleeping quietly on the sofa. Presently Mrs. Clay went upstairs and Benton told Clay "that, in whatever concerned his life and honor, my best wishes were with him." Apparently, Clay gave Benton no opening through which the duel might be averted.

At midnight General Hamilton and Colonel Tatnall repaired to Randolph's lodgings, where they found the senator reading Milton's "Paradise Lost," on which he immediately launched an animated disquisition. Presently Tatnall told Randolph that it might be well for him to impress another friend to take his, Tatnall's, place as second.

"Senator, I am told that you have determined not to return Mr. Clay's fire. I can't go out there only to see you shot down."

Replied Randolph: "Well, Tatnall, I promise you one thing: if I see the devil in Mr. Clay's eye and that with malice prepense, he intends to take my life, I may change my mind."

On the morning of the duel Senator Benton hurried to Randolph's lodgings and pictured the tranquil scene he had found in Clay's home the night before. He told of the sleeping child and Mrs. Clay's grief. In a tone of rebuke, Randolph exclaimed: "I shall do nothing to disturb the sleep of the child or the repose of the mother." In an adjoining room Randolph's seconds were making last codicils to his will, bequests slight in value, but priceless in sentiment.

About two o'clock Randolph sent his servant, Johnny, to the Corcoran and Riggs bank to get a few gold pieces. When

John came back to report that the bank had none, Randolph mounted his horse and hustled down Pennsylvania Avenue to the bank, where he threatened to withdraw his entire account, four thousand dollars in gold, unless the cashier gave him what he wanted.

"I want my money," he screeched.

"Have you a cart to put it in?" asked the cashier, who assured Randolph there was a mistake.

Randolph compromised. He took nine pieces of gold coin and a New York draft for the balance of his account. Putting the coins in his breeches pocket, Randolph returned to his lodgings where he gave Benton a sealed paper instructing him, in the event of his death, to feel in his left breeches pocket for the gold pieces. Three were for Tatnall, three for Hamilton, and three for Benton. With the coins they were to have seals made and wear them in remembrance of Randolph.

As the hour for the duel approached the two principals, with their seconds, entered carriages and set out for the rendezvous. Senator Benton followed on horseback, as did the celebrated surgeon, Dr. Hunt.

The afternoon sun was sinking behind the Virginia hills as the two carriages, a few minutes apart, clattered across the Chain Bridge and pulled up on the Virginia shore. The woods along the river were greening with early April. First to arrive was John Randolph who, before alighting, scribbled a penciled note which he handed out to Senator Benton. Randolph had learned from his seconds that Clay, a trifle out of practice, had expressed concern that he might not be able to take aim, much less fire, if the "word" was to be given as fast as the seconds had agreed.

To Randolph it now appeared as if Clay were actuated by a cold-blooded, deliberate intention to kill him. This realization unsettled Randolph's purpose. He apparently modified his intention of not firing at Clay. In the note he handed to Benton, Randolph expressed his feelings:

"Information received from Colonel Tatnall since I got into the carriage *may* induce me to change my mind, of not returning Mr. Clay's fire. I seek not his death. I would not have his blood upon my hands—it will not be upon my soul if I shed it in self-defence—for the world. He has determined, by the use of a long, preparatory caution by words, to get time to kill me. May I not, then, disable him? Yes, if I please."

The carriage bearing Clay and his seconds soon came to a halt. Randolph was just alighting. The eccentric Virginian was clad in a vast, flowing white flannel dressing gown which trailed to his heels. On his hands were thick buckskin gloves. He looked like something out of a sideshow rather than the mighty Virginia senator about to present himself as a bull's eye for the Secretary of State's pistol. So ridiculous was Randolph's get-up that Clay and his seconds were forced to repress their smiles. Randolph's costume violated the rules of the code, but Clay made no protest. Randolph knew that, enveloped as he was in a long gown, his adversary might find difficulty in aiming at vital parts. Clay later said: "I might as well have tried to shoot at a pair of tongs as at Randolph."

Rigid code formalities now took over. The principals stiffly bowed to each other and the two little groups vanished into the woods, pausing at a small glade near the river. Quickly stepping off an east-west line of ten paces, the seconds tossed a coin for choice of positions. Menacing long-barreled pistols were taken from their shiny cases. Colonel Tatnall won and picked the west stand for Randolph with his back to a bank of gravel. Clay faced the last rays of the setting sun filtering through the woods. An old stump stood just behind him.

Tatnall having won the position, code etiquette prescribed that Clay's second, Jesup, must deliver the fatal word, "Fire!" Like two fighters called to the center of the ring for last-minute instructions by the referee, Clay and Randolph listened while their seconds rehearsed the manner in which the "word" would be given. Clay was all business. It was apparent he wanted satisfaction and time in which to exact it. To Randolph, still uncertain whether to fire or not, the fast count was naturally not displeasing.

Now, two of the most extraordinary men in our history took their stands and courteously saluted each other. Such politeness! Having loaded Randolph's pistol, Tatnall set it on a hair-trigger, although Randolph had objected to this because he was wearing heavy gloves. While Randolph was adjusting the butt of the pistol to his hand the weapon ex-
ded, the ball digging up the ground at his feet. It was
ling.
y's second, General Jesup, immediately called out: "I
stantly leave the ground with my friend, if that oc-
in!" Randolph exclaimed: "I protested against that
r." The seconds went into a quick huddle. It was
much delicacy, this untimely fire, and the code
ut Clay broke in: "It was clearly an accident.
ed."
nd, to Randolph, painful interlude over, these
antagonists faced each other at ten paces. The
d back out of the line of fire. Clay and Ran-
ld a pistol at his side, muzzle down. Benton,
er, perched himself "on a piece of rising
ich I could see what passed and hear what
surgeon opened his instrument case. Ran-
nt, Johnny, peered wide-eyed through a clump
andolph's small eyes bored into Clay's. If he
led "a devil in Clay's eye," he gave no indi-
ay apparently was sizing up the voluminous
of Randolph's freakish dressing gown for a
aim. It was impossible to tell just where
rame was located.
t; "Fire! One, Two. . . ."
he silence. They had fired simul-
."

Randolph had aimed low, firing only to disable Clay and spoil his aim, not to kill him. His bullet struck the stump behind Clay, whose bullet whizzed through Randolph's gown near the waist and dusted the gravel behind him. Not a scratch on either man. Benton said both bullets were so true and close it was a marvel that they missed their marks.

Now Benton rushed between the principals and begged them to consider the affair settled, but Clay waved him aside: "This is child's play. I demand another fire." Randolph made a similar demand. While the seconds reloaded the pistols, Benton pressed Randolph to agree to an "acco modation," but he refused. The accidental firing of his p preyed on his mind. It was the immediate cause, he sa his firing at Clay. He regretted it instantly. To Ben declared: "I would not have seen him fall mortally doubtfully, wounded, for all the land that is wate King of Floods and all his tributary streams." averred that in firing he had not sought to tak not even to shoot as high as his knees "for it w to shoot a man in the knee," but only to dis spoil his aim.

Pistols in hand, the principals faced eac more. Again the word "Fire!" and the quic Three, Stop." Clay aimed more carefully th his bullet ploughed through Randolph's Having received Clay's fire, Randolph raised discharged it in the air.

"And then," said Senator Benton in his vivi this romantic duel, "I saw him (Randolph) of Mr. Clay, saw the gravel knocked up in saw Mr. Randolph raise his pistol—and disc air; heard him say, 'I do not fire at you, M mediately advancing and offering his h the same spirit. The moment Clay s thrown away his fire, advancing said with emotion, 'I trust in God, my dear sir, you are untouched. After what has occurred, I would not have harmed you for a thousand worlds!' They met halfway, shook hands, Mr. Randolph saying, jocosely, 'You owe me a new coat, Mr. Clay' (the bullet had passed through the skirt of the coat, very near the hip)—to which Mr. Clay promptly and happily replied, 'I am glad the debt is no greater.' "

Henry Clay and John Randolph had settled their long feud. The happy outcome of the grim business brought congratulations all around. Good humor prevailed as the gentlemen climbed into their carriages and hurried back to Washington. The exchange of shots was followed two days later by an exchange of cards. Social relations were courteously restored.

News of the duel flew through Washington, creating a sensation. Randolph was the hero of the day. He and his seconds went back to his lodgings to celebrate, but as Senator Benton put it, "none of us wanted dinner that day." Digging into his pocket, Randolph produced the gold coins remarking, "Gentlemen, Clay's bad shooting sha'n't rob you of your seals. I am going to London and will have them made for you," which he did.

Clay's carriage rattled back to his Ninth Street home where he told his beloved Lucretia the fortunate termination of the affair he had kept secret from her. It was Clay's last duel. It was the first and only time a member of the Cabinet faced a pistol at ten paces.

But Clay's honor was satisfied. For the time being, at least, Randolph's tongue avoided the Clay-Adams partnership, although the Jackson newspapers depicted him as a bloodthirsty duelist. He felt no qualms of conscience over this affair. To a clergyman he wrote: "My regrets are limited to the countenance which a pernicious practice may receive from one example, and to the apparent violation of religious obligation. I must, however, say that my present feelings are in a state of composure and satisfaction, which I should not have enjoyed, if the occasion had not occurred. We are strange beings!"

This bloodless duel was the most famous affair of its kind ever staged in the United States. To it Benton, the duel connoisseur, pinned this accolade of semi-glory: "It was about the last high-toned duel I have witnessed, and among the highest-toned that I have ever witnessed, and so happily conducted to a fortunate issue—a result due to the noble character of the seconds as well as to the generous and heroic spirit of the principals. Certainly dueling is bad, and has been put down, but not quite so bad as its substitute—revolvers, bowie-knives, blackguarding and street-assassinations under the pretext of self-defense." Benton did not explain what he meant by a "high-toned duel." Nor did he indicate what a low-toned affair might be.

The years hurried by. In April, 1833, John Randolph's sands were fast running out. Fevered and restless of mind, he set out for Philadelphia in quest of health he never found.

It was a long, arduous road for a man so broken. As he passed through Washington, Randolph was borne on a stretcher into the Senate Chamber. It was evening, the candles were flickering in the chandeliers, and Henry Clay, still superb, still the idol, held the center of the stage. He was speaking on his famous Tariff Compromise.

Suddenly, during a pause Clay heard a ghostly, familiar voice, shrill and piercing as of old.

"Raise me up!" said Randolph to his attendants. He was too feeble to sit up. "I want to hear that voice again."

Clay was startled. Could it be John Randolph of Roanoke? It came again. A voice out of the turbulent past.

"Raise me up!" Randolph was more insistent.

Then Clay saw the spectral figure on the stretcher, "looking as if he were not long for this world." Slowly he walked to the rear of the chamber and took Randolph's emaciated hand.

"Mr. Randolph, I hope you are better, sir."

"No, sir," replied Randolph in a whisper. "I am a dying man, and I came here expressly to have this interview with you."

For long moments Clay stood there clasping Randolph's hand in cordial salutation. Then, with tears in his eyes, he watched as they bore the fast-ebbing Randolph out of the chamber. These two amazing figures had parted forever. Four weeks later Randolph's untamable spirit forsook its wasted habitation.

The story goes that, shortly before he died, Randolph asked to be buried with his face to the West so that he could see Henry Clay on Resurrection Day. In 1879 the State of Virginia brought the ashes of her fantastic yet illustrious son, from his home, Roanoke, to rest forever in Richmond amid others of his stature. When they found him—under eight feet of earth as he had requested in his last wild moments— he was looking westward. And thus they re-buried him, facing West, on a hill above a river, the James, as restless and as unpredictable as the man himself.

4

KING ANDREW AND THE SPOILSMEN TAKE OVER

ANDREW JACKSON

On July 4th, 1828, ninety-year-old Charles Carroll of Maryland, sole surviving signer of the Declaration of Independence, broke ground for the first railroad in America, thirteen miles of track between Baltimore and Ellicott Mills. As he lifted the first spadeful of dirt, the venerable patriot said he considered the event as second in importance to signing the charter of America's freedom.

But this massive landmark of progress, origin of the world's transportation system, was eclipsed by the sulphurous clouds of personal abuse arising from the most ferocious mud-slinging election campaign in American history. Charles Carroll's prophetic words were forgotten as President John Quincy Adams and General Andrew Jackson began tossing epithets at each other.

Center of this saturnalia of political scurrility was Washington, the Versailles of the Western Hemisphere, and fast becoming the capital of the world. Washington was growing up, yet it was still far from being the City Beautiful, or a city at all. The standard joke of the day was "everyone knows that Washington has a Capitol, but the misfortune is that the Capitol wants a city." Capitol Hill and the President's mansion were the chief ornaments of this town of 15,000 that still wallowed amid muddy streets, "looking as if it had rained naked buildings upon an open plain." In 1828 Washington quite verified the good Abbe Correa's apt bon mots, "Washington, the City of Magnificent Distances."

In the White House English-bred Louisa Catherine Adams' "drawing rooms" reached a new high in social grandeur, attracting crowds as sweet syrup draws flies. Actually they were the afterglow of a dying colonial glitter. "Her doors were open to men of every sort of political opinion; and whatever rancors Congressional debate or executive office interviews begot, all were left behind at her threshold." Her stately affairs called for knee breeches for men. Women wore Paris gowns of finest material. Headdresses were fearfully and wonderfully made.

No social lion was old John Quincy Adams. On his diplomatic missions covering a quarter-century, he had sampled the splendors of all the courts of Europe, and that was sufficient for his puritanical soul. Reading the Bible before retiring and getting up at 5 A.M. (in winter to make his own fire, in summer to go swimming in the Potomac) seemed to have been his chief diversions. Dutifully though, he undertook the numerous chores required by his wife's ambitious entertainments. Tired and bored one evening in 1828, he turned to his diary: "This evening was the sixth drawing room. Very much crowded; sixteen Senators, perhaps sixty members of the House of Representatives, and multitudes of strangers. These parties are becoming more and more insupportable to me."

But in 1828 Adams was running for re-election against the man he had defeated in 1824 and who would not be denied. It is certain that if the people had not elected Andrew Jackson in 1828, they would have picked a man much like him. Democracy was coming in. Control of the national government by "eastern gentlemen of the old school in wigs, ruffles, knee breeches and silver buckles" was coming to an end. It was the old against the new, and Andrew Jackson, the gaunt stormy petrel from Tennessee, the duelist, cock-fighter, horse racer, slave owner, hard swearer, bad grammarian, was the spokesman *extraordinaire* for the new and for eleven new states in which male suffrage was universal.

In 1828 the American people had their first real chance to vote for president. Religion, property-ownership, and other qualifications for voting were being discarded as state after state removed restrictions on white male suffrage. There were plenty of opponents, notably, in Virginia, James Monroe and James Madison. John Randolph of Roanoke referred to it as giving the presidency over to "King Numbers." But old political ideas were going by the board. Americans were discarding them just as they did their courtly colonial costumes and powdered hair-dos for more practical long trousers and short-cropped hair. The rise of the common man was at hand. He was literally being pulled up by Andrew Jackson's bootstraps.

Nothing was left unsaid in the election of 1828. For the first time elaborate party machinery was set up with smart politicians at the throttle. Rallying around the "brawler from Tennessee," Andrew Jackson, were the Democrats,

actually an old party with a new look. At the helm of the
Jackson ship was "the most elegant man in the United
States," Senator and erstwhile Governor of New York, Martin Van Buren, whose sartorial grandeur and captivating
manners devastated Washington drawing rooms.

If the Jackson propaganda was to be believed, President
Adams was a thief, gambler, and procurer. Had he not, while
Minister to Russia, sold a beautiful American girl to a lech-
erous Muscovite Czar? Had he not for years cheated the
government on his expense accounts? Had he not turned
the White House into a gambling den by installing a billiard
table at public expense?

As for Jackson, Adams' supporters plumbed the depths of
political mud to bring up the blackest, most malignant vituperation. Jackson was a "bastard," his mother "a common
prostitute . . . afterwards married to a mulatto man with
whom she had many children of which General Jackson is
one." Jackson had killed thirteen men. Notorious "Coffin
Handbills" were circulated, depicting Jackson as a cold-
blooded, military tyrant who had hanged seven of his own
Tennessee militiamen in the War of 1812.

The Adams people trotted out the ancient scandal of
Jackson's marriage to his adored Rachel before she was le-
gally divorced from her first husband. Asked a pro-Adams
pamphlet: "Ought a convicted adulteress and her paramour
husband to be placed in the highest offices of this free and
christian land?" Jackson reached for his pistol to strike a
blow for the woman he loved and was so soon to lose. But he
yielded to those who counseled patience. This time he had
to control himself, though "how hard it is to keep the cowhide from those villains."

On March 4th, 1829, Washington witnessed a sight it had
never dreamed of. Jackson rode into the presidency following a wave of protest votes and on the shoulders of the
people, thousands of them packing the Capitol Plaza to
watch his swearing-in. "King Mob seemed triumphant,"

groaned Justice Story, but poet-lawyer, Francis Scott Key, murmured ecstatically, "It is beautiful. It is sublime."

"It seemed as if half the nation had rushed at once into the capital," said an eyewitness. Wrote another: "The noisy and disorderly rabble brought to my mind descriptions I have read of the mobs at the Tuileries and in Versailles." Said Daniel Webster, "I never saw such a crowd here before. Persons have come five hundred miles to see the General, and they really seem to think the country has been rescued from some dreadful danger."

Democrats surged through Washington streets. As the lean, grizzled soldier stepped to the platform on the east portico of the Capitol to take the oath, the crowds screamed with delight. The solemn ceremony over, Jackson mounted his horse and slowly rode toward the White House, trailed by crowds of his adoring countrymen—farmers, gentlemen, men, women, and boys, black and white.

Into the mansion rushed the crowds. Old Hickory had invited them all to his open house. Tubs of orange punch were placed in the wondrous East Room, in the foyers, on the lawn. Jackson tried to shake hands with all. So hilarious grew the festivities that the tubs of punch were overturned, glasses smashed, china broken. Fights broke out, eyes were blacked, noses bloodied. Women fainted and men felt suffocated. Still they came in by the doors, even the windows. "Black, yellow and gray, poured in in one uninterrupted stream of mud and filth . . . many subjects for the penitentiary . . . tyros from Liberia . . . a stout black wench eating jelly with a gold spoon. We had a regular Saturnalia."

Men with muddy boots stood on tapestried chairs and divans. Curtains were torn down. Thousands of empty whisky flasks lay broken on the floor. Jackson himself had to be rescued. He was forced to climb out of a window and escape to the sanctuary of his rooms at Gadsby's Tavern.

Old Hickory was himself the product of a social revolution. He had said, "If I am elected to fill the presidential chair, it must be by the people; and I will be President of the nation, and not of a party." Now for the first time a man of the people was president. Into office with Jackson went Vice-President John Caldwell Calhoun of South Carolina. In 1824 the total presidential vote was only 356,000. By 1828 it had swelled to 1,500,000; by 1840 it would be 2,400,000. This tremendous upsurge can be traced to the unshackling of the ballot and the ever-mounting interest of the public in politics.

America was on the march and Jackson was leading it. He brought change. Primping up the White House was not the least of his efforts. He had the now familiar north and south porticoes completed and, after a manner, turned the mansion around. Hereafter the formal front entrance would be the massive north doors opening on Pennsylvania Avenue. The East Room was given a final going-over of splendor. To impart a frontier, yet necessary touch, Jackson distributed twenty spittoons (at $12.50 each) at advantageous points around the stately room. Plumbing was modernized by a novelty, an iron pipe which introduced running water into the mansion. New glassware was bought, including nine sizes of wine glasses. Also, a new dinner service of French china, decorated with gold and blue and American eagles. At the suggestion of the new Secretary of State, Martin Van Buren, Jackson fenced in the front lawn of his new domicile.

In his first annual address Jackson announced a new patronage maxim which the "outs" translated into "Spoils System." Public office, he averred, had come to be looked on as a "species of property." Long continuation in office had bred indifference to public welfare. He made it clear that many of the "ins" would soon be out. Fear struck the hearts of thousands of officeholders. "Rotation in office" was a necessity of democratic government, said Jackson.

Into the dusty recesses of government departments went the Jackson broom sweeping out civil servants, left-overs from older administrations, who felt they "owned" their jobs. Many were dismissed for partisan reasons, others for long-continued, carefully hidden misconduct and malfeasance in office. The headsmen cut deep into the post-office, customs, and diplomatic services. At the same time postmasterships were given to fifty-six editors of influential papers. In his eight years in office it is estimated Jackson changed about one-fifth of all Federal officeholders.

At the height of the "proscription" outcry one day an elderly gentleman, Solomon Van Renssalaer, postmaster at Albany, New York, appeared at a White House reception. Asking to have a personal talk with the President, he was told to seat himself in the East Room until the numerous guests had cleared out.

"General Jackson," said Van Renssalaer, "I have come here to talk to you about my office. The politicians want to take it from me, and they know I have nothing else to live on."

Jackson listened but remained silent until suddenly the aged postmaster began excitedly stripping off his clothes.

"In heaven's name, what are you going to do?" exclaimed Old Hickory. "Why do you take off your coat in a public place like this?"

"Sir, I am going to show you my wounds which I received in fighting for my country against the British."

"Put on your coat at once, sir," commanded Jackson. "I am surprised that a man of your age should make such an exhibition of himself."

But the iron President's eyes filled with tears as Van Renssalaer pointed to this scar and that and held out his first commission signed by George Washington.

Next day Congressman Silas Wright brought Jackson a list of Federal officials recommended for dismissal. The elderly postmaster's name led the list. Jackson was seated before the fireplace, puffing a clay pipe. Why dismiss the man, he asked. Because, argued Wright, the postmaster had actively supported Adams in the late election. Wright's words were hardly out of his mouth before Jackson sprang to his feet, flung his pipe into the fire and exclaimed with much vehemence, "I take the consequences! I take the consequences! By the Eternal! I will not remove the old man—I cannot remove him. Why, Mr. Wright, don't you know that man carries almost a pound of British lead in his body?"

That settled it. The old postmaster was not dismissed, at least not by Jackson.

In 1830 a crisis was in the making, one that Jackson would meet and demolish as was his fighting nature. In the last days of the Adams administration Congress had enacted the "Tariff of Abominations," designed primarily to help New England woolen manufacturers although John Randolph of Roanoke charged it was "intended to rob and plunder one half of the nation for the benefit of the residue." It was to bear bitter fruit. In Congress the "American System" of a high, protective tariff wall, advocated by Henry Clay and reinforced by Daniel Webster, met with violent assault. In South Carolina long pent-up hostility to tariffs exploded in what James Madison called the "colossal heresy," Nullification, fathered by John Calhoun, now Vice-President of the United States.

1830, and the golden age of oratory was flowing in full. The fierce clashes on tariffs, states rights, slavery, and abolition were mirrored in fervid outbursts that rose in spectacular, eloquent clouds above Capitol Hill.

Foremost orator of the South was John Calhoun, the model of the intellectual debater, polished, coldly logical like the blade of a steel knife. To his followers, golden-voiced Henry Clay of Kentucky was a demigod possessing all the arts of enchanting men with the spoken word. But master of rhetoric and of them all was the poor New Hampshire boy who rose, by his voice, to the commanding position he now occupied in the Senate. His diction moved like the rhythmic tread of armies, magnificent, mighty, compelling. It was of Daniel Webster's plea before the Supreme Court in the Dartmouth College case—"It is, sir, as I have said, a small college. And yet there are those who love it"— that Justice Story wrote, "We listened for the first hour with perfect astonishment, the second hour with perfect delight, and for the third hour with perfect conviction."

5

LIBERTY AND UNION, NOW AND FOREVER . . ."

It was said of Daniel Webster that he was "a living lie because no man on earth could be as great as he looked." Certainly, as he rose in the Senate at noon on January 26th, 1830 for the transcendent effort of his career, he looked greater than his humblest admirer had ever dreamed. He was truly the Godlike Daniel.

No scene in our history was endowed with finer drama or more prophetic of the nation's destiny. Like a gladiator of old, Webster stood foursquare beside his desk, a robust, picturesque, magnetic figure, tossing eloquent thunderbolts at the senator from South Carolina, who had dared champion nullification of the laws of the Federal Union.

To those who witnessed it, this was an unforgettable panorama. The small semicircular Senate chamber was packed to the walls. Visitors had come from even as far away as Boston. The fair sex, in profusion, embellished the occasion with gay bonnets and bright gowns. Audaciously, they monopolized the galleries and swarmed onto the Senate floor, usurping the chairs of the more gallant members of the upper house. When Webster rose to speak, he gave his seat to an overeager lady who plopped into his chair.

The galleries, the floor space behind the desks of the forty-eight senators, the aisles, the lobbies, the halls, and even the stairways were thronged. All roads led to Capitol Hill that cold, blustery January morning. Coach after coach lumbered up the hill to discharge bevies of fashion and beauty.

The Great Debate would reach its grand finale today. A

great and perplexing question would be answered: What was the United States—a Federal Union or a loose compact of states which could interpret and nullify its laws as they saw fit?

But it was not the question or its answer which drew jostling crowds to Capitol Hill. The irresistible magnet was the man. Today Webster would reply to—and demolish— Senator Robert Young Hayne who, with power and fire, had defied the validity of the Constitution and set above it the impious doctrine of nullification.

From that observant lady, Margaret Bayard Smith, came this enthusiastic description of the historic occasion:

"Almost everyone is thronging to the Capitol to hear Mr. Webster reply to Col. Hayne's attack on him and his party. A debate on any political principle would have had no such attraction. But personalities are irresistible. It is a kind of moral gladiatorship in which characters are torn to pieces and arrows, yes, poisoned arrows, are hurled by the actors against each other. The Senate Chamber is the present arena and never were the amphitheatres of Rome more crowded by the highest ranks of both sexes than the Senate Chamber is. Every seat, every inch of ground, even the steps, were compactly filled, and yet not space enough for the ladies—the Senators were obliged to relinquish their chairs of State to the fair auditors who literally sat in the Senate. Yesterday there were 300 ladies besides their attendant beaux on the floor of the Senate."

In the presiding chair sat Vice President John C. Calhoun, grave, slender, handsome, and square-jawed. He was the passionate father of nullification; Senator Hayne was his representative and spokesman.

Dominating the arena by word, gesture, and appearance was Daniel Webster, one of the most commanding figures ever to tread the Senate floor. For this most crucial moment of his career the burly, barrel-chested Webster was arrayed in his favorite dress of Revolutionary colors: a blue, swallow-tailed coat with gilt buttons, blue trousers, buff waistcoat, and a high white cravat. His raven hair, his massive dome-like forehead, his dark, sunken eyes glowing beneath his craggy brows, his leonine grace, the rich tones of his voice, all blended splendidly into the dramatic spectacle which Healy immortalized on the colossal canvas which now hangs in Boston's Cradle of Liberty, Faneuil Hall. Healy may have erred in the accuracy of a few figures in the gallery, but not in his portrayal of Webster standing like the archangel of the Senate on guard at the portals of the Constitution.

For hours the thunder of his voice vibrated through the chamber. With arguments of power and beauty, rich imagery, glowing figures of speech, happy phrases, unmatched rhetoric, bursts of sheer brilliant eloquence, and sublime appeal to patriotism, Webster cast his spell as he flowed on to his majestic closing words, the most eloquent passage in the English language and certainly one of the finest ever uttered on the floor of Congress: "Liberty and Union, Now and Forever, One and Inseparable!"

Unhurried, self-possessed, Webster had begun speaking in low, impressive, scarcely audible words to which every ear in the Senate was keenly attuned. Every head inclined forward to catch the faintest inflection of his voice. A sudden, deep, and almost mysterious silence fell on the assemblage as Webster began his familiar exordium:

"Mr. President—When the mariner has been tossed, for many days, in thick weather, and on an unknown sea, he naturally avails himself of the first pause in the storm, the earliest glance of the sun, to take his latitude, and ascertain how far the elements have driven him from his true course. Let us imitate this prudence; and before we float further on the waves of this debate, refer to the point from which we departed that we may, at least, be able to conjecture where we now are. I ask for the reading of the Resolution before the Senate."

The Foote Resolution! How few Americans know that this innocent, relatively unimportant resolution on public lands—now buried deep in Senate annals—touched off this historic controversy on the nature of the Union and brought charging into the Senatorial lists, with lances leveled for the kill, these two Knights of the Great Debate, Senator Hayne of South Carolina, the "Achilles of the South," and Senator Webster of Massachusetts, Expounder and Defender of the Constitution.

Unfurling their respective banners of "States Rights" and "The Nation and the Constitution," these two warriors tilted for days until Hayne went down under the sledge-hammer impact of Webster's crushing eloquence.

In 1830 mighty forces were stirring in the United States, a prelude to the new and turbulent era which would end in civil war.

Since 1800 the population of the nation had doubled and now one-third of the people lived west of the Alleghenies. The nation was pushing toward the setting sun. Thus, the West, beyond the mountains and the Mississippi, was rising in importance and the frontier was a force to be reckoned with in American politics. They were individualists, these people of the West. With their own hands they had carved a civilization out of a wilderness. They had come from many states, even from lands across the sea, to turn virgin wilds into an empire of which they might be proud. They were jealous of their rights and fought for them even as they had fought for the land on which they lived.

In 1830 the sectional struggle between North and South was widening. The bitter dispute which began with the Missouri Compromise had blazed out again with the Tariff of Abominations, which Vice-President Calhoun had denounced as unconstitutional, unjust, oppressive, and destructive of liberty. In what he called the South Carolina Exposition, Calhoun had secretly enunciated his pernicious doctrine that South Carolina—or any state—had the right to nullify the tariff law or any other law which it decided was unconstitutional.

The Twenty-first Congress opened in a blaze of oratory on December 7th, 1829. Once again giants sat on Capitol

Hill. Like three gods assembling on America's political Mount Olympus, the Great Triumvirate—Webster, Calhoun, and Clay—strode, one after the other, into the Senate, which had succeeded the House of Representatives as the nation's political coliseum.

New stars shone in the political firmament. Brightest of these was a Westerner, Andrew Jackson, who had come to the Presidency in 1829, bringing with him the age of the common people. His enemies called it the "millennium of minnows." The Jackson Men, now emerging as the Democratic Party, controlled both houses of the national legislature.

In his first message to Congress President Jackson foreshadowed things to come, notably his forthright attack on the Bank of the United States which would convulse the Congress and the nation.

On the Senate floor sat John Tyler of Virginia, destined to become President in 1841; Thomas Hart Benton of Missouri, "Old Bullion," champion of the expanding West; Daniel Webster, Massachusetts' brightest orb. Upholding South Carolina's laurels was Robert Young Hayne, handsome, persuasive, and fluent in debate, a patrician to his finger tips. He was Calhoun's most ardent disciple.

Such, in brief, was a picture of the nation when on December 29th, 1829 Senator Samuel Foote of Connecticut, offered his historic resolution to inquire into the expediency of limiting the sale of public lands, for a period, to those already on the market and still unsold.

To Westerners, eager to draw new settlers by cheap lands, the resolution was clearly a deliberate attempt to restrict emigration to the West and slow down its growing importance. To Southerners, smarting under the protective tariff policies forced on them by the North, here was an opportunity to join hands with the West against Northern dictation.

The West, speaking through the passionate, vigorous voice of Senator Benton, was quick to resent the resolution.

On January 18th, 1830, in a speech of great merit, Benton lit the conflagration. Fanatically, he laid the issues on the fire, fanning it with sectional animosities, denouncing New England for endeavoring to prevent the settlement of the West, searching history for grievances to lay at her door. He tied the tariff so hated by the South and the public lands resolution into a package: "A most complex scheme of injustice which taxes the South to injure the West, to pauperize the poor of the North."

In an incredible broadside of words Benton made a strong case for an alliance between the South and the West. "The West," said he, "must look to the solid phalanx of the South for succor." When at last Benton yielded the floor he had set the tone and pace of the Great Debate which would range the whole gamut of public questions, past and present: the tariff, the Ordinance of 1787, slavery, internal improvements, the loyalty or disloyalty of New England in the War of 1812, the fundamental principles of the Constitution, and the hitherto untouched issue of nullification.

Next day, January 19th, Senator Hayne joined the attack on the Foote Resolution. No one present underestimated the power of this handsome, formidable orator from South Carolina, who dealt out killing blows with such charming grace.

Senator Webster had not up to this moment followed the public lands debate with any too great interest. On the afternoon when Benton fired the tinder, Webster was on the floor below, pleading an important case before the Supreme Court, before which he had a lucrative practice. On the next day, after court adjourned, Webster sauntered up the marble stairs to the Senate to find Hayne unleashing challenging accusations. Webster was lounging against a pillar in the rear of the chamber, but he perked up instantly. Soon he went to his seat and paid strict attention. Asserting that "the South would always sympathize with the West," Hayne suddenly and savagely turned his fire on New England, characterizing the attitude of the Eastern states on the public lands question as "selfish and unprincipled."

Openly, Hayne advocated an entente between the South and the West to combat the Northern protective tariff. The warmth and fury of Hayne's onslaught on New England took Webster by surprise. He felt that Hayne was shooting directly at him without provocation. Hayne fiercely charged that the policies of the Eastern states "to consolidate the government" would be fatal to the "sovereignty and independence of the states."

At this point Hayne apparently received from Vice-President Calhoun in the presiding chair the signal to raise the curtain which had hidden Nullification from view and to inject the issue into the debate.

"Sir," said Hayne, "I am one of those who believe that the very life of our system is the independence of the state, and that there is no evil more to be deprecated than the consolidation of this government."

Webster caught the significance of the words instantly. He sensed at once that this was the real gauntlet Hayne was tossing at his feet. Day was dying when Hayne sat down. Candles were lighted. Three Senators—Bell of New Hampshire, Chambers of Maryland, and his Massachusetts colleague, Nathaniel Silsbee—went to Webster's desk and urged him to make an immediate reply to Hayne's attack on New England. Webster, they said, was the logical spokesman. But the late hour brought adjournment until the morrow. While Hayne was speaking, Webster had filled three small sheets of paper with notes which he later failed to use.

Overnight news of the head-on collision between two such powerful combatants spread through the city. On January 20th a crowd greater than usual flocked to the Senate. Important drama was in the making. At 12:30, Daniel Webster began his First Reply to Hayne, so little known to most Americans. This speech fills twenty-one pages of his works. It was a point-blank speech, deliberately meant to be irritating. It was not a legitimate reply at all, but rather a refutation of Hayne's charges against the East and a personal attack which ricocheted on South Carolina. Webster was adroitly changing the subject, maneuvering to place Hayne in an indefensible position from which he could controvert the powerful South Carolinian. Webster selected his points carefully, but apparently without too great preparation, for which there was really no time. Webster's real purpose in this First Reply was to lay treason at the door of South Carolina.

Webster himself said: "Owing to other engagements, I could not employ even the interval between the adjournment of the Senate and its meeting next morning, in attention to the subject of this debate."

In this first reply Webster directed much of his speech at Calhoun rather than at Hayne. Answering Hayne's charges of consolidation, Webster said:

"Consolidation, that perpetual cry of both terror and delusion—consolidation! This, sir, is General Washington's consolidation. This is the true constitutional consolidation. I wish to see no new powers drawn to the general government; but I confess I rejoice in whatever tends to strengthen the bond that unites us and encourages the hope that our Union may be perpetual. I am a Unionist.

"I would strengthen the ties that hold us together. Far, indeed, in my wishes, very far distant, be the day when our associated and fraternal stripes shall be severed asunder, and when that happy constellation under which we have risen to so much renown shall be broken up and be seen sinking, star after star, into obscurity and night!"

Eloquently Webster went to the defense of the East:

"I come to that part of the gentleman's speech which has been the main occasion of my addressing the Senate. The East: the obnoxious, the rebuked, the always reproached East! . . . We are charged with the crime of a narrow and selfish policy, of endeavoring to restrain emigration to the West, and having that object in view, of maintaining a steady opposition to Western measures and Western interests. And the cause of this selfish policy the gentleman finds in the tariff.

"Sir, I rise to defend the East. I rise to repel both the charge itself and the cause assigned for it. I deny that the East has ever manifested hostility to the West, and I deny that she had adopted any policy that would naturally lead her in such a course. But the tariff! the tariff! Sir, I beg to say, in regard to the East, that the original policy of the tariff is not hers whether it be wise or unwise. New England is not its author."

Webster closed by moving that consideration of the Foote Resolution be indefinitely postponed. Hardly was he seated before Benton took the floor and charged that Webster's request for postponement was an admission of weakness. Next day, Wednesday, January 21st, Webster had urgent business before the Supreme Court which would compel his absence from the Senate. His friend, Senator Chambers, therefore requested that the debate be deferred until Monday next. Angry, burning to reply to Webster's strictures on South Carolina, Hayne objected:

"I see the gentleman from Massachusetts in his seat and presume he could make an arrangement which would enable him to be present. I will not deny that some things have fallen from the gentleman which rankle here (touching his breast), from which I would desire at once to relieve myself. The gentleman has discharged his fire in the face of the Senate. I hope he will now afford me the opportunity of returning the shot."

With much dignity, Webster rose, arms folded, to say: "Let the discussion proceed. I am now ready to receive the gentleman's fire."

Good sportsmanship demanded that Webster do nothing less. Hastening to the Supreme Court, he obtained postponement of his court business and returned to find the floor held by Benton, who yielded at once to the confident Hayne.

Of the millions who have read with glowing hearts Webster's Second Reply to Hayne how few have ever scanned the powerful passages of Hayne's magnificent speech which took the better part of two days to deliver.

Excited throngs now filled the galleries in anticipation of fireworks which were not long delayed. Members of the House deserted their seats to come and listen. Boyishly slender, clad in coarse South Carolina homespun instead of Northern broadcloth, Hayne was the Knight Errant of the South rising to slay the ponderous Dragon of the North. So thought the Southerners who rallied around Hayne. Never was Hayne's mellifluous voice so well modulated, rising and falling like music at the touch of a master.

Leaning forward in his chair, Vice-President Calhoun drank in every word as it fell from Hayne's lips. Calhoun was taut and grim-faced. His whole theory of states rights was at stake on the issue. It was his doctrine which Hayne was forcefully expounding and his dark eyes glowed approvingly as his pupil drove home his plausible and persuasive arguments. Time after time Calhoun scribbled hasty notes of advice and argument which a page boy ostentatiously carried down the aisle to the orator.

Hayne spoke for an hour, then paused. He was midway in his speech, the day was far spent, and he agreed to an adjournment until Monday, January 25th. That day dawned brightly for the South. The impending clash had been widely publicized. It was to be Victory Day; Hayne would complete his triumph. By eight o'clock a mass of humanity struggled for entry at the Senate chamber. Over the long weekend Hayne had refreshed his ammunition chests.

A New York Congressman, who sat glued to his seat in the gallery, said: "Hayne bore down in a strain of eloquence alternately grave, indignant and witty, upon the Senator from Massachusetts, the like of which I have never witnessed and which, as I thought, completely demolished him. Webster suffered. He seemed uneasy in his seat; sometimes he took notes—then audibly dissented, anon assented, and occasionally leaned back in his chair."

With unanswerable repartee and scorn Hayne turned his fire on the semi-treasonable acts of the Massachusetts Federalists in the War of 1812, praising the patriotism of South Carolina, castigating the dubious loyalty of Massachusetts and even casting doubts on Webster's own fidelity. Webster was an easy prey on this score. In the War of 1812 he and his New England Federalists had intemperately opposed the administration.

"At this dark period of our national affairs, where," Hayne asked with fine sarcasm, "was the Senator from Massachusetts? How were his political associates employed? 'Calculating the value of the Union?' With what justice or propriety can the South be accused of disloyalty from that quarter?"

"Sir, the war affected in its progress a union of all parties at the South. But not so in New England; there great efforts were made to stir up the minds of the people to oppose it. Nothing was left undone to embarrass the financial operations of the government, to prevent the enlistment of troops, to keep back the men and money of New England from the service of the Union, to force the President from his seat.

"When I think of the measures adopted in Boston to deprive the government of the necessary means for carrying on the war, and think of the success and the consequences of these measures, I feel my pride as an American humbled in the dust.

"Of the same character with these measures was the conduct of Massachusetts . . . In some places on the coast neutrality was declared and the enemy was suffered to invade the soil of Massachusetts . . .

"And now, sir, I must be suffered to remark, that at this awful and melancholy period of our national history, the gentleman from Massachusetts, who now manifests so great a devotion to the Union, and so much anxiety lest it should be endangered from the South, was 'with his brethren in Israel' [the Federalists].

"And are we, Mr. President, who stood by our country then, who threw open our coffers, who bared our bosoms, who freely periled all in that conflict, to be reproached with want of attachment to the Union? If, sir, we are to have lessons of patriotism read to us, they must come from a different quarter. The Senator from Massachusetts, who is now so sensitive on all subjects connected with the Union, seems to have a memory forgetful of the political events that have passed away."

In a merciless tirade of then-and-now accusations Hayne raked Webster fore and aft for his inconsistency on the tariff question: opposing it in 1820 and 1824 only to support the Tariff of Abominations in 1828. He followed this with fair warning to Webster of the fate that awaited him in this debate:

"Now, Mr. President, I call upon every one who hears me to bear witness that this controversy is not of my seeking. . . . But, sir, the gentleman has thought proper, for purposes best known to himself, to strike the South, through me, the most unworthy of her servants. He has crossed the border, he has invaded the State of South Carolina, and is making war upon her citizens and endeavoring to overthrow her principles and institutions. Sir, when the gentleman provokes me to such a conflict, I meet him at the threshold; I will struggle, while I have life, for our altars and our firesides; and, if God gives me strength, I will drive back the invader discomfited. Nor shall I stop there. If the gentleman provokes war, he shall have war."

Now Hayne lowered his guard for Webster's sharpest lance by plunging into an explanation and defense of the South Carolina doctrine of nullification. States rights were the traditional American doctrine, he said. Nullification was the doctrine of Jefferson, of Madison, and even of Webster when he protested against the Embargo. Thus, Hayne pioneered nullification on the floor of Congress. He upheld it as having been promulgated by the "fathers of the faith":

"The Senator from Massachusetts, in denouncing what he is pleased to call the Carolina doctrine, has attempted to throw ridicule upon the idea that a State has any constitutional remedy, by exercise of its sovereign authority, against 'a gross, palpable and deliberate violation of the Constitution.'

"Mr. President, the South Carolina doctrine is the republican doctrine of 1798; it was promulgated by the fathers of the faith; it was maintained by Virginia and Kentucky in the worst of times; it constituted the very pivot on which the political revolution of that day turned; it embraces the very principles of triumph which, at that time, saved the Constitution at its last gasp. . . . Sir, as to the doctrine that the federal government is the exclusive judge of the extent as

well as the limitations of its powers, it seems to me to be utterly sub-
versive of the sovereignty and independence of the States.

"In all the efforts that have been made by South Carolina to resist
the unconstitutional laws which Congress has extended over them,
she has kept steadily in view the preservation of the Union by the
only means by which she believes it can be long preserved—a firm,
manly and steady resistance against usurpation.

"It is the principle involved in the contest, a principle which, sub-
stituting the discretion of Congress for the limitations of the Constitution, brings the States and the people to the feet of the federal
government, and leaves them nothing they can call their own.

"The South is acting on a principle she has always held sacred—resistance to unauthorized taxation. These, sir, are the principles which
induced the immortal Hampden to resist the payment of a tax of
twenty shillings. 'Would twenty shillings have ruined his fortune?
No! but the payment of half twenty shillings, on the principle on
which it was demanded, would have made him a slave.'

"Sir, if, acting on these high motives—if, animated by that ardent
love of liberty which has always been the most prominent trait of
Southern character—we should be hurried beyond the bounds of a
cold and calculating prudence, who is there, with one noble and
generous sentiment in his bosom, that would not be disposed, in the
language of Burke, to exclaim, 'You must pardon something to the
spirit of liberty!' "

It was a mighty effort, seemingly unanswerable to many
who heard it. Hayne was done. The hands of the Senate
clock pointed to the hour of four. Darkness was coming on.
There was excitement enough for one day—even on Capitol
Hill—and the Senate adjourned, but not before Webster had
obtained the floor for the morrow.

Throughout Hayne's superb arraignment Webster sat immobile as a sphinx, making notes now and then on bits of
paper. The debate had veered far away from public lands.
He had sought from the start to lure Hayne into a defense
of nullification, to swing the debate to the greatest issue—
States Rights versus supremacy of the national government.
Webster had been expounding the doctrine of national supremacy before the Supreme Court for a decade. On this
constitutional issue Webster knew that he had no master.

Fears and doubts assailed Webster's Northern friends whose "timid eyes and depressed bearing" betrayed their anxiety over Webster's ability to cope with Hayne's onslaught. That night Hayne was the toast of the town wherever Southerners foregathered. Congratulations poured in on him. Taverns rang with his praises as Southern patrons quaffed glass after glass of steaming punch. Daniel Webster and the tariff were downed never to rise again! Nullification had emerged from its chrysalis in glorious raiment!

Early that evening Judge Story called at Webster's home and offered to help in looking up material to answer Hayne's arguments.

"Give yourself no uneasiness, Judge Story," assured Webster. "I will grind him as fine as a pinch of snuff."

Later Edward Everett called. He said he had never seen Webster "more calm or self-possessed or in better spirits."

"Did you take notes of Mr. Hayne's speech?" asked Everett.

"Yes," replied Webster, producing a small slip of paper. "I have it all. This is his speech."

To Everett, Webster said he regarded Hayne's speech as an entirely unprovoked attack upon the Eastern states which it was impossible for him as a New England senator to leave unnoticed. He felt also that, even more important, Hayne had advanced a theory of politics which could go far to change the form of government established by the Constitution. He expressed his determination to put that theory to rest forever as far as it could be done by an argument in the Senate chamber.

To a friend of Hayne's who praised the South Carolinian's speech, Senator Iredell of North Carolina gave this prophetic view: "He has started the lion, but wait till we hear his roar and feel his claws."

During the evening Webster scribbled twelve pages of loose notes, but so saturated was he with his subject that he was to find little use for them. Next day, January 26th,

1830 it was near noon when Webster climbed the Capitol steps. Summoning his friend, Senator Bell, into the robing room he said: "You know my constitutional opinions. There are, among my friends in the Senate, some who may not concur in them. What shall I do?"

With vigor Bell urged him to speak out: "It is a critical moment, sir, and it is time, high time, that the people of this country should know what this Constitution is."

"Then, by the blessing of Heaven," declared Webster solemnly, "they shall learn, this day, before the sun goes down, what I understand it to be."

Before entering the Senate, Webster arranged with his friend, Joseph Gales, editor of the *National Intelligencer,* to take down his speech in shorthand.

Crowds were already flocking to the Capitol. By noon there was not even standing room. The House of Representatives was soon deserted, leaving the Speaker presiding over a baker's dozen of the more fatihful.

An eyewitness left us this vivid description of the scene:

"The floor of the Senate was so densely crowded, that persons once in could not get out or change their position. In rear of the Vice-Presidential chair the crowd was particularly intense. A Representative from Alabama became wedged in here. From his enormous size it was impossible for him to move without displacing a vast portion of the multitude. Unfortunately, too, for him, he was jammed in directly behind the chair of the Vice-President, where he could not see, and hardly hear, the speaker. By slow and laborious effort—pausing occasionally to breathe—he gained one of the windows, which, constructed of painted glass, flanked the chair of the Vice-President on either side. Here he paused, unable to make more headway. But determined to see Mr. Webster as he spoke, with his knife he made a large hole in one of the panes of the glass; which is still visible as he made it. Many were so placed as not to be able to see the speaker at all."

Webster entered the Senate with slow, stately steps, the observed of all observers. He was the warrior in full panoply. In the aisle he was greeted by Senator Clayton of Delaware with whom he had dined the night before.

"Are you well charged, Senator?" asked Clayton.

"Seven fingers," replied Webster confidently—referring to the charge of a muzzle-loading gun for which four fingers were deemed ample.

At noon the tap of the Vice-President's gavel brought an expectant hush over the excited assemblage. Webster rose and began his Second Reply to Hayne, who was seated barely ten feet from him. On the rostrum Calhoun's eyes roamed restlessly. He was a sombre figure.

With consummate artistry Webster enchained attention instantly and set his audience at ease by his simple, opening request that the original Resolution be read. On that day Webster spoke for over two hours. Two-thirds of his speech —the part delivered on the first day—were devoted to a vindication of himself and refutation of the slurs Hayne had cast on New England and Massachusetts. That day he displayed little of the boasted power of uplifting his audience to emotional heights. His only gestures were the up-and-down motions of his right arm. He hardly moved from the spot on which he set his feet when he began his speech. On his desk lay his scant notes to which he gave hardly a glance.

As Webster advanced into his mighty appeal, bowling Hayne's arguments over one by one like tenpins, Calhoun's face grew dark; he was restless in his chair. Time after time Calhoun sought to interrupt Webster. Suddenly the orator swung his forensic battle-axe directly at Calhoun as he pointed to the inconsistencies of the South Carolina politicians on the subject of internal improvements.

"I now may safely say, I think," thundered Webster, "that we have had the authority of leading and distinguished gentlemen from South Carolina in support of the doctrine of internal improvement. I repeat that, up to 1824, I, for one, followed South Carolina; but when that star in its ascension veered off in an unexpected direction I relied on its light no longer."

It was more than Calhoun could endure. Agitated by this

direct thrust Calhoun broke all parliamentary rules and cut
in with the curt demand:

"Does the chair understand the gentleman from Massachusetts to say that the person now occupying the chair of
the Senate has changed his opinions on the subject of internal improvements?"

It was unparliamentary, un-Senatorial. The Vice-President has no voice in the Senate save to preserve order and
enforce rules. He cannot participate in debates or proceedings, but it made no difference to the harassed Calhoun.
Good-naturedly Webster rebuffed the excited presiding officer.

"From nothing ever said to me, sir, have I reason to know
of any change in the opinions of the person filling the chair
of the Senate. If such a change has taken place, I regret it."

Webster paused at a fitting point in his discussion of the
tariff and asked adjournment until the following day. He
was two-thirds through. Why he left off at this point, no
one knows although Gales' shorthand report would indicate
that he closed his first day with a passage not found in the
published version of the speech and not with the generally
accepted paragraph ending with the sentence: "And there is
another sort to which I lay as little, and that is, a kind of
consistency by which persons feel themselves as much
bound to oppose a proposition after it has become a law of
the land as before."

Hayne's adherents were still jubilant. Webster had not yet
met and mastered the South Carolinian's chief arguments.
Refreshed, more confident than ever, Webster resumed on
January 27th before a hushed, expectant throng which was
not to be disappointed. Today Webster closed in on Hayne,
turning first to sentiment. In an inspired burst of eloquence,
he pronounced his immortal eulogium on Massachusetts:

"Mr. President, I shall enter no encomium upon Massachusetts;
she needs none. There she is. Behold her, and judge for yourselves.
There is her history; the world knows it by heart. The past, at least,

is secure. There is Boston and Concord and Lexington and Bunker Hill; and there they will remain forever. The bones of her sons, falling in the great struggle for independence, now lie mingled with the soil of every State from New England to Georgia, and there they will lie forever. And, sir, where American liberty raised its infant voice, and where its youth was nurtured and sustained, there it still lives in the strength of its manhood and full of its original spirit. If discord and disunion shall wound it, if party strife and blind ambition shall hawk and tear it, if folly and madness, if uneasiness under salutary and necessary restraint, shall succeed in separating it from that Union by which alone its existence is made sure, it will stand, in the end, by the side of that cradle in which its infancy was rocked; it will stretch forth its arm, with whatever of vigor it may still retain, over the friends who gather round it; and it will fall at last, if fall it must, amid the proudest monuments of its own glory and on the very spot of its origin."

As he uttered those words Webster raised his eyes toward the galleries where a group of Massachusetts men "shed tears like girls." Emotion swept the assemblage. There was hardly a dry eye in the Senate. No man appreciated love of state more than discomforted Calhoun, who found it hard to conceal his emotions. Tears shone in his eyes.

The variety of Webster's speech kept his audience in continued wonder. It was a complete drama: comedy, banter, scorn, pathos, irony, sarcasm. He struck every chord of the human heart.

Now Webster drove on toward his goal: his explanation and understanding of the nature of the Federal Union and the Constitution which bound it together. This question transcended all others. Was Hayne justified in asserting that a state had the right to decide what laws enacted by Congress were unconstitutional and to disobey them if it did not approve them? On this question the American people had long needed enlightenment. For the people Webster held the lantern high so that all might see—and hear—his simple, powerful, understandable conception.

The grandeur of the man as he warmed to this subject so close to his heart defied expression and electrified his audience. It was breathtaking. This was what the spectators were waiting for, what many had come hundreds of miles to hear and feel:

"There yet remains, Mr. President, by far the most grave and important duty which I feel to be devolved on me by this occasion. It is to state and to defend what I conceive to be the true principles of the Constitution under which we are here assembled. . . .

"I understand the honorable gentleman from South Carolina to maintain that it is a right of the State legislatures to interfere whenever, in their judgment, this government transcends its constitutional limits, and to arrest the operation of its laws.

"I understand him to maintain this right as a right existing under the Constitution, not as a right to overthrow it on the ground of extreme necessity, such as would justify violent revolution.

"I understand him to maintain an authority, on the part of the States, thus to interfere for the purpose of correcting the exercise of power by the general government, of checking it, and of compelling it to conform to their opinion of the extent of its powers.

"I understand him to maintain that the ultimate power of judging of the constitutional extent of its own authority is not lodged exclusively in the general government or any branch of it; but that, on the contrary, the States may lawfully decide for themselves, and each State for itself, whether, in a given case, the act of the general government transcends its power.

"I understand him to insist that, if the exigencies of the case, in the opinion of any State government, require it, such State government may, by its own sovereign authority, annul an act of the general government which it deems plainly and palpably unconstitutional.

"This is the sum of what I understand from him to be the South Carolina doctrine, and the doctrine which he maintains. I propose to consider it, and compare it with the Constitution."

Denying the right of a State to annul a law save "on the ground of the inalienable right of man to resist oppression" Webster admitted:

". . . there is an ultimate violent remedy, above the Constitution and in defiance of the Constitution, which may be resorted to when a revolution is to be justified. But I do not admit that, under the Constitution and in conformity with it, there is any mode in which a State government, as a member of the Union, can interfere and stop the progress of the general government, by force of her own laws, under any circumstances whatever.

"This leads us to inquire into the origin of this government and the source of its power. Whose agent is it? Is it the creature of the State legislatures, or the creature of the people? If the government of the United States be the agent of the State governments, then they may control it; if it be the agent of the people, then the people alone can control it, restrain, modify, or reform it. . . . It is, sir, the people's Constitution, the people's government, made for the people, made by the people, and answerable to the people. The people of the United States have declared that this Constitution shall be the supreme law. We must either admit the proposition, or deny their authority.

"The people, then, sir, erected this government. They gave it a Constitution, and in that Constitution they have enumerated the powers which they bestow on it. They have made it a limited government. They have defined its authority. They have restrained it to the exercise of such powers as are granted; and all others, they declare, are reserved to the States or the people."

Quoting the clause of the Constitution which declares the Constitution, or any law passed under its pursuance, to be the supreme law of the land, Webster asked:

"But who shall decide this question of interference? To whom lies the last appeal? This, sir, the Constitution itself decided also by declaring 'that the judicial power shall extend to all cases arising under the Constitution and laws of the United States.' These two provisions cover the whole ground. They are, in truth, the keystone of the arch! With these it is a government, without them a confederation. In pursuance of these clear and express provisions Congress established, at its very first session, in the judicial act, a mode for carrying them into full effect, and for bringing all questions of Constitutional power to the final decision of the Supreme Court. It then, sir, became a government. It then had the means of self-protection; and but for this it would, in all probability, have been now among things which are past.

Webster now thundered his historic warning that State resistance to the execution of a federal law was tantamount to revolution and that the South Carolina doctrine, incompatible as it was with peaceful government, would lead directly to civil strife and disunion. But, he said:

"Let it be remembered that the Constitution of the United States is not unalterable. It is to continue in its present form no longer than the people who established it shall choose to continue it. If they shall become convinced that they have made an injudicious or inexpedient partition and distribution of power between the State governments and the general government, they can alter that distribution at will.

"If anything be found in the national Constitution either by general provision or subsequent interpretation, which ought not to be in it the people know how to get rid of it. If any construction unacceptable to them be established so as to become practically a part of the Constitution, they will amend it at their own sovereign pleasure. But while the people choose to maintain it as it is, while they are satisfied with it and refuse to change it, who has given, or who can give, to the legislatures a right to alter it, either by interference, construction or otherwise? . . .

"The people have preserved this, their own chosen Constitution, for forty years, and have seen their happiness, prosperity and renown grow with its growth and strengthen with its strength. They are now, generally, strongly attached to it. Overthrown by direct assault it cannot be; evaded, undermined, nullified it will not be if we, and those who shall succeed us here, as agents and representatives of the people, shall conscientiously and vigilantly discharge the two great branches of our public trust faithfully to preserve and wisely to administer it. . . ."

"No one ever looked the orator, as he did, in form and feature how like a god. His countenance spake no less audibly than his words. His manner gave new force to his language. As he stood swaying his right arm, like a huge tilt-hammer, up and down, his swarthy countenance lighted up with excitement, he appeared amid the smoke, the fire, the thunder of his eloquence, like Vulcan in his armory forging thoughts for the Gods."

"I profess, sir, in my career hitherto, to have kept steadily in view the prosperity and honor of the whole country, and the preservation of our Federal Union. It is to that Union we owe our safety at home and our consideration and dignity abroad. It is to that Union that we are chiefly indebted for whatever makes us most proud of our country. That Union we reached only by the discipline of our virtues in the severe school of adversity. It had its origin in the necessities of disordered finance, prostrate commerce and ruined credit. Under its benign influences these great interests immediately awoke as from the dead, and sprang forth with newness of life. Every year of its duration has teemed with fresh proofs of its utility and its blessings; and although our territory has stretched out wider and wider, and our population spread farther and farther, they have not outrun its protection or its benefits. It has been to us all a copious fountain of national, social and personal happiness."

The grandeur of his voice fairly lifted his hearers from their seats. It penetrated every recess and corner of the Senate. Every eye was riveted on the orator whose gleaming torrent of words seemed to leap as they raced toward his glorious climax. His eyes burned as if "touched with fire."

Friend and foe alike knew that Webster was forging a masterpiece. They knew, and Webster knew, that he was speaking not merely to those within the sound of his voice, but to the thirteen millions of Americans throughout the length and breadth of the land—and to the millions of Americans who would follow in their train. For these, the unseen and the unborn, this greatest of American orators was making the greatest oration of his life. His message would be understood by sailors and tradesmen, by farm hands and clerks, by woodsmen and professors. He was expounding the Constitution so clearly and inspiringly that it was to become a living document which every citizen might understand.

Webster's audience now sat as if held by some mesmeric witchery. How high could this man reach! There was no stopping him. The very walls of the Senate must have thrilled as he began his immortal peroration so often compared with Demosthenes' Oration On the Crown:

"I have not allowed myself, sir, to look beyond the Union, to see what might lie hidden in the dark recess behind. I have not coolly weighed the chances of preserving liberty when the bonds that unite us together shall be broken asunder. I have not accustomed myself to hang over the precipice of disunion, to see whether, with my short sight, I can fathom the depth of the abyss below; nor could I regard him as a safe counsellor in the affairs of this government whose

BORN TO COMMAND.

OF VETO MEMORY.

HAD I BEEN CONSULTED.

KING ANDREW THE FIRST.

This cartoon, KING ANDREW THE FIRST, was published by President Jackson's political enemies. It depicts him in kingly robes, armed with veto and sceptre, trampling on the Constitution and Supreme Court decisions. Once when the Supreme Court handed down a decision that displeased him Jackson defiantly exclaimed, "John Marshall has made his decision; now let him enforce it." He refused to execute and the State of Georgia to obey the mandate of the Supreme Court in this case which involved the rights of the Cherokees in Georgia. The Supreme Court was powerless to enforce its own order.

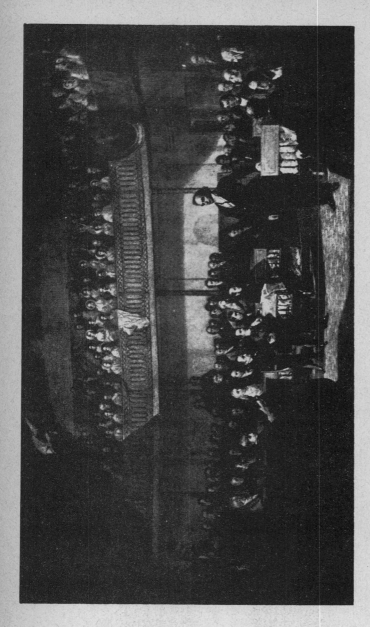

This massive painting, "Webster's Reply to Hayne," by G. P. A. Healy, hangs in Fanueil Hall, Boston. It shows the old semicircular Senate Chamber, January 1830, as Senator Daniel Webster rose to reply to Senator Hayne's powerful nullification speech. Vice-President Calhoun occupies the dais. The artist introduced into the gallery several of his friends, who were not actually there on this historic occasion. Mrs. Daniel Webster, the orator's recently-taken second wife, sits prominently in the first row. (*Courtesy Fanueil Hall*)

This famous scene in the Senate, painted by Peter Rothermel, shows Henry Clay, the Great Compromiser, making the last eloquent appeal of his career for his Omnibus Bill in 1850. This bill precipitated by California's appeal for entrance into the Union as a free state, compromised the bitter slavery issues which divided the nation.

John Randolph of Roanoke, "Mad Jack" (*left*), was perhaps the most unique figure in Congressional history. Tall, cadaverous, rapier-voiced, he had the face of a boy of fifteen. His sarcasm stung like an adder's tongue. He was President Jefferson's first-term floor leader in the House. (*Old contemporary print*) Incensed by the coarse remarks Senator Sumner had aimed at his kinsman, goateed Congressman Preston Brooks of South Carolina (*right*) walked into the Senate chamber and floored Sumner with a heavy gutta-percha cane. Southern admirers acclaimed him as a hero; Southern belles crowded the Capitol and smothered him with kisses. (*Contemporary sketch*)

This turbulent scene in the House of Representatives during the bitter debates over Kansas and slavery in 1858, was precipitated by South Carolina's Laurence Keitt, who called Pennsylvania's Galusha Grow a "black Republican puppy." Grow retaliated with "slave driver." Fists began to fly, spittoons sailed through the air; an excited Southerner is seen snatching off a Northerner's wig. Keitt's hot blood never cooled. He died storming Grant's lines in the Wilderness in 1864. (*Harper's Weekly sketch*)

President Andrew Johnson was the first and only President ever impeached by Congress. The Senate acquitted him of "high crimes and misdemeanors" by a single vote. His only "crime" was his effort to carry out Lincoln's more moderate reconstruction policies in the South. In light of history Johnson's impeachment was a fabricated injustice, chargeable almost entirely to one man, Thaddeus Stevens, who hated him implacably. (*Brady print*)

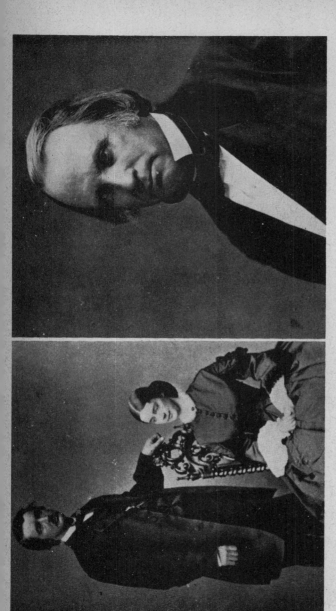

Beauteous, witty Kate Chase Sprague, daughter of Chief Jusice Chase who presided, was queen of the gala audience at President Johnson's state trial by the Senate in 1868. Her husband, William Sprague, former "Boy Governor" of Rhode Island and at the time Senator, stands beside her. Washington's Civil War glamor girl, she dazzled the city with her jewels, clothes and entertainments, competing with Mrs. Lincoln for best-dressed honors. Unhappily married, she had many masculine admirers, resulting in scandalous complications. She died in abject poverty. (*National Archives Brady print*)

Senator Henry Wilson of Massachusetts was not romantic looking, as this picture will testify, but it appears that he loved well and unfortunately not wisely. His passion for the Confederate spy, Rose O'Neal Greenhow, apparently led to the loss of the Battle of Bull Run though it cannot be actually proved. She claimed that she obtained information from him that brought the Union defeat. Love letters to her, intercepted by the government, were signed "H." The red-dotted map, used by the Senate Military Affairs Committee, apparently also found its way into her hands. (*National Archives Brady print*)

B-4278

These are the House Impeachment Managers who trumped up the eleven Articles of Impeachment against President Johnson. Frothing with hate they failed to make a plausible case even though the Senate cards were stacked against the President. Seated left to right: Pop-eyed "Beast" Ben Butler; Old "Thad" Stevens looking like a corpse; Thomas Williams, a Radical henchman; tricky John Bingham who resembled a church deacon; and, standing, James Wilson, another Stevens henchman; George Boutwell, faithful "lobbygow" for Stevens; John A. Logan, great soldier and no mean statesman who belonged in better company. Logan's statesmanlike nose and incomparable handlebar mustache are things to conjure with. (*National Archives*)

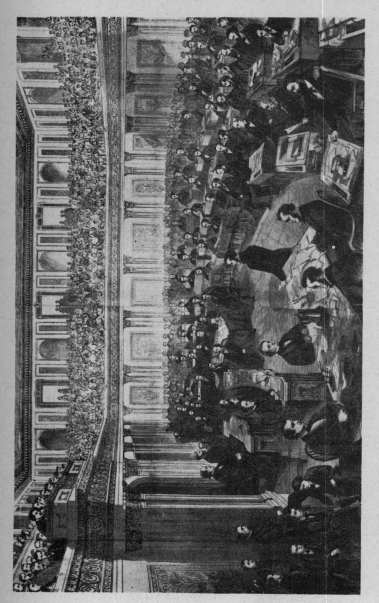

This was the great pay-off scene in the Senate—President Johnson's trial, *in absentia*, by the Senate sitting as a court. Presiding is Chief Justice Salmon P. Chase. Johnson's staff of lawyers occupies the table in the immediate foreground; the Impeachment Managers are seated around the table opposite. The *Harper's Weekly* artist, who sketched this scene on the spot, did his best to depict the glitter and glamor of the galleries which were packed to the walls. (*Harper's Weekly*)

thoughts should be mainly bent on considering, not how the Union
may be best preserved, but how tolerable might be the condition of
the people when it should be broken up and destroyed. While the
Union lasts we have high, exciting, gratifying prospects spread out
before us, for us and our children. Beyond that I seek not to penetrate the veil. God grant that in my day, at least, that curtain may
not rise! God grant that on my vision never may be opened what
lies behind! When my eyes shall be turned to behold for the last time
the sun in heaven, may I not see him shining on the broken and
dishonored fragments of a once glorious Union; on States dissevered,
discordant, belligerent; on a land rent with civil feuds, or drenched,
it may be, in fraternal blood! Let their last feeble and lingering
glance rather behold the gorgeous ensign of the Republic, now known
and honored throughout the earth, still full high advanced, its arms
and trophies streaming in their original lustre, not a stripe erased
or polluted, nor a single star obscured, bearing for its motto no such
miserable interrogatory as 'What is all this worth?' nor those other
words of delusion and folly, 'Liberty first and Union afterwards'; but
everywhere, spread all over in characters of living light, blazing on
all its ample folds, as they float over the sea and over the land, and
in every wind under the whole heavens, that other sentiment, dear to
every true American heart: 'Liberty and Union, now and forever,
one and inseparable!'"

He was finished. With an ever so slight bow to the chair,
a bob of his head toward the galleries, and a glance at
Hayne, Webster sat down. His audience sat in absolute
silence, spellbound. Angrily rapping his gavel as he sought
to break the spell cast by Webster's words, Calhoun called
"Order! Order!", but there was no disorder, only deep stillness, not a movement, not a gesture, not a whisper. Was
Calhoun apprehensive lest forbidden spontaneous applause
break out and insult the dignity of the Senate? Hardly.
Again Calhoun rapped sharply. Rousing from their spell,
the spectators slowly filed out. One and all knew that what
they had heard would reverberate down the centuries.

As Webster took his seat a Southern senator, overcome
with emotion, went to him: "Mr. Webster, I think you had
better die now and rest your fame on that speech." Over-

hearing this, Hayne turned to say: "You ought not to die. A man who can make such speeches as that ought never to die."

Webster's colleagues, friend and foe, surrounded him, shaking his hand. Making her way slowly through the milling crowds was a comely young woman with tears in her eyes. She was Caroline LeRoy Webster, the orator's second wife, a bride of five weeks, who, seated in the balcony, had thrilled to her husband's magic words. Even the phlegmatic, watery-eyed John Quincy Adams, who sat listening in the gallery, went home in a daze to set down in his *Diary:* "Remarkable . . . it demolished the whole fabric of Hayne's speech, so that it leaves scarcely a wreck to be seen."

Hayne rose instantly, but his feeble rebuttal was lost in the tide of Webster's words that seemed still to be surging through the Senate chamber.

That evening the two protagonists met at a brilliant White House levee. Here Webster outshone even Old Hickory himself. Hayne, courteous as always, extended his hand in congratulations to his rival.

"How are you this evening, Colonel Hayne?"

"None the better for you, sir," responded Hayne gallantly.

The Great Debate was to continue for weeks, but the two greatest actors had spoken their magnificent lines and left the stage. What came now was anticlimax.

Yet another debate continued: Had Webster overnight prepared this great speech which fills seventy-three pages of the National Edition of his works? Could even the Godlike Daniel do such a thing?

To a young preacher who inquired whether his Reply to Hayne was extemporaneous, Webster gave this oracular reply: "Young man, there is no such thing as extemporaneous acquisition."

To a friend, he once said: "The materials of that speech had been lying in my mind for eighteen months, though I had never committed my thoughts to paper, or arranged them in my memory."

In 1851 the city of Boston purchased for forty thousand dollars from the artist, G. P. A. Healy, his famous painting inspired by Webster's Reply to Hayne. This is the most celebrated of all paintings of great scenes in the American Congress. A colossal canvas, sixteen by thirty feet, it hangs over the platform in Faneuil Hall. One hundred and fifty of those present on this great occasion appear in the portrait. Most of these faces were drawn from life. Healy erred slightly in introducing the faces of several of his friends who were not in the gallery at the time. Webster stands in the center, foursquare as usual, his clenched fist resting on his desk, dominating the scene. Calhoun and Hayne are nearby. Benton, the man who started it all, leans against a pillar. Nor did the artist forget the page boy who carried Calhoun's notes to the fighting Hayne.

In this great speech Webster had asked that his dying eyes might "behold the gorgeous ensign of the Republic." In this he was gratified. As he lay dying in October of 1852, the Stars and Stripes were nailed to the mast of a little boat moored on a pond beneath his window so that he could see the flag from his bedside. He asked that at night a ship's lantern be lighted and hung beside the flag so that, even in the darkness as his life flickered out, his eyes could fondle the banner of his beloved country. In a whisper he said: "I want to keep my flag flying and my light burning till I die."

6

JACKSON CONFOUNDS THE NULLIFIERS

From 1831 to 1832 the nation was presenting this picture.

In Illinois, a rawboned young fellow of twenty-three—"I am humble Abraham Lincoln"—making his political debut. . . . In Washington, society agog over the wedding of Arlington heiress, Mary Custis, to penniless Second Lieutenant Robert E. Lee . . . From England, steel pens cutting in on America's goose-quill business . . . At West Point, a young cadet, George G. Meade, learning the rudiments of war for a rendezvous with destiny at Gettysburg . . . Across the nation Junius Brutus Booth delighting playgoers with his impersonations of Richard III, King Lear, Othello, and Sir Giles Overreach . . . *Godey's Lady's Book* making its bow with new ideas on fashions, etiquette, and home economics . . . In the Shenandoah Valley young farmer, Cyrus McCormick, demonstrating a crude reaper which would revolutionize agriculture . . . At Harvard, a young graduate, Oliver Wendell Holmes, writing a poem, "Old Ironsides," that saved a famous ship from the scrap heap . . . At Monticello, Thomas Jefferson five years under the sod but more vocal than ever. . . . On the Mississippi, Black Hawk leading the Sauks and Foxes in a last fight against the white man . . . Mr. and Mrs. America reading Cooper's newest bestseller, *Last of the Mohicans* . . . In fractious South Carolina, Nullifiers pondering Old Hickory's defiant pronunciamento that he intends to uphold Federal authority . . . Shocked America reading British Mrs. Frances Trollope's scorching caricature, *The Domestic Manners of the Americans* . . . Brimstone matches supplanting the oldtime tinderbox with flint and steel . . . Ex-President John Quincy Adams taking his seat in the House of Representatives . . . At Boston a new weekly newspaper, the *Liberator,* demanding total and immediate abolition of slavery . . . At Bladensburg the President of the United States watching a "main" of his Hermitage fighting cocks . . . From Baltimore the first clipper ship, *Anna McKim,* setting new speed records for ocean commerce . . . In New York, James Monroe dying in poverty . . . In Washington a resolute old soldier threatening to hang John Calhoun for treason.

In December, 1832, a crisis confronted the White House. Andrew Jackson's whole career was set in crises. In the President's study a solitary lamp cast its feeble beam on the haggard face of a determined old man, writing. His pen went scrawling across the page. "Nullification means insurrection and war. I will meet it at the threshold and have the leaders arrested and arraigned for treason. In forty days I can have within the limits of South Carolina fifty thousand men, and in forty days another fifty thousand. Grenades and rockets are excellent weapons in a street fight." This was written to Unionist leader, Joel R. Poinsett, in South Carolina.

Already a ship had sailed out of Charleston harbor with the Stars and Stripes flying upside down. When told of it Jackson blazed out, "For this indignity to the flag she ought to have been instantly sunk no matter who owned or commanded her."

To Sergeant (now General) Sam Dale, old companion in arms, who came visiting, he said, "They're trying me here, Sam. You will witness it. But, by the God in heaven, I will uphold the laws."

South Carolina had precipitated the crisis by her Ordinance of Nullification proclaiming the Federal tariff acts void and not "binding upon this State or its citizens." It was tantamount to secession. Vowing he would uphold the sovereignty of South Carolina or "perish beneath its ruins," Governor Robert Y. Hayne rushed war preparations. Bands played and banners waved in the streets of Charleston. Blue cockades were everywhere.

The nation turned to Andrew Jackson for the next move. What would the man in the White House do? The nation did not have long to wait. On December 6th, 1832, Jackson and his Secretary of State, Edward Livingston, sat in the President's study drafting the answer. Peering over the Secretary's shoulder, Jackson watched every word Livingston wrote. "Let it receive your best flight of eloquence," he urged Livingston. "The Union must be preserved without blood, if this be possible, but it must be preserved at all hazards and at any price."

To the paper Livingston transcribed his "best flight of eloquence." The words were mostly his, but the drive and spirit behind this great state paper, President Jackson's proclamation against Nullification addressed to the people of South Carolina, came from the fighting heart of a man who had dealt in gunpowder all his life.

The hour was late when Livingston rose to go. The proclamation was finished. Jackson looked tired and wan. He was about to retire, though before snuffing his candle he would read a chapter in Rachel's worn Bible, say good night to her picture beside his bed. He stood up and his keen eyes met Livingston's. Then he said, "I should like Mr. Madison to read this before I make it public. You will carry it to him, Mr. Secretary . . . at once, if possible."

The "at once" had a soldierly snap. Old Hickory was a military man in all things.

"At once, Mr. President," repeated Livingston.

At dawn Livingston took the wintry road toward Montpelier, Virginia, where the aged father of the Constitution, James Madison, was soon to make his adieu, burdened with the infirmities he bore with a philosophy and fortitude matching that of Benjamin Franklin in his last days. It was after midnight and bitterly cold when the Secretary of State reached Montpelier. The house was dark, its occupants asleep, but a knock on the door ushered Livingston into the presence of a sleepy but gracious lady, Dolly Madison, still charming and exquisite in her violet *robe de chambre*. Madison had been in bed since twilight, but he was awakened and agreed to receive Livingston in his chamber.

Painfully Madison climbed out of his ancient curtained four-poster bed. His frame was wasted, his face shrunken and pain-wracked. His archenemy was rheumatism from which there seemed no escape. The winters were long miseries to him.

As Livingston entered, Madison was seated before a glowing fire, clad in a loose-fitting flannel nightgown and woolen cap Dolly had made for him. At his side was a small table on which burned a single tallow candle.

With apologies for the lateness of the hour, Livingston said, "The President has sent me to you, sir, for advice, or rather, for assistance. It is quite urgent. You are familiar with the state of affairs in South Carolina."

"This colossal heresy has gone too far," said Madison. "It must be stopped." He was deeply aroused. He knew the Nullifiers were leaning heavily on the Virginia and Kentucky Resolutions attacking the Alien and Sedition laws he and Jefferson had written thirty years back. He would scotch them if he could.

Livingston continued, "The President has prepared a paper on this miserable business. He wishes you to offer such thoughts and suggestions as you may deem advisable."

"I am flattered, sir," said the wizened patriot. His face brightened. Another candle was lighted. At Madison's suggestion, Livingston slowly read aloud Jackson's proposed proclamation, holding the document close to the two flickering candles. Twice he read it. The ex-President listened attentively. Now silence, save for the logs crackling on the hearth. Madison sat long minutes in deep thought. Calling for quill and ink, he took the paper and in a fine, legible hand made a number of interpolations.

Dawn was breaking before the revision was completed. Following an early breakfast, Livingston bade the Madisons farewell. Late that day he reached the White House to find Jackson waiting. Next day Jackson issued his famous proclamation, embodying Madison's suggestions.

It was a thunderbolt. He meant every word he said. The nation knew it. South Carolina knew it. The Nullifiers knew it. Had Jackson put a bugle to his lips and sounded the call to arms he could not have electrified his fellow-countrymen more. Like martial music, his words sent the blood leaping through patriot veins. It struck confusion to the hearts of men who had counseled Nullification. Across the nation men paraded and lit bonfires. The Governor of South Carolina issued a counter-proclamation, but to little avail. To South Carolina's order for 125,000 pounds of gunpowder, Ireneé du Pont, powder-maker on the Brandywine, said flatly no. If gunpowder was needed, the government could get all he could make. He would have none of South Carolina's $24,000 cash offer for the explosive.

Even John Quincy Adams and Daniel Webster fell in with the President, while Henry Clay began pressing a compromise tariff as the way out. Thousands who thought Jackson a backwoods' devil with horns overlooked their personal antipathies and applauded his sledgehammer blow at Nullification.

Jackson's proclamation had a single theme: THE UNION WILL BE PRESERVED—"The United States is a government, not a league." It was not a threat, nor a broadside of vituperation full of highly polished constitutional theories. Basically it was an appeal to reason and the patriotic love of America. But it was firm, foursquare, aflame with Jackson's determination to maintain Federal authority at all and any cost.

Striking directly at the heart of Nullification, Jackson sounded his trumpet:

> "I consider then the power to annul a law of the United States, assumed by one State, incompatible with the existence of the Union, contradicted expressly by the letter of the Constitution, unauthorized by its spirit, inconsistent with every principle on which it was founded, and destructive of the great object for which it was formed."

There were no mincing words. He branded Nullification as an "impractical absurdity. . . . If this doctrine had been established at an earlier day the Union would have been dissolved in its infancy . . . admit this doctrine and every law for raising revenue may be annulled. . . . To say that any State may at pleasure secede from the Union is to say that the United States is not a nation."

Then he levelled his sword straight at Nullifiers, but spoke directly to the people of South Carolina:

> "The laws of the United States must be executed. I have no discretionary power on the subject; my duty is emphatically pronounced in the Constitution. Those who have told you that you might peaceably prevent their execution, deceived you—they could not have deceived themselves. Their object is disunion; but be not deceived by names; disunion, by armed force, is TREASON. Are you ready to incur its guilt?"

Jackson did not stop with his proclamation. He went ahead preparing for emergencies: assembling regiments at strategic points, massing ships outside Charleston Harbor, clearing near-by forts for action while Nullification struggled for breath against his clutching hands.

One man, Jackson's favorite, had remained aloof in this national crisis, but he was the best political tightrope walker in America, Vice-President elect Martin Van Buren. From Albany where he lingered during the Nullification tumult,

he had written Jackson, urging, "Caution, caution, caution."
For Van Buren had other fish to fry. He was not so sure but
that Jackson had gone too far in his proclamation. He feared
alienation of his Southern political allies. This Nullification
business might ruin his hopes of evoluting to a higher office
than the vice-presidency. His secret political motto, like that
of his native state, was "Excelsior, Higher."

Jackson had written back, "No, my friend, your policy
would destroy all confidence in our government both at
home and abroad."

But Martin Van Buren, founding father of American politics, knew there was always more than one way of getting
what you wanted out of politics, which at this moment was
the presidency when Old Hickory stepped out.

7

THE LITTLE MAGICIAN CLINCHES THE PRESIDENCY

Vice-President John Caldwell Calhoun was jubilant. This was his day. It was nearing noon on January 25th, 1832 when he, Senator Daniel Webster, and Senator Henry Clay —the Great Triumvirate—met in the privacy of the Vice-President's office for a last-minute conference. In a quarter of an hour Calhoun would mount the rostrum and call the Senate to order.

"It will kill him off," enthused Calhoun. His dark, variegated eyes glowed. "He'll never kick again."

Senator Clay took a pinch of snuff and sneezed heartily. It was his first entente with the gloomy-browed, spiky-haired statesman from South Carolina.

"But we don't want to kill him too dead," cautioned Clay, brushing a bit of snuff from his flowered waistcoat. His blue eyes twinkled. "There is such a thing in politics, you know."

"Very true," agreed magnificent, portly Senator Webster, "but we must do as we had planned. We'll finish it today." The Expounder of the Constitution poured himself three fingers of Madeira from the Vice-President's decanter. "Here's to success," he breathed as he tossed off the fragrant, amber liquid.

All three had scores to even up with Martin Van Buren. Now, at last, they had run the Red Fox to earth and today they would skin him and nail his political hide to the walls of the Senate chamber. With barefaced delight they would perform the last rites over the ablest trickster in American politics.

Calhoun panted hardest for revenge. His grudge was deep. To Van Buren, Calhoun laid the scheme which had blasted his hopes of becoming President of the United States, the thing he desired above all else in this world.

The vengeance hatched by Clay and Webster and Calhoun to dim the prestige and popularity of the Little Magician appeared to be flawless. Today, by a prearranged vote, the Senate would reject Van Buren's appointment as Minister to Great Britain. First, however, they would discredit Van Buren in the eyes of the American people by airing his iniquities on the Senate floor, showering him with charges of evil-doing, and even of semi-treason. Thus besmirched, Van Buren would forever be ineligible for public office, his goose cooked and his political capers stilled. It looked as simple and as adroit as if the Red Fox himself had contrived it.

It would also be an affront to President Jackson who, in the summer of 1831 during the Congressional recess, had appointed his recent Secretary of State as Minister to the Court of St. James. On December 7th, soon after Congress convened, Jackson sent Van Buren's nomination to the Senate for confirmation. At about the same time the National Republicans, soon to transform themselves into the Whigs, nominated Clay for President. That gentleman naturally welcomed an opportunity to throw mud at the administration of Jackson who, seeking a second term, would be his rival in the coming election.

With licking of chops the three "conspirators" evolved the plot to destroy Van Buren. They failed to see that rejecting him was bad politics, at least for them. Nor did they take seriously the warning of Whig editor Thurlow Weed that, with Van Buren in London, he was at least out of the way. If rejected, he "would return a prosecuted man, throw himself on the sympathy of the party, be nominated for Vice-

President and he huzzahed into office on the heels of General Jackson."

While the statesmen on Capitol Hill were meditating his political destruction, Van Buren was in London. He had hurried to England soon after Jackson notified him of his recess appointment.

Van Buren swirled through the upper social brackets of London like a veteran courtier, lapping up champagne and fine food and consorting with the King and Queen, who were captivated by the dapper, diminutive, exquisitely groomed—though still unconfirmed—American Minister. Van Buren knew that his many enemies would turn his career inside out before confirming him, but Old Hickory had sent this reassurance: "The opposition would, if they durst, try to reject your nomination as Minister, but they dare not—they begin to know that if they did the people in mass would take you up and elect you Vice-President without a nomination. Were it not for this, it is said, Clay, Calhoun & Co. would try it."

Yet, try it Clay, Calhoun & Co. did. On January 10th, 1832 the Senate Foreign Relations Committee, controlled by Jackson Democrats, reported Van Buren's nomination favorably. On January 17th the galleries were cleared and the Senate went into executive session to take action on the appointment. The doors were hardly closed before Senator Holmes of Maine, an ally of the Clay faction, moved that Van Buren's nomination be returned to the committee with instructions to investigate the causes of the dissolution of Jackson's first Cabinet and "also whether the said Martin Van Buren, then Secretary of State, had participated in any practices disreputable to the national character, which were designed to operate on the mind of the President of the United States and calculated to smooth his way to his appointment to the high office to which he has been nominated."

The insinuation in Holmes' resolution was that Jackson

had not given the true reason for his Cabinet dismissal. This would open up the celebrated Peggy Eaton affair to the prying eyes of Jackson's enemies and expose Van Buren's part therein.

Considerable legislative byplay preceded the big show. First came a four-point "indictment" of Van Buren designed fully to explore that gentleman's nefarious political conduct. Little Van was accused on these counts:

1. The instructions drawn up and signed by Mr. Van Buren as Secretary of State, under the direction of the President and furnished to Mr. McLane, for his guidance in endeavoring to reopen the negotiations for the West Indian trade.

2. Making a breach of friendship between the first and second officers of the Government—President Jackson and Vice President Calhoun—for the purpose of thwarting the latter and helping himself to the Presidency.

3. Breaking up the Cabinet for the same purpose.

4. Introducing the system of "proscription" (removal from office for opinion's sake) for the same purpose.

Next, the Red Fox trappers arranged twelve carefully rehearsed speeches against Van Buren, with special, blister-raising blasts by the three oratorical giants, Clay, Webster and Hayne, Calhoun's mouthpiece on the Senate floor. Obligingly enough, several Senators agreed, if desired, to absent themselves so that the vote on the nomination would be a tie. This would give Vice-President Calhoun the opportunity for which his soul yearned: to cast the vote which rejected Martin Van Buren as Minister to Great Britain.

Count number one was silly. The "conspirators" hoped to arouse public indignation against Van Buren by depicting him as a second Benedict Arnold. They based this count on the instructions then-Secretary of State Van Buren had given Jackson's new Minister to Britain, Allen McLane, to reopen negotiations for the West Indian trade and to inform the British government that Jackson's election was a repudiation by the American people of the past foreign policies of President John Quincy Adams and his Secretary of State, Henry Clay. For this, and other clawings, Clay naturally desired revenge.

Count number four was probably true. Van Buren was America's original political spoilsman. Most of the tricks of that trade were the product of his fertile mind. When Jackson drafted him for the State portfolio, the Little Magician was Governor of New York and boss of the state's Democratic machine. America's first professional politician, Van Buren showed the "boys" how to squeeze the most out of politics. Astute, wily, always a jump or two ahead of his rivals, he had well earned the sobriquet of Red Fox by his craftiness in extricating himself from many a political ambush.

Nicknames he had aplenty: the Red Fox of Kinderhook, the Little Magician, the Flying Dutchman, the American Talleyrand, Matty, Little Van. Calhoun called him "The Weazle." His round, florid face always wore a smile; his enemies called it smirking. His bald head was relieved by pink side whiskers. He was the good-humored, easy boss.

His smallish figure was always fastidiously garbed. His tastes ran to snuff-colored coats with lace cuffs, white trousers, silk cravats, yellow gloves, and morocco shoes. He abounded in social graces. Son of a Dutch tavernkeeper at Kinderhook on the Hudson, his friends and even his enemies wondered where he acquired such elegance of manner. When the Queen of Holland asked Van Buren how far back he could trace his ancestors, he replied democratically: "As far back as Kinderhook, may it pleasure Your Majesty."

Vanity and love of luxury were laid at his door. His enemies charged that he posed so long and so often before a large White House mirror that he wore the carpet threadbare. Worse still, he perfumed his whiskers—or so went the allegation.

A widower without strings, Van Buren was ambitious. When he joined Jackson's official family, he began considering the possibilities of climbing higher. Four Secretaries of State before him had ascended to the Presidency. He might do likewise were it not for John C. Calhoun, second in command in the Democratic ranks and indicated successor to Old Hickory's mantle. "To be President," once wrote Van Buren, "has ever been my most earnest desire . . . the great goal . . . the Ultima Thule of political life." His only chance was to head off Calhoun—and he found a golden opportunity awaiting him the moment he became Secretary of State.

Count number two of the "indictment" smacked of Calhoun's bitter disappointment. He probably wrote it. Calhoun had made two mis-steps. In the campaign of 1828 Jackson had toasted his running mate up and down the land as "John Calhoun—An honest man's the noblest work of God," but Calhoun's espousal of nullification had brought to Old Hickory's lips another toast, "Our Federal Union— It must be preserved," aimed directly at Calhoun and his partners, who threatened to nullify Federal laws in South Carolina. To Jackson, nullification was simon-pure treason. No longer were President and Vice-President to see eye to eye.

Calhoun's second error was taking the wrong, or rather the anti-Jackson, side of the Peggy Eaton imbroglio. He, the Vice-President, joined her detractors while Andrew Jackson, President, rallied to her defense.

Count number three also stemmed from Calhoun, who thus ushered onto the Senate forum luscious Peggy Eaton, the Gorgeous Hussy. Though her name appears not once in the record of this bitter debate, the swish of her petticoats could almost be heard in the Senate aisles as the "conspirators" sharpened their knives to flay Van Buren.

When Andrew Jackson entered the White House in 1829, the Peggy Eaton tempest blew right in after him. All at once this voluptuous female became the storm center of a petticoat war which swept social and political Washington, blasting Jackson's first Cabinet out of office and dividing the nation's capital into two hostile camps.

Everybody who was anybody in Washington was sucked into the maelstrom of gossip which swirled around the question of Peggy's chastity. Newspapers defended or defamed her according to their political persuasion. Rival politicians found in Peggy's morals, good or bad, new reasons to revile each other.

Whatever her virtue or lack of it, Peg Eaton has at least gone into history as having broken a cabinet, made a Vice-President who later became President, and had her foibles put on public record by a vote of the House of Representatives. An unparalleled record!

Peggy was the toast—or the roast—of the town. To her divine form wagging tongues pinned a profusion of appellations: Gorgeous Hussy; Bellona; Goddess of War; Adulteress; Scarlet Woman of the Administration; Pothouse Peg; American Pompadour; and others even less flattering.

When Old Hickory declared of Peggy, "She is as chaste as a virgin," Henry Clay, wittily improvising on Shakespeare, replied, "Age cannot wither nor custom stale her infinite virginity." Washington laughed at Clay's wisecrack, but not the tempestuous old gentleman who had so recently occupied the White House. Jackson rushed to Peggy's support with all the zeal of his ardent nature. In the malicious gossip aimed at Margaret O'Neale Timberlake Eaton, the President saw the same injustice which had been meted out to his beloved Rachel, hounded to a recent grave by the tongues of her traducers. He saw also in this brawl, for such it was, an effort to discredit his new administration.

Leading the feline pack which snapped at Peggy's pretty heels was sprightly Floride Calhoun, social queen of Washington, wife of Vice-President Calhoun, then at his zenith as heir apparent to the Presidency. Could Calhoun have peered into the future, he might have read in his wife's refusal to accept Peggy into the charmed and virtuous circle of cabinet matrons the wreckage of his own political ambitions.

Peggy was the innkeeper's daughter who simply had no business marrying a cabinet minister. Social climbing, it appears at this distance, was her greatest sin. Daughter of William O'Neale, who ran the Franklin House, Washington's most popular hostelry, she had grown up with politicians, who came to roost under her father's roof. Jackson, a frequent guest, had known Peg since she ran about the place in pigtails. Lafayette made O'Neale's place his headquarters on his famous visit in 1825. When business was rushing, Peg helped out as barmaid. Her saucy back talk and fetching smiles were prime attractions.

At twenty-one, she was too beautiful; Daniel Webster vouched for it, and the Godlike Daniel was no mean judge of pulchritude. Her large, dark, restless eyes, full lips, and willowy figure were too much for most men. Women envied her her haunting beauty, her success with men, and her conversational charm. To her physical endowments nature had added another—a witty tongue. She reeled off bright repartee by the yard. Her frequent "damn it" was too cute to be resented.

To Peggy, Edward Coates Pinckney dedicated his well-known poem lyricizing her beauty. The poet need not have written another line beyond this first stanza:

> "I fill this cup to one made up
>   Of loveliness alone—
> A woman, of her gentle sex
>   The seeming paragon;
> To whom the better elements
>   And kindly stars have given
> A form so fair, that, like the air,
>   'Tis less of earth than heaven."

A young newspaper man of the day, Ben Perley Poore, left this ecstatic description:

"Her form, of medium height, straight and delicate, was of perfect proportions. Her skin was of delicate white, tinged with red . . . her dark hair, very abundant, clustered in curls about her broad, expressive forehead. Her perfect nose, of almost Grecian proportions, and finely curved mouth, with a firm, round chin, completed a profile of faultless outlines. She was in Washington City what Asphasia was in Athens—the cynosure by whose reflected radiance

> 'Beauty lent her smile to wit,
> And learning by her star was lit.' "

A rejected suitor had already killed himself for unrequited love of Peggy when she married Naval Purser John Timberlake, whose ship, the *Constitution*, was soon ordered on a Mediterranean cruise on which Timberlake died mysteriously. Rumor said he took his life when told of his pretty wife's indiscretions in his absence. Peggy was, so ran the gossip, too affectionate with Senator John Eaton of Tennessee, close friend of Andrew Jackson and long-time patron of her father's hostelry.

In 1829 the widow, Peggy O'Neale Timberlake, was married to the senator whose premarital intimacies with her had already provided Washington with tattling chitchat. This was surprising enough, but shocking indeed to upper social Washington was Jackson's appointment of Eaton, his one-time companion in arms of fighting days, as Secretary of War in the new cabinet soon to take office. A barmaid in the cabinet family . . . and a scandalous one at that! Unthinkable!

When Vice-President-elect Calhoun complained to Jackson that Washington society would not countenance the Eaton pair in such high places, Jackson flared back: "Do you suppose that I have been sent here by the people to consult the ladies of Washington as to the proper persons to compose my cabinet?"

So it started. At the inauguration, the rest of the cabinet and their wives gave the Secretary of War and his shapely wife the perfect snub . . . they refused to associate with her. Mrs. Calhoun took the lead. But Peggy had learned the art of give-and-take the hard way—bantering with politicians, high, low, rich and leering, who patronized her father's tavern. She smiled through the insults blithely, but she poured it all into the ears of Andrew Jackson, who thought her the most wonderful and persecuted woman in the world.

Two weeks after Jackson moved into the White House, he received a letter from a busybody Philadelphia cleric imploring him, "for your own sake, for your dead wife's sake, for your administration, for the credit of the government and the country you should not countenance a woman like this." In short, rid yourself of your new, sinful Secretary of War and his adulterous wife.

Jackson, however, never turned his back on friends, and both Eaton and his Peggy were his friends. Back at the cleric Jackson shot a three-thousand-word, fulminating denial of the charges against Peggy. He sent government sleuths snooping through hotel registers in New York where, it was alleged by the clergyman, Peggy and Eaton, before their marriage, had frequently put up as man and wife.

Finding no proof of Peggy's indiscretions, Jackson summoned the accusing clergymen (there were two of them) to the White House where he cross-examined them before his cabinet, refuted the charges, and handed down his blunt, take-it-or-leave-it verdict: "She is as chaste as a virgin."

But the cabinet ladies refused to be placated: they simply would not associate with Peggy. Jackson asked the Secretary of the Treasury, and the Attorney General to intercede with their wives on Peggy's behalf, but the ladies were adamant. Peggy must go . . . or burn. Floride Calhoun's edict ostracizing Peggy was carried out to the letter and John Calhoun moved up to support his wife's challenge to Old Hickory.

It was not long before the cabinet was so split that it did not meet at all.

When Jackson appealed to Vice-President Calhoun to ask his wife to visit Mrs. Eaton, Calhoun refused.

"Then I shall ask her myself," declared Jackson.

"Well, sir, I would advise you not to try," warned the Vice-President.

It was another nail in the coffin of the South Carolinian's aspirations to the Presidency.

Into this tangle of petticoats and politics now moved the wily Secretary of State, Martin Van Buren, who had arrived in Washington determined to treat all members of the cabinet with equal courtesy. Van Buren soon found that there was no neutral ground; he must espouse one side or the other. If he joined the Calhoun forces against Peggy, he would thus array himself against his chief, the President. Van Buren made his choice at once, arraying himself beside Old Hickory in his fight for Peggy's place in the cabinet social sun. By so doing, Van Buren virtually assured Calhoun's political destruction and his own succession as heir apparent. In Van Buren Jackson now saw another champion of a much-persecuted, virtuous woman.

Van Buren entered the fray by showering attentions on Peggy. He whirled Peggy through a kaleidoscopic round of dinners, dances, routs, and balls at which she was the honored guest. It made little difference to Van Buren that the wives of the Secretaries of the Treasury and of the Navy and the Attorney General boycotted his affairs. Van Buren went right ahead. At his request, the Russian Minister, Baron Krudener, gave an elaborate reception at which Peggy was the ranking American woman present. The wives of the three recalcitrant cabinet members had declined to attend. Giving his arm to Peggy, the Baron led her into dinner, so enraging the wife of the Netherlands Minister, who was in collusion with the anti-Peggy brigade, that the lady went home in a huff.

When Peggy, who reported every snub to Jackson, told Old Hickory of this occurrence, he snorted: "I'd sooner have live vermin on my back than the tongues of the women of Washington on my reputation."

Smoothly and quietly, Van Buren played his game. To Peggy he confided, "President Jackson is the greatest man who ever lived," but he warned her not to tell Jackson he had said it. Peggy, of course, could hardly wait to repeat it to Old Hickory who, with tears in his eyes, averred, "That man loves me." It was exactly what Van Buren wanted.

Try as he might to force Washington society to "accept" Peggy by showers of parties in her honor, Van Buren found himself up against a stone wall of femininity which refused to budge an inch. There was apparently no cure for "Eaton Malaria" as it was called. Still, he was entrenching himself deeper and deeper in the heart of "King Andrew I," as Henry Clay dubbed the tempestuous old gentleman from Tennessee.

Soon Peggy became a national, or rather a Jackson, headache. He could order the ladies of the cabinet to be nice to Peg, but that was as far as he could go. Old Hickory, used to cutting Gordian knots, found this one too tough for his mettle.

Van Buren now came under attack as the juggler behind the scenes who was conspiring, through the Peggy Eaton business, to destroy Calhoun. Foxlike, he laid low and said nothing, although he knew something must be done to extricate Jackson from a situation which was daily becoming more ridiculous and unbearable. The cabinet crisis was a drag on the administration; it could not continue without wrecking Jackson's Presidency.

Out of his political hat the Little Magician now pulled his masterpiece. He decided to resign as Secretary of State. He reasoned shrewdly. Throwing himself to the wolves was martyrdom, but he felt it would bring its reward. At least, if he stepped out, it would lift a vast burden from Jackson's

sh .ders and give him an excuse for a Cabinet houseclean-
ir . Automatically, with the three Calhoun sympathizers
(.t, it would eliminate that gentleman's influence in Jack-
n's inner circle. Jackson could then select a new cabinet
.nd go ahead untrammeled, with a harmonious administra-
ion. Having shown Jackson how to finesse his way out of
:he Eaton impasse, Van Buren would earn Old Hickory's
eternal gratitude—and simultaneously the Vice-Presidency.

Jackson and Van Buren often found recreation in horseback riding. On a canter through the Virginia hills, Little
Van unfolded his unique plan.

"We shall, I hope, soon have peace in Israel," observed
Jackson as they rode along.

It was the opening Van Buren was waiting for. "No, General, there is only one thing that can give you peace."

"What is that, sir?"

"My resignation."

Jackson reined in his horse quickly. His sharp features
flushed. "Never, sir," he protested. "Even you know little
of Andrew Jackson if you suppose him capable of such a
humiliation of his friend by his enemies."

"It is the only safe way out of this . . . this affair, General.
It is my duty, sir, to you as my friend and my President and
to the country."

"I cannot and will not hear of it, sir," Jackson's voice
trembled.

"But, General, as you know, I am attracting assaults on
your administration that may mean harm to your legislative
program."

"And I know who is making these assaults," flashed Jackson. "By the Eternal I will stand by you to the end . . . just
as you have stood by Mrs. Eaton."

Van Buren argued for hours. Jackson finally consented to
Van Buren's stratagem, but he insisted that the Secretary
of State, in resigning, be prepared to accept the mission to
England.

In a previous burst of gratitude for Van Buren's espousal of Peggy's cause, Jackson had already offered to make the Little Magician President by proposing to run for re-election with Van Buren as Vice-President and resigning after a few months, leaving Van Buren to succeed him to the highest office. This Van Buren had rejected.

Now it was different. He told Jackson, "I should consent to run for the office of Vice-President against my will." That was hardly true. In the meantime he would go to Britain until recalled by the "voice of the people" and Andrew Jackson to become Vice-President.

Van Buren submitted his resignation at once. Secretary of War Eaton followed suit. Jackson would soon send him and his pretty Peggy to represent the United States at the Spanish court.

Now Jackson demanded the resignation of the three ministers who, with their wives, had held the social ramparts against Peggy. Van Buren's masterpiece was complete. The cabinet was dissolved and the nation stood aghast for the while. Postmaster General Barry alone remained. He and his wife had gallantly stood beside Peggy throughout the "war."

In the crash of Jackson's official family Calhoun saw his last, fleeting hope of the Presidency evaporate. Had Peggy ordered it, she could not have asked sweeter revenge on the Calhouns, who had spearheaded the fight against her.

To a friend farseeing, woman-wise Daniel Webster opined: "It is odd enough that the consequences of this dispute in the social and fashionable world are producing great political effects, and may very probably determine who shall be successor to the present Chief Magistrate."

Unconsciously or consciously, it was Peggy Eaton's affair, plus a bit of political sleight of hand by the Little Magician of Kinderhook, New York.

At noon on January 25th, 1832 the stage was set for Martin Van Buren's political execution. When chief executioner Calhoun rapped for order, forty-six Senators were in their chairs. The Senate Star Chamber was highly charged for this grim yet ludicrous piece of business.

Clay, Calhoun & Co. had counted and arranged the votes meticulously. They knew from the first that they were masters of the nomination, with votes to spare, but rejection and humiliation of Van Buren was not enough. He must be degraded before dying the political death he had so often meted out to others. And Calhoun must have his pound of flesh!

They knew, of course, that the Jacksonian Senators would defend Matty with salvos of words and hot rejoinders, although, in the clinching two-day debate, only four rose to battle for him. Against the absent Van Buren, three thousand miles away in London, the "conspirators" had brought up an unprecedented array of talent. The dozen set speeches from as many Senators was double the number of those who spoke against Warren Hastings at his celebrated impeachment trial in the House of Lords.

The implacable Calhoun had labored diligently for this retribution. It was really his show. Resentment against the Red Fox burned deep in his soul. Two years ago he had taken his seat on the rostrum of the Senate, acclaimed as the acknowledged successor of Andrew Jackson and dreaming of the day when he would take the sceptre and give the South, his beloved South, its place in the sun and its rights as he interpreted them under the Constitution. Now the prize had slipped from his grasp.

Van Buren's death march began on January 24th when Senator William L. Marcy of New York moved that the Senate resume consideration of the appointment which had been tabled ten days before by the casting vote of Vice President Calhoun.

The attack on Van Buren was nicely arranged. He would be arraigned on all four counts of the "indictment." Clay and his particular confederates would aim at the pusillanimous instructions Van Buren, as Secretary of State, had given to Minister Allen McLane. Webster would level his cannon at the unAmerican, unpatriotic, almost treasonable, character of these instructions. Calhoun, speaking through his man Friday, Senator Robert Hayne, would attack Van Buren's nefarious conduct in creating discord between Jackson and Calhoun. Lesser lights would rake Van Buren for introducing the New York spoils system into the Federal government.

Senator Holmes set the pace:

"Yes, sir, the honor and dignity of the nation has—the heretofore unsullied diplomatic character of the American Republic has been stained, its lofty pride has been humiliated—unnecessarily, wantonly humbled—by the man who is now proposed as its guardian, and protector, and advocate, and, as an American Senator, I am not content barely to put upon him the seal of reprobation in a secret session of this body. No, sir, let the American Government, let the American people, proud of their national honor, know that no ruthless hand shall desecrate it with impunity; and let foreign nations and all the world know that even an American Secretary of State dare not pollute its ermine."

Next came the Kentucky charmer, Henry Clay, at his very best. There was grace in his tall form, grace and power in his flowing words. Once chief of the War Hawks, the very idea of submitting to Britain on anything—as Van Buren had supposedly told Minister McLane to do—was anathema to Clay. Van Buren had sullied the national honor. He must be punished. He was not worthy to represent the United States anywhere.

"On our side, according to Mr. Van Buren, all was wrong; on the British side, all was right. We brought forward nothing but claims and pretensions. And Mr. McLane was commanded to avail himself of all the circumstances in his power to mitigate our offence, and to dissuade the British government from allowing their feelings, justly incurred by the past conduct of the party driven from power, to have an adverse influence towards the American party now in power. Sir, was this becoming language from one independent nation to another? Was it proper in the mouth of an American Minister? Was it in conformity with the high, unsullied and dignified character of our previous diplomacy? Was it not, on the contrary, the language of an humble vassal to a proud and haughty lord? Was it not prostrating and degrading the American eagle before the British lion?"

Ponderously Senator Webster rose to fulminate at Van Buren's lack of public devotion. In instructing McLane, Van Buren had told him to tell the British that a new administration had come in power. Webster took as his text Van Buren's actual words to McLane: "I will add nothing to the impropriety of any feelings that find their origin in the past pretensions of this government to have an adverse influence upon the present conduct of Great Britain." Quoting this, Webster took off on a thunderous flight:

"Sir, I submit to you, and to the candor of all just men, if I am not right in saying that the pervading topic, through the whole, is not American rights, not American interests, not American defence, but denunciation of past pretentions of our own country, reflections on the past administration, and exultation and a loud claim of merit for the administration now in power.

"Sir, I would forgive mistakes; I would pardon the want of information; I would pardon almost anything where I saw true patriotism and sound American feeling; but I cannot forgive the sacrifice of this feeling to mere party.

". . . And, sir, however unimportant may be the opinion of so humble an individual as myself, I now only wish that I might be heard by every independent freeman in the United States, by the British minister, and the British King, and by every minister and every crowned head in Europe, while, standing here in my place, I pronounce my rebuke, as solemnly and as decisively as I can, upon the first instance in which an American minister has been sent abroad as the representative of his party, and not as the representative of his country."

Elegant, powerful Senator Hayne arose. Calhoun was his idol. He had hoped to see Calhoun step from the Senate rostrum into the White House and he reviled the Red Fox who had outmaneuvered the eminent South Carolinian:

"I have arrived at the following conclusion: that when Mr. Van Buren came into the Cabinet he found a state of circumstances here that opened a door to the establishment of an influence favorable to his own personal views; that, instead of exerting himself to remove the causes of discord and dissension by which the executive was unhappily surrounded, he dexterously availed himself of them, and wielded them for the promotion of his own personal and political interests, and for the advancement of his friends and supporters to office, to the exclusion of almost all others.

"I firmly believe, sir, that he determined to break up the Cabinet, by withdrawing himself, and driving his colleagues from their stations; taking care, however, to provide a safe retreat for himself in this mission to England."

Although he did not know it, Hayne had hit the nail on the head. History was to prove he had guessed the secret known then only to the Little Magician himself.

Now it was fast-shooting Senator Poindexter of Mississippi, who boldly paraded the Peggy Eaton affair before his colleagues: Van Buren had engineered the cabinet meeting at which President Jackson had applied his verbal whitewash, "She is as chaste as a virgin" to the luscious Bellona. For this Van Buren must go.

Miller of South Carolina, another Calhoun ally, took up the strain to say that Van Buren had confessed to friends in New York that the dissolution of the cabinet was the result of a conspiracy between Calhoun and Secretary of the Treasury Ingham "to exclude a virtuous woman from society." Loudly the Senator proclaimed his "determination to hold anyone as criminal, who boldly, and openly, and indecently invades public sentiment and public morals. As the guardians of female character we must sustain the majesty and supremacy of female virtue. For my part I am ready to put the seal of condemnation on him who shall attempt, knowingly, to narrow down the distance in society which separates the suspected from the modest woman," which was the Senator's way of interpreting Van Buren's effort to elevate Peggy to the social front rank.

The attack was carefully cued as the "conspirators" rose to horsewhip Van Buren. Hawklike, Calhoun followed every word. When vigorous Senator Forsyth of Georgia lashed out at the Calhoun-controlled press for their attacks on Van Buren, the Vice-President gave way to the pressure from within. He broke in sharply.

"Does the Senator from Georgia allude to the present occupant of the chair?" he inquired.

"By what authority, sir, do you ask that question?" demanded Forsyth, challenging the Vice-President's right to speak at all.

"The allusion appeared so direct I felt I had a right to ask the question."

"I deny the right," thundered Forsyth. He paused. His gaze roved the Senate chamber. "And if it is considered a question of order, I appeal to the judgment of the Senate."

There was silence. Even the conspirators recognized that the Vice-President had breached the rules of the Senate and violated his Constitutional prerogative as presiding officer.

Awed by the Senate's silent response to Forsyth's appeal, Calhoun retreated with a Parthian shot. "If the allusion was directed at me, there is no foundation for it."

Next, there came to Van Buren's support a fellow New Yorker, Senator William L. Marcy, who carried the fight for the nomination. In this bitter debate Marcy introduced the historic doctrine which has since echoed on every political wind that blows. Marcy's rendering of the old Brennic cry, *"Vae Victis,"* Woe to the Conquered, were the only words of this virulent debate which attained immortality.

With considerable spirit Marcy denied the charge that Van Buren had intrigued against Jackson to advance his own

political interests but, in expiation of the accusation that
Van Buren had introduced political proscription in the Federal government, Marcy made a bland admission which has
become a household saying and which has forever attached
Andrew Jackson's name to the spoils system:

"I know, sir, that it is the habit of some gentlemen to talk with
censure or reproach of the politics of New York. Like other States,
we have contests, and, as a necessary consequence, triumphs and
defeats.

"It may be, sir, that the politicians of the United States are not
so fastidious as some gentlemen are, as to disclosing the principles
on which they act. They boldly preach what they practice. When they
are contending for victory they avow their intention of enjoying the
fruits of it. If they are defeated, they expect to retire from office. If
they are successful, they claim, as a matter of right, the advantages of
success. They see nothing wrong in the rule, that to the victor belong
the spoils of the enemy."

The case was in, before the highest jury in the land. When
the veil of secrecy was lifted from the Senate proceedings,
the American people would gaze in horror on Martin Van
Buren, traitor, villain and general all-out political scamp!

The Senate timepiece pointed to four o'clock of January
25th, 1832. The question before the Senate was now read
again: "Will the Senate advise and consent to the nomination of Martin Van Buren of New York to be Envoy Extraordinary and Minister Plenipotentiary of the United States
at the court of the United Kingdom of Great Britain and
Ireland?"

Slowly the yeas and nays were called, forty-six of them.
Not a Senator had left his seat. Vice-President Calhoun
could be seen jotting down each vote as it was called. Webster's booming nay seemed to shake the chamber walls.
There was no mistaking how he felt. The minutes dragged.
The roll call was finished and the clerk handed the paper
tally up to the Vice-President.

"The vote on the question is tied, 23 Nays, 23 Yeas," announced Calhoun in a graveyard voice hardly audible on the outer edge of the rows of Senators.

Calhoun's great moment had come. His casting vote would decide the issue. He had yearned for this. He had helped arrange it. Here it was. Triumph at last over the man who had defrauded him of his succession to the Presidency. Forty-six pairs of eyes were fixed on him. All knew the satisfaction which at the moment flooded his gaunt frame as, pale with emotion, the blood drained from his face, he rose and descended the half-dozen steps from the rostrum to the Senate floor. He paused before the rostrum and faced his colleagues. An eyewitness said there was a "barbaric leer" in his eyes.

"On the question of the nomination of Martin Van Buren, hair votes Nay!"

eed was done! Van Buren was a political corpse. As urned to ascend the rostrum he could not restrain on. To a Senator friend he shot a historic aside, him, sir, kill him dead. He will never kick, sir,

litical-wise Senator Benton of Missouri, over- ark, thought differently. To Alabama's Sena- had voted against Van Buren, Benton ked, "You have broken a Minister and elected t."

sked Moore.

will see nothing in it but a combination of competitor," said Benton. "They will pull and set Van Buren up."

" exclaimed Moore, who only twenty minutes red the last of the prearranged blasts at the uren. "Why didn't you tell me that before uld have voted the other way."

ate. The Great Triumvirate had created martyr, who would soon usurp the very chair occupied by the arch-executioner Calhoun and would later follow Andrew Jackson into the White House. Clay, Calhoun & Co. did not then realize that the Red Fox was the most willing martyr the world has ever known. Nor were they aware that being a martyr was part of his plan to promote himself to the great office which he called "the Ultima Thule of political life."

How did the illustrious trio arrange the tie so that Calhoun could exact his pound of Van Buren's flesh with such nicety? In his *Thirty Years' View* Senator Thomas Hart Benton explains it this way:

"How those tie-votes, for there were two of them, came to happen twice, 'hand-running,' and in a case so important, was a matter of marvel and speculation to the public on the outside of the locked-u֊ senatorial doors. It was no marvel to those on the inside, who how it was done. The combination had a superfluity of votes, Mr. Van Buren's friends were every one known, and woul᷍ it required the superfluous votes on one side to go out; a equilibrium between the two lines was established. When ished the injunction of secrecy was taken off the pro᷍ the dozen set speeches delivered in secret session i᷍ lished—which shows that they were delivered for eff᷍ Senate, but upon the public mind."

On the evening of the day the news of Va᷍ tion reached London, the Little Magician, f᷍ in the best Pall Mall tailoring, was lionized a᷍ at the home of Prince Talleyrand, French ᷍ British court. Distinguished attentions were ᷍ What pleased him most was the wise and p᷍ tion of Lord Auckland, "It is an advantage ᷍ to be the subject of an outrage."

So it would seem. Van Buren came home t᷍ successively Vice-President and President, wh᷍ Triumvirate, Calhoun, Clay and Webster, w᷍ ately sought to be President, none ever ᷍ ished goal.

Once when the Little Magician strolled off the rostrum to avoid casting a vote on a tied question, Calhoun leaped up "eagerly and loudly," calling for the Sergeant-at-Arms to overhaul Matty and drag him back into the chamber by force. Daily, the Great Triumvirate and their allies invoked every parliamentary trick or indignity they could think of to harry the presiding officer and make his task more difficult and embarrassing, even to staging commotions in the gallery among the spectators.

If Van Buren felt these barbs, his demeanor failed to reveal it. Suave, unruffled, and apparently undismayed, he lounged back in his comfortable chair, twiddling his mallet and refusing to lose his temper at even the most annoying rebuff. His placid, bland countenance was wreathed in perpetual smiles. It would seem as if he enjoyed being the target of the butts of Clay, Calhoun & Co.

Reporter Ben Perley Poore jotted down this on-the-spot description of the scene: "He (Van Buren) received the fusillade of snubs and sneers as the ghost of Creusa received the embraces of Aeneas—he heeded them not. He leaned back his head, threw one leg over the other and sat as if he were a pleasant sculptured image, destined for that niche for life."

To the observant British visitor, Harriet Martineau, who watched these turbulent scenes from the gallery, "The American Senate is a most imposing assemblage" where sat "the cast-iron Man, Mr. Calhoun, who looks as if he had never been born and never could be extinguished. . . . Mr. Calhoun's countenance first fixed my attention; the splendid eye, straight forehead, the inflexible mouth . . . one of the most remarkable heads in the country—his colleague, Mr. Preston, in singular contrast, stout in person, with a round, ruddy, good-humored face, large blue eyes and a wig, orange today, brown yesterday and golden tomorrow—the transcendant Webster, with his square forehead and cavernous eyes—the homely Clay, with his face and figure of a farmer, but something of the air of a divine, from his hair being combed straight back from his temples—then there was the bright bonhommie of Ewing of Ohio, the most primitive looking of the Senators; the benign, religious gravity of Frelinghuysen—the gentlemanly air of Buchanan—the shrewdness of Poindexter—near them sat Colonel Benton, a temporary people's man, remarkable for his pomposity . . . swelling among his piles of papers and books, looking like a being destined by nature to be a good-humored barber or innkeeper but forced by fate to make himself into a mock-heroic Senator . . ." As for the Vice-President Miss Martineau said "he yawned ostentatiously."

She should have added that Senator Thomas Hart Benton of Missouri, "Old Bullion," was the "fiercest tiger in the Senate." Leader of Jackson's battles in the upper house, he was a poseur, but an implacable foeman, vain but valiant. Daily, for the edification of the gallery, he strutted the Senate aisles, a stalwart, eye-filling figure, clad in a long double-breasted bright blue coat with a huge rolling collar. With a roar he would plunge into a parliamentary battle-royal like a free-swinging prizefighter. Fearlessly, he took on Clay or Calhoun or Webster or all three at once, if need be.

To make the scene complete, the British lady might have mentioned the "supers" in this great Jacksonian drama, the little Senate pageboys who, clad in Etonesque collars and plumcolored jackets, dashed in and out of the hectic scenes —"the rushing, dancing, little Pucks," as Charles Dickens called them—scurrying hither and yon, filling snuffboxes, keeping the sand-dusters filled with blotting sand, sharpening goosequills, running a thousand and one errands through the dark Capitol corridors. She might have noticed, too, the blind adoration these scampering young fellows gave Senator John Calhoun because, as one of them told James Parton, he was "as polite to a page as to the President of the Senate and as considerate of their feelings." Perhaps, the pages failed to notice that Calhoun was anything but polite to the President of the Senate.

In 1834 Jackson's war on the Bank of the United States was at its zenith. Repercussions of this tussle were shaking the very desks on Capitol Hill. Having beaten the "Bank Monster" to its knees, Jackson had proceeded to drain its lifeblood by removing the government deposits from that institution and putting them into smaller state banks which his enemies nicknamed "Pet Banks."

One day in January, 1832, a Philadelphia surgeon came to the White House, took out his scalpel and proceeded to extract an old dueling bullet from the President's left shoulder. This missile was fired by Jesse Benton, brother of the great Senator from Missouri, back in 1813 during a four-way fracas between the Benton brothers and Old Hickory and his friend, John Coffee. Baring his shoulder and taking a grip on his walking stick, Jackson told the surgeon to start probing for the bullet, which had troubled him periodically. The operation over, Jackson summoned a messenger and dispatched the leaden souvenir to Senator Benton on Capitol Hill. But Benton politely declined the token and sent it back to Jackson who, he said, "had acquired a clear title to it in common law by twenty years' peaceable possession."

Oddly enough, when the bullet was delivered at the Senate chamber, it found Benton engaged in the opening skirmish of Jackson's war on the Bank of the United States.

This institution was semi-governmental. It had twenty-seven branches. In a sense it was the Reconstruction Finance Corporation of its day. It was the sole depository of government funds on which it paid no interest. The government's average monthly balance was seven million dollars, a large figure for that time, making the bank the nation's leading financial institution. Enjoying many special blessings not accorded other banks, it was really a "privileged corporation," with a monopoly of the nation's banking business, and it was through this weak spot in its armor that Andrew Jackson attacked and destroyed it.

Presiding over the bank in a Greek-temple architectural masterpiece at Philadelphia was suave, alert Nicholas Biddle, who had a flair for literary expression and propaganda. Biddle actually controlled credit in the United States. By increasing or diminishing loans he could make money abundant or scarce, business good or bad. The bank's shortcomings were many, but it had served usefully by financing business, promoting industry, and stabilizing currency.

Next to Andrew Jackson, in 1832, Biddle was the most powerful man in America. He once boasted, "In half an hour I can remove all the constitutional scruples in the District of Columbia" by distributing "half a dozen Presidencies, a dozen Cashierships, fifty clerkships and one hundred Directorships, to my worthy friends who have no character and no money."

The Bank of the United States, chartered in 1816, had seven years to run when Jackson became President. Old Hickory sincerely believed the bank was corrupt or, at least, corrupting to government, although certain of his charges were fantastic. His cabinet was divided on the wisdom of attacking the bank. Jackson wanted a government-owned bank, an arm of the Treasury, with no lending power. Up to 1832 he had contented himself with sniping at the bank, which he felt had used its money and influence against him in the 1828 election.

At Jackson's behest, the House of Representatives appointed a committee to investigate its affairs. The disclosures of this committee lit up the political sky by revealing that large loans had been made to members of Congress and others in positions of power on unsecured notes. In 1830, the bank's outstanding loans to fifty-nine lawmakers totalled $192,000; in 1831, $322,000 to fifty-nine lawmakers; in 1832, $478,000 to forty-four. Senator Daniel Webster dipped in the bank's till for $32,000, in addition to receiving a hand-

some retainer. Henry Clay was on the payroll for years.
The chairman of the House Ways and Means Committee
enjoyed an accommodation of $100,000; John Calhoun's
son-in-law borrowed $20,000; the Chief Clerk of the Treas-
ury had a yearly gratuity; and there were numerous others.
The bank often advanced Congressmen and other officials
their entire year's salaries at no interest. It had a long list
of most-favored government officials, editors, journalists,
and even a college president.

The majority report, studded with such shocking disclosures, called the bank "a monster of corruption." A minority
report, prepared by the bank's subsidized friends, declared
just the opposite.

1832 was an election year. Henry Clay, the bank's best
friend on Capitol Hill, was the National Republicans' nominee for the Presidency. Needing an election issue, he decided that rechartering the bank was one on which Old
Hickory could well hang himself. The bank's charter still
had four years to run. Clay felt certain of the votes to pass
such a bill. If Jackson signed it, he would reverse his previous stand and alienate many supporters; if he vetoed it,
he would lose the support of Pennsylvania, a Jackson strong-
hold, where the bank was powerful and popular.

By concert, no doubt, at this time in January of 1832,
Nicholas Biddle, president of the bank, memorialized Congress for recharter of the bank. Clay quickly introduced a
bill for this purpose and the war was on. Jackson romped
to battle. Thus was the bank injected as the leading campaign issue in the race between Clay and Jackson for the
Chief Executiveship.

On July 3rd, 1832, the rechartering bill was driven through
the Senate and the House of Representatives. Biddle himself had come to Washington and set up headquarters in a
committee room where he could personally take command
of the fight on the Senate floor. He openly announced he
was ready to barter loans for votes. Roger B. Taney, later

Chief Justice of the Supreme Court, once said that Biddle
lent twenty thousand dollars to a Representative who
changed his vote from nay to yea on the rechartering bill.

On July 10th Jackson hurled the bill back at Congress
with a flaming veto, one of the most vigorous ever written
by a President. Try as they might, Clay and his friends
were unable to override the veto in which Old Hickory
summed up his objections to the bank in a single word:
monopoly.

Clay and Biddle were jubilant over the veto message.
They felt it would cost Jackson the election. Biddle exulted:
"It has all the fury of a chained panther, biting the bars of
his cage. It is really a manifesto of anarchy." Gleefully, the
bank distributed thousands of copies of the message which,
to Biddle's amazement, turned into as many boomerangs.
Overnight Jackson became the champion of the downtrod-
den against the forces of monopoly. The masses believed
him when he called the bank a "monster" and reelected him
overwhelmingly in November.

Interpreting his election as a mandate to destroy the bank,
Jackson ordered Secretary of the Treasury McLane to remove the government deposits and re-deposit them in good
state banks. McLane demurred. Jackson changed Treasury
heads twice before finding one, Roger B. Taney, willing to
carry out his instructions.

Biddle fought back. His weapon was contraction of credit
in the nation. The bank war became personal: Jackson
versus Biddle, who yelled: "This worthy President thinks
because he has scalped Indians and imprisoned judges he
can have his own way with the bank. He is mistaken."

Shortening of credit brought on a mild panic, an artificial
depression which threw thousands out of work. Business
languished. Congress was engulfed in bitter partisan disputes
on the wisdom of removing the government funds from the
bank. Distress spread like a galloping plague. Stock values
melted, money became scarce. Biddle's propaganda machine

flooded Congress and the White House with wild protests.

"Damn your old soul," wrote an enraged Ohio Whig to Jackson, "remove them deposits back again, and recharter the bank, or you will certainly be shot in less than two weeks and that by myself."

Jackson was immovable. "Go to the Monster, go to Nicholas Biddle," he roared back. "I will not bow down to the golden calf."

Propaganda broke in waves over the adamant old gentleman in the White House. A congressional delegation came to warn him that a "Baltimore mob" planned to lay siege to the Capitol until the deposits were restored. Jackson sputtered: "I will be glad to see this mob on Capitol Hill. By the Eternal, I will hang the leaders as high as Haman to deter forever all attempts to control Congress by intimidation."

On went the fight; the recriminations continued unabated. Meanwhile, the Whigs emerged as a political coalition. Chief luminaries of the "party" were Clay, Calhoun, and Webster. Product of hatreds, jealousies, and ambitions, it was a strange grouping to which Clay brought his National Republicans, Webster his followers, and Calhoun his Nullifiers. Everybody had an axe to grind and to one purpose: lopping off the political head of "King Andrew I." Dominating this odd alliance of factions—as they did the Senate—was the Great Triumvirate. All three had Presidential aspirations, but Clay felt the prize really belonged to him, if ever they could get past the Jackson hurdle.

On December 26th, 1833, Henry Clay introduced in the Senate a historic resolution censuring President Jackson for removing the deposits from the Bank of the United States. The castigating words of this Resolution brought on a storm:

"Resolved, that by dismissing the late Secretary of the Treasury because he would not, contrary to his sense of duty, remove the money of the United States in deposit with the Bank of the United

States and its branches, in conformity with the President's opinion, and by appointing his successor to effect such removal, which has been done, the President has assumed the exercise of a power over the Treasury of the United States not granted to him by the Constitution and laws, and dangerous to the liberties of the people."

Clay supported his resolution in a three-day, slashing speech. Before a tense Senate and galleries overflowing with excited spectators, Clay smote Jackson furiously. Clay's condemnation has seldom been surpassed in the history of Congress. Clay charged Jackson with seizing the public purse much as "Julius Caesar had seized the public treasury of Rome." It was an act of "open, palpable, and daring usurpation."

When Clay's words were brought to the White House that evening, Old Hickory blew up: "If I live to get these robes of office off me, I will bring this rascal, Henry Clay, to a dear account."

The fight on Clay's Resolution ran for three months, the longest single debate since the government was launched in 1789.

On March 7th, 1834, Vice-President Van Buren rolled up to the Capitol in his gorgeous English coach. Debonair, polished, and apparently pleased with himself and the world, the Little Magician mounted the Senate rostrum and rapped for order.

The Millboy of the Slashes rose at once to present a memorial from a group of Philadelphia mechanics imploring the President to restore the deposits to the bank and thus relieve the nation's economic distress. These memorials were part of the bank's high-pressure propaganda campaign. Congress was flooded with them.

As Clay warmed to his task, tears ran down his cheeks. His voice quavered with emotion as he pictured the miseries of the nation. Clay was past master of this sort of business. He was never better than when pouring out pathos. Ladies in the gallery sobbed into their handkerchiefs. Men sniffled. Even Webster bent his head over his desk and wept.

Leaving his desk, Clay advanced to the foot of the rostrum and addressed his lachrymose appeal directly to Vice-President Van Buren, who was apparently drinking in Clay's words. Matty's admiration for the Kentuckian's eloquence was sincere, although the two men seldom saw eye to eye politically. The more doleful Clay waxed, the more eagerly Van Buren appeared to drink in his words. Point-blank, Clay tearfully implored Van Buren to intercede with the President and rescue the people from their anguish. Apostrophizing Van Buren, Clay inundated the rostrum with his supplications:

"No one, sir, can perform that duty better than you. You can, if you will, induce him to change his course . . . I make this appeal.

"Go to him and tell him, without exaggeration, but in the language of truth and sincerity, the actual condition of his bleeding country.

"Depict to him, if you can find language to portray the heartrending wretchedness of thousands of the working classes out of employment.

"Tell him of the tears of helpless widows, no longer able to earn their bread, of unclad and unfed orphans . . .

"Tell him he has been abused, deceived, betrayed by the wicked counsel of unprincipled men around him . . .

"Tell him that in his bosom alone, under actual circumstances, does the power reside to relieve the country; and that unless he opens it to conviction, and corrects the errors of his administration, no human imagination can conceive, no human tongue can express the awful consequences that may follow. . . .

"Tell him to guard against an odious comparison with that worst of Roman emperors who, contemplating with indifference the conflagration of the mistress of the world, regaled himself during the terrific scene in the throng of his dancing courtiers. . . .

"Entreat him to pause and reflect that there is a point beyond which human endurance cannot go, and let him not drive this brave, generous, and patriotic people to madness and despair."

It was terrific, splendid, fascinating oratory, Clay's level best, punctuated with every amazing gesture in his repertory. Exhausted, Clay all but fell into his seat. A deep, dramatic hush fell over the Senate. Every eye was focused on the Vice-President. It was incumbent on him to say something, but whatever he said could only be anticlimactic.

Somehow the Red Fox knew something was "up." He must pull a masterpiece out of his hat, if he could, and quickly too. He decided to act, not to speak. Laying aside his gavel, he beckoned a Jacksonian Senator to take the chair. Rising, he descended with stately tread to the floor. He was going to speak! Webster and Calhoun exchanged elated glances. Matty had fallen into the trap! They would tear him to pieces for anything he said.

Yet, instead of veering about to address the chair, Van Buren, to the utter amazement and confusion of Clay *et al*, stalked slowly up the Senate aisle, a veritable fashion parade in his Pall Mall tailoring, and paused beside the drooping Clay.

"Senator Clay," he said nonchalantly, "may I borrow a pinch of your fine Martinique snuff."

It was annihilating. The frustrated Clay fumblingly offered his snuffbox to Van Buren, who took a pinch of the rose-scented powder, inhaled it deeply, and walked serenely out of the chamber. Van Buren had pulled the very carpet from under Clay's tragic, appealing admonition. It was a triumph only Matty could have thought up. A titter ran through the gallery as he vanished.

On the night of March 28th, 1834, by a vote of twenty-six to twenty, Messrs. Clay, Calhoun, and Webster steamrollered the resolution of condemnation through the Senate. Debate had abbreviated it to:

"Resolved, that the President, in the executive proceedings in relation to the public revenue, has assumed upon himself authority and power not conferred by the Constitution and laws, but in derogation of both."

Clay, Calhoun & Co. had a triumph over Jackson at last. They would complete it on the spot. In silence the Secretary of the Senate brought the *Journal* into the chamber. On the proper page the Secretary wrote the stinging words of the Resolution and Andrew Jackson went into history as the first President to be rebuked publicly by a vote of the United States Senate.

As the goose quill scratched across the *Journal* page, Senator Benton rose to avow that he would one day wipe the slur on Jackson from the official record of the Senate of the Twenty-third Congress.

Angry to his marrow, Old Hickory threw back a fiery protest, declaring that the resolution was tantamount to impeachment. "Without notice, unheard and untried," he shouted, "I thus find myself charged on the records of the Senate, and in a form hitherto unknown in our country, with the high crime of violating the laws and Constitution of my country."

January, 1837. The scepter was passing. In his upstairs study in the White House a gaunt, scarred-face old warrior was counting the days till March 4th when he could lay aside the burdens of state and head back to Tennessee—and the Hermitage. Andrew Jackson's eight-year reign was closing.

On Capitol Hill the last Jackson battle was raging. It was a sullen, dogged fight. Overhead the great chandelier shone down on a crowded, embattled Senate chamber. Grim, determined, interminably vocal, Senator Benton was forcing the fight to erase from the official record Henry Clay's historic resolution censuring Jackson for removal of the deposits. Session after session, Benton had sought to redeem his irrevocable vow to prosecute deletion of the offending resolution until he had succeeded.

By 1835 five state legislatures had instructed their Senators "to use their untiring efforts to cause to be expunged from the *Journal* of the Senate the Resolve condemnatory of President Jackson." It was a burning political issue. By 1837, as Jackson made ready to retire from office, a majority of the states had "revealed the public voice and in an imperative form." Jackson's popularity had given him a majority in the Senate, and Benton cracked the political whip mercilessly. Clay, Calhoun, and Webster read the handwriting on the wall, but they determined to fight off the inevitable to the last ditch.

On December 26th, 1836—the third anniversary of the day on which Senator Clay had moved his resolution of censure—Benton, for the fourth and last time, introduced his long-familiar resolve that would clear the Senate record and let Old Hickory go home publicly vindicated. The Great Triumvirate had already offered compromises which Benton had refused. One word only would satisfy him: "Expunge," not "Rescind," or "Abrogate," or anything less. To blot out the deed, the obnoxious Resolution must be physically expunged, actually obliterated. Clay decided to meet Benton head on, to oppose his motion by filibuster, "consumption of time, delay and adjournment."

In his deep, booming voice Benton opened the fight with this resolution, preceded, of course, by various whereases:

"Resolved, That the said Resolve be expunged from the Journal; and, for that purpose, that the Secretary of the Senate, at such time as the Senate may appoint, shall bring the manuscript *Journal* of the session of 1833-34 into the Senate, and, in the presence of the Senate, draw black lines round the said Resolve, and write across the face thereof, in strong letters, the following words: 'Expunged by order of the Senate, this . . . day of . . . . . in the year of our Lord, 1837.'"

It was tabled, but on January 12th, 1837, Benton called it up. Feelings ran high. Presiding over this momentous setting was not Vice-President and President-elect Van Buren, but

Senator King of Alabama. King, acting President of the Senate, had felt Benton's party lash and had fallen in behind the Benton Resolution which he first opposed.

"And now, sir," roared Benton, "I finish the task which three years ago I imposed on myself. Solitary and alone, and amidst the jeers and taunts of my opponents, I put this ball in motion. The people have taken it up, and rolled it forward, and I am no longer anything but a unit in the vast mass which now propels it. In the name of the mass I speak. I demand the execution of the edict of the people; I demand expurgation of that sentence which the voice of a few Senators and the power of this confederate, the Bank of the United States, has caused to be placed on the *Journal* of the Senate; and which the voice of millions of freemen has ordered to be expunged from it."

To Benton, Senator Preston of South Carolina cried back: "It is not in the power of your black lines to touch us. Remove us. Turn us out. Expel us from the Senate. Would to God you could. Call in the praetorian guard. Take us, apprehend us. March us off!"

Marshalled by Benton, the impassioned expurgators rose to demand that the "polluted page" be stricken from the Senate *Journal*. All day and far into the next night the debate ran on with increasing violence. Twilight was falling on Friday, January 13th when gaunt, stubborn, sallow-faced John Calhoun took the floor. All day he had sat silent, watching, listening, gloomy. In the dimness of the chamber he looked unearthly. His short, incisive, compact sentences began slicing through the gloom like red-hot knives.

Sweeping the darkening Senate chamber with his flashing, sunken eyes, he excoriated his colleagues who had yielded to Benton's goad:

"Sir, there are some questions so plain that they cannot be argued; nothing can make them more plain; and this is one. No one not blinded by party zeal can possibly be insensible that the measure proposed is a violation of the Constitution. I know perfectly well that gentlemen have no liberty to vote otherwise than they will. They are coerced by an exterior power. They try, indeed, to comfort their consciences by saying that it is the voice of the people. It is no such thing.

"We all know how these legislative returns have been obtained. It is by dictation from the White House. The voice of the PEOPLE! I see before me Senators who could not swallow that Resolution when it was first introduced: has it changed its nature since? Not at all. But executive power has interposed. Talk to me about the voice of the people! It is the combination of patronage and power which coerces this body to a palpable violation of the Constitution.

"But why do I waste my breath? I know that is all utterly vain. The day is gone; night approaches, and night is suitable to the dark deed meditated. The act must be performed; and it is an act which will tell on the political history of this country forever. The act originates in pure, unmixed, personal idolatry. It is the melancholy evidence of a broken spirit, ready to bow down at the feet of power. The removal of the deposits was an act such as might have been perpetrated in the days of Pompey and Caesar, but an act like this could never have been consummated by a Roman Senate until the times of Caligula and Nero."

On that bitter note the Senate adjourned to Monday, January 16th. Fearing defections in the Democratic ranks, Senator Benton on Saturday night played host to the administration Senators at Boulanger's famous restaurant on G Street. Of this historic, gastronomic get-together Benton said:

"Saturday, the 14th of January, the Democratic Senators agreed to have a meeting, and to take their final measures for passing the expunging resolution. They knew they had the numbers; but they also knew that they had adversaries to grapple with to whom might be applied the proud motto of Louis the Fourteenth—'Not an unequal match for numbers.' They also knew that members of the party were in process of separating from it and would require conciliating. They met in the night at the then-famous restaurant of Boulanger, giving to the assemblage the air of convivial entertainment.

"There were serious differences upon the mode of expurgation, while agreed upon the thing; and finally, obliteration, the favorite of the mover, was given up; and the mode of expurgation adopted which had been proposed in the resolutions of the General Assembly of Virginia, namely, to inclose the obnoxious sentence in a square of black lines—an oblong square; a compromise of opinions to which the mover agreed upon condition of being allowed to compose the epitaph, 'Expunged by order of the Senate.'"

At noon on Monday, January 16th, the galleries were densely packed. Clay and Webster had agreed to hold their fires until the lesser figures had volleyed, but to drag out the affair for hours on end, if need be—anything to stave off a final vote. The scene was grand, impressive, solemn, bitterly contested every word of the way. Forty-three Senators held their seats as if bolted to them.

In the late afternoon Henry Clay took the floor. A nervous bustle ran through the chamber. Mover of the original hated resolution, he would stand by it till the last shot was fired. Never was he grander, more indomitably defiant, as he poured out his wrath and grief. Benton himself admitted "Clay was grand and affecting":

"I put it to the calm and deliberate consideration of the majority if they are ready to pronounce for all time that, whoever may be President, the Senate shall not dare to remonstrate against any Executive usurpation whatever. For one, I will not.

"In one hand he [the President] holds the purse and in the other brandishes the sword. He has swept over the government during the last eight years like a tropical tornado. What object of his ambition is unsatisfied? When disabled from age any longer to hold the scepter of power, he designates his successor, and transmits it to his favorite.

"What more does he want? Must we blot, deface and mutilate the records of the country to punish the presumptuousness of expressing an opinion contrary to his own? Is it your design to stigmatize us? You cannot.

"Black lines! Black lines! Sir, let the Secretary preserve the pen with which he may inscribe them. And hereafter, when we shall lose the form of our free institution, some future monarch, in gratitude to those by whose means he has been enabled upon the ruins of civil liberty to erect a throne, and to commemorate this expunging resolution, may institute a new order of knighthood, under the appropriate name of THE KNIGHTS OF THE BLACK LINES.

"But why should I detain the Senate? The decree has gone forth. The deed is to be done—that foul deed, which, like the blood-stained hands of the guilty Macbeth, all the ocean's waters will never wash out. Proceed, then, with the noble work which lies before you. And when you have perpetrated it, go home to the people and tell them what glorious honors you have achieved for our common country!"

However, the expungers, in full force and "masters of the chamber," held on doggedly against the talent and eloquence arrayed against them. Benton's strategy was to let the Clay-Calhoun-Webster filibuster run on endlessly, but to keep the Senate in continuous session until the delaying action faltered. When it came, he would crack the party whip for the finale. Since four o'clock a nearby committee room had bulged with the finest, tastiest viands which Boulanger could provide—turkey, ham, beef, wine, cakes, and coffee—supplied by Benton, who determined that hunger should cost him no absentees.

The afternoon waned and night came on. Above the dramatic scene the massive chandelier burned with a hundred candles. Clay, Calhoun, and Webster knew the inevitable was at hand, "that the damnable deed was to be done that night."

"The night was wearing away: the expungers were in full force—masters of the chamber—happy and visibly determined to remain. It became evident to the opposition leaders that the inevitable hour had come: that the damnable deed was to be done that night: and that the dignity of silence was no longer to them a tenable position. The battle was going against them, and they must go into it without being able to re-establish it."

As the Senate clock struck eleven, Daniel Webster's massive frame bulked up from his desk. Webster set the scene and the mood, almost paraphrasing his celebrated summation to the jury which had hanged the Knapp brothers at Salem years before. Midnight, he said, was coming on, a fitting hour for such a deed as the expungers were committing. Webster made, not a speech, but a stately, deep-toned, measured protest against defacing the *Journal* by the Benton Resolution.

"But this resolution is to pass. We expect it. We make up our minds to behold the spectacle which is to ensue. We collect ourselves to look on, while a scene is exhibited which, if we did not regard it as a ruthless violation of a sacred instrument, would appear to us to be little elevated above the character of a contemptible farce. This scene we shall behold; and hundreds of American citizens, as many as may crowd into these lobbies and galleries, will behold it also: with what feelings I do not undertake to say."

Dramatically Benton described what followed:

"Midnight was now approaching. The dense masses which filled every inch of room in the lobbies and galleries remained immovable. No one went out: no one could get in. The floor of the Senate was crammed with privileged persons and it seemed that all Congress was there. Expectation, and determination to see the conclusion, was depicted upon every countenance. It was evident there was to be no adjournment until the vote should be taken—until the deed was done; and this aspect of invincible determination had its effects upon the ranks of the opposition.

"They began to falter under the useless persistence, for they alone now did the speaking; and while Mr. Webster was reciting his protest, two Senators from the opposite side, who had best been able to maintain their equanimity, came round to the author and said, 'This question has degenerated into a trial of nerves and muscles. It has become a question of physical endurance; and we see no sense in wearing ourselves out to keep off for a few hours what has to come before we separate. We see that you are able and determined to carry your measure: so call the vote as soon as you please. We shall say no more.'

"Mr. Webster concluded. No one rose. There was a pause. A dead silence and an intense feeling. Presently the silence was invaded by the single word 'Question'—the parliamentary call for a vote—rising from the seats of different Senators. One blank in the resolve remained to be filled—the date of its adoption. It was done. The acting President of the Senate, Mr. King of Alabama, then directed the roll to be called."

The Expunging Resolution passed, twenty-four to nineteen.

"Nothing remains, sir, but to execute the order of the Senate," said the exultant Benton. "I move that it be done forthwith."

"It is so ordered," said chair.

As if to avoid witnessing the "desecration" of the record, Clay, Calhoun, Webster and their confederates, who had voted against the resolution, filed dramatically from the chamber. Clerk Asbury Dickens now brought in the bulky manuscript *Journal.* Opening to the page on which the condemnatory resolution of March 28, 1834 was written, Dickens drew around it a square of heavy, black lines. Vertically, across the face of the censuring sentence, Dickens, using Benton's own pen, next wrote in bold script these words: "Expunged by order of the Senate, this 16th day of January 1837."

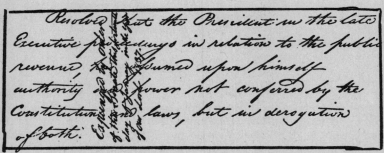

The expunged resolution as it appeared on the Journal of the Senate. This original page of the Journal vanished years ago. Boxed in black lines, the expunging words were written across the face of the original resolution condemning President Jackson for removal of the deposits of the Bank of the United States in 1834. Unobtrusive to gaze on these few lines are reminiscent of one of the fiercest scenes in Senate history.

Hardly had the Secretary finished his expunging task when loud hisses and groans broke from the left of the gallery directly over Benton's head. The presiding officer ordered the galleries cleared, but Benton opposed it:

"I hope the galleries will not be cleared, as many innocent persons will be excluded, who have been guilty of no violation of order. Let the ruffians who have made the disturbance alone be punished: let them be apprehended. I hope the Sergeant-at-Arms will be directed to enter the gallery and seize the ruffians . . . Let them be taken and brought to the bar of the Senate. Here is one just above me, that may easily be identified—the bank ruffians!"

A single spectator was arrested by the Sergeant-at-Arms, brought to the bar of the Senate, and quickly discharged.

Thus, dramatically and in a flurry of bitterness, perished the Senate's rebuke to President Jackson. The original manuscript of the *Journal* of the Senate bearing the Expunging Resolution vanished years ago. In the Library of Congress there is a facsimile of it, the only record left of this tremendous scene in the old Senate chamber.

Two nights later Old Hickory invited the expungers and their wives to a victory dinner at the White House. Too weak to sit long at the table, Jackson came in briefly to express his gratification and to receive from head-expunger Benton the pen the clerk had used in the ceremony of deletion. Pleased and touched, Jackson placed Benton in his chair at the head of the table. With tears in his eyes, the old gentleman withdrew to his sickroom.

It was Jackson's sunset triumph over his political enemies —a tribute to his invincibility and to the unflinching loyalty of Thomas Hart Benton to the man with whom he had once exchanged bullets on the streets of Nashville.

The next day a leading Whig newspaper in Virginia printed the names of the twenty-four expungers in large capital letters, enclosed in a box with heavy black borders. Above the names ran this legend: "The following individuals received from the hands of Martin Van Buren the accolade, on the night of January 16th, 1837, and are received into the order as KNIGHTS OF THE BLACK LINES."

But the outcries of the Whigs made little difference to Old Hickory and less to Old Bullion. The expunging resolution was written where posterity could read the vindication of Andrew Jackson by the United States Senate.

9

MARTIN THE FIRST OCCUPIES THE "PALACE OF THE CAESARS"

In December, 1836, while the electoral votes for the Eighth President were being counted Senator Henry Clay sauntered down to the rostrum to remark with courteous significance, "It is a cloudy day, sir."

"But the sun will shine on the Fourth of March, sir," beamed Vice-President Martin Van Buren, whom the electoral count had just made President-elect.

So it did. The day was glorious. Not a cloud marred the sky as four dappled grays spanked out of the White House driveway, pulling an elegant phaeton made of wood from the frigate *Constitution* and presented to the retiring President by the idolatrous Sons of Tammany.

Seated in the phaeton were two picturesque personalities: Old Hickory risen from a sick bed for the occasion and "Martin the First" to whom he was passing the scepter. As the carriage rolled down Pennsylvania Avenue toward the Capitol, the crowds went wild. There was no mistaking that the boisterous plaudits were meant for the grizzled old soldier now bowing out of the presidency. The wind tossed his whitened locks and tears ran down his cheeks as he raised his hat again and again to cheering admirers.

For many it was an unforgettable scene as Jackson stood on the east portico of the Capitol bestowing the presidency and his parting blessing on his incoming favorite. Sartorially

Van Buren was in rare form, wearing the latest fashion from London. The ailing patriarch's affection for Van Buren was plain to be seen. His cheeks glowed with pleasure as the Little Magician, in his inaugural address, sounded Jackson's praises and promised to walk in the path of his "illustrious predecessor."

Administering the oath to the Eighth and first President not born a British subject was Chief Justice of the United States Roger B. Taney, a Jackson appointee. No sooner had Van Buren kissed the Bible and pledged himself to uphold the Constitution than the ex-President came forward and shook his hand cordially. Then, leaning on his cane, Jackson descended the Capitol steps to his carriage. Instantly the dense crowds in the Capitol plaza broke into thunderous applause and surged forward for a farewell glimpse of the old chieftain. Deeply moved as he watched the scene, Senator Benton exclaimed, "It is the acclaim of posterity!" He was later to say, "For once the rising was eclipsed by the setting sun."

That evening Jackson, much restored to health, attended the inaugural ball at Carusi's. His cup of happiness overflowed. His protégé was in. Van Buren's administration has often been called "Jackson's third term."

In his inaugural address Van Buren had pointed with pride to the achievements of Jackson's two terms. Well enough. The national debt was extinguished. Jackson had paid it off. The Treasury had a surplus. Harvests were good. The nation's goose hung high. Still, speculation was running riot. So, on the surface at least, was prosperity.

In 1839 the Sultan of Morocco sent President Van Buren a lion and lioness whose nightly roars were most alarming to the Philadelphia Navy Yard where they landed. Inasmuch as the Constitution prohibited acceptance of presents from "any King, Prince or Foreign State," this gift posed a ferocious problem whose solution required a joint resolution of Congress authorizing the Chief Executive to receive the royal pair, sell them and deposit the proceeds in the Treasury.

But the roars of the king of beasts and his consort were faint whispers compared to those of the people and press as financial delirium tremens began rocking the nation a few weeks after Van Buren took office. Suddenly the economic structure of the nation came tumbling down on the President's head. "Jackson prosperity" vanished like a bubble in the devastating panic of 1837, first major depression in the long cycle of boom and bust. Van Buren was merely reaping the whirlwind. This crisis, born of the orgy of speculation, was at least hastened by several measures enacted during Jackson's last year in office.

The Distribution Act, apportioning the government's $37,000,000 surplus among the states, touched off a fresh speculative splurge. Then came the "Specie Circular." Alarmed by the amount of doubtful bank paper the government was receiving for public lands, President Jackson had issued his famous "Specie Circular," requiring gold and silver in payment for government lands—"hard money" which was scarce. This acute check on land speculation cast discredit on all bank notes. It was the straw that toppled the tower.

Credit fell, trade vanished, real-estate prices shot up, bankruptcies multiplied, cotton dropped, bread riots broke out in the large cities while landlords demanded rent in gold or silver, "no rag money." Textile mills closed their doors. Thousands were thrown out of work overnight. On May 10th, 1837, every bank in New York City closed its doors. In a fortnight banks in Philadelphia, Baltimore, Boston, New Orleans, and a dozen leading cities suspended payments. The depression gathered momentum, swept the nation. Paper money became worthless. Hard times knocked at thousands of doors.

"Immense fortunes melted away like snows under the April sun," wrote Philip Hone, diarist extraordinary. "Where will it all end? In ruin, revolution, perhaps civil war." Declared Oliver Wendell Holmes, "Society has played out its last stake."

Under the impact of economic disaster the Democratic Party split in two, one faction emerging as the Locofocos, radical leftwingers whose curious name originated in a fight for control between the conservatives and the radicals at a meeting in Tammany Hall, New York: the conservatives had turned off the gaslights to prevent a radical victory whereupon the radicals utilized a new invention, locofoco friction matches, to keep the meeting going. Abolition of banks and monopolies were the chief creed of the Locofocos, who blamed the panic of 1837 on the reckless doings of banks and bankers.

In the White House, Van Buren sat apparently unconcerned, vainly predicting an early return of prosperity while the deluge of misery lapped at the threshold. To many he seemed oblivious of the sad state of the Union, for he busied himself restoring the glories of the mansion and reviving the court life of former occupants. What had been the people's house under Jackson became a sort of palace. New decorations, floral carpets, delicately tinted chinaware and a thousand lovely objects blossomed like flowers in the spring. Jackson's perpetual open house had really left the mansion in a sad state.

Wrote Frederick Marryat, a visiting British literary lion, "A few years ago a fellow would drive his hackney coach up to the door, walk into the saloon in all his dirt and force his way to the President." Now Mr. Van Buren "has prevented mobacracy from intruding itself upon his levees. The police are now stationed at the door to prevent the intrusion of any improper persons."

Van Buren's Saturday-night dinners were models of culinary art set off by sherry, port, brandy, and "Supreme Court" Madeira. The President would name the vintage of each bottle as it made the rounds. "Supreme Court" Madeira had wide renown. It was a special importation of the justices of the high court who would sip it as they discussed the cases before them.

To his lush gatherings Van Buren invited his political brethren as well as his ill-wishers. Amnesty began at the White House portals. Van Buren was not called the "Red Fox" for nothing. Clay, Webster, Calhoun, his archenemies came with gusto, drank the Little Magician's wine and partook of his gastronomic delights.

One evening amid wine and good cheer a servant interrupted the festivities to say, "The house is on fire." Excusing himself, Van Buren dashed out to help quench the flames with a few buckets of water. On his return, up rose irrepressible Henry Clay. Hand over his heart and with rare good nature, Clay assured Van Buren, "Mr. President, I am doing all I can to get you out of this house, but I assure you I do not want to burn you out." The Little Magician bowed and smiled his famous enigmatic smile.

In September, 1837, Van Buren summoned Congress for a special panic session to seek remedies for the depression. His message to this Congress was a pronouncement of first rank; it is among the best ever penned by a Chief Executive. He followed this with his celebrated Sub-Treasury or "Divorce" Bill, which proposed to separate "Bank and State," private and public business, and to establish an independent Treasury, with Sub-Treasuries in certain large cities having their own vaults, keeping government bullion and issuing their own notes. Van Buren's plan is today an integral part of the nation's monetary system. His Sub-Treasury Bill was no panacea. Three years elapsed before the Whig-controlled Congress enacted it.

Meanwhile other problems rose to disturb the harassed Little Magician. The slavery question would not die down. In Florida the Seminoles, led by Osceola, offered bloody resistance to removal beyond the Mississippi. Sabres rattled as the Maine farmers disputed boundary claims with the

New Brunswick lumberjacks. This bloodless "Arostook War"
was later settled by the Webster Ashburton Treaty. Texas
had won her revolution. Now the independent Lone Star
Republic was knocking at the door of the Union, threatening
complications with Mexico.

Slowly the depression receded though it would be felt for
five years. Van Buren was the "whipping boy" for it all. The
blame rested squarely on his shoulders, and a presidential
election was coming up.

John Randolph of Roanoke once described Van Buren as
a man who "rowed to his object with muffled oars." The
remark was apt, to be sure, but posterity has never really
given Van Buren his just dues. Son of a Dutch tavernkeeper
at Kinderhook-on-the-Hudson, he began life as a potboy in
his father's taproom, rising through a dozen public offices
to the presidency. The nation knows little of this man save
the ridicule he got in the Log Cabin Campaign of 1840. Yet
he was President, Vice-President, Secretary of State, United
States Senator, Minister to England, Governor and Attorney
General of New York. He was also czar of the New York
political empire he created, the Albany Regency, and to
make the story complete, Grand Sachem of Tammany Hall.
Quite a record!

The Americans had a word for Van Buren's political code
of noncommittalism. In the jargon of the day it was *van-
burenish*. The story goes that a senator once wagered he
could trap Matt into giving a positive answer on *something*,
no matter what. Accordingly he sidled across the senate
chamber to the exquisitely dressed Van Buren. "Matt, it has
always been said that the sun rises in the east. Do you believe it?"

"That's the common impression, Senator," replied Little
Van. "But as I always sleep till after sunrise I really can't
say it's true."

No American politician was ever his equal. He set the
style of straddling public issues so much favored by modern

politicians. It was born in him, this political adroitness that raised him from nothing to chief magistrate of the American people. The patronage system, now so vast as to defy calculation, was his brainchild. The "Spoils System," for which Jackson himself has been so often blamed, was whispered into Old Hickory's ear by the wily Van Buren. The "smoke-filled hotel-room" political routine for selecting candidates originated with Van Buren, though it was not so named till years later.

His enemies—and he had scores of them—have given unfair pictures of him. Most unjust of these was Davy Crockett's *Life of Martin Van Buren,* written the year before the backwoodsman was killed at the Alamo. The book sold far and wide, doing Van Buren much damage with its salty, picturesque slang and crude wit at Matt's expense. Wrote Crockett:

"Van Buren is as opposite to General Jackson as dung is to diamond. It is said that at a year old he could laugh on one side of his face and cry on the other at one and the same time. His mind beats round like a tame bear tied to a stake in a little circle no bigger than the head in which it is placed. When entering the Senate Chamber he struts and swaggers like a crow in the gutter. He is laced up in corsets, such as women of the town wear, and, if possible, tighter than the best of them. It would be difficult from his personal appearance to say whether he was man or woman, but for his large red and gray whiskers."

Lambasted and ridiculed Van Buren was still a significant figure in the presidential cavalcade as the nation entered the Fabulous Forties.

10

CONGRESS PICKS THE FIRST MISS AMERICA, BUT ALAS!

Walking through the Capitol on January 29th, 1839 one could read signs, prominently placed, requesting statesmen to squirt the essence of their tobacco quids into the "national spittoons" and not around the bases of the lovely marble columns.

Climbing the narrow stairway which led from the lobby to the gallery of the House of Representatives, one gazed down on a scene of perfect decorum. Below, on the floor of Latrobe's beautiful Hall of Representatives, 243 statesmen, for eight dollars a day and traveling expenses, were making the laws of the nation. In handsome, well-stuffed chairs they lolled at their labors amid a welter of papers and cuspidors. At least two score were engaged in pursuits concomitant with lawmaking: whittling, carving their initials on their desks, snoozing head-down or feet-up on desktops, writing letters home, aiming at spittoons and missing, and yawning.

A long-winded member held the floor. With threshing gesticulations he was haranguing his colleagues about nothing in particular, "talking for Buncombe," as they said in those days. Speaker James K. Polk was twiddling his gavel listlessly. The orator gushed like a Roman candle, emitting "Star Spangled Banners," "sovereign people," "tariff," "spirit of Seventy-six," "executive tyranny," and other political catch phrases.

At this moment, when the legislative mill had seemingly stalled, a lady, luscious and eye-catching, entered the gallery and seated herself in the front row. Escorting her and snuggling into a seat close beside her was, of all people, the patriarch of the House, the venerable ex-President, Representative John Quincy Adams of Massachusetts.

There was immediate and audible rejuvenation on the floor of the chamber. The spare-visaged Speaker perked up and raised his eyes towards the gallery. Whittlers suspended their tasks. Chewers shifted cuds to locations more convenient for looking. Sleepers opened their lids. The orator, beflustered and excited, addressed his remarks to the fair newcomer rather than to the Speaker. The House of Representatives was on the *qui vive* instantly.

It was hard to believe yet yonder, in the gallery, was the austere Mr. Adams, Old Man Eloquent himself, gurgling half-French, half-English blandishments into the lady's ear as he pointed out this statesman and that on the floor below.

But the lady! She was the first Miss America. Her face was wreathed in the adorable smile which had devastated both Houses of Congress. Lovely to look at was she; such dark, liquid Italian eyes, such inviting curves, such lustrous, midnight hair, such everything—if we are to believe Senator Daniel Webster, who was captivated by her. And the Godlike Daniel was an excellent judge of liquor and femininity.

Little wonder that the House of Representatives sat and stared and that the wheels of government ceased turning. The Speaker's stern countenance softened. A dozen members left their seats and hurried to the gallery where they swarmed about the charming, glamorous visitor.

Could America do other than honor this lady whose appearance in Washington in the winter of 1839 created such a social sensation? Did not the blood of Amerigo Vespucci, the Italian navigator-discoverer, flow in the veins of Helena Maria America Vespucci? Was she not a direct descendant of the man who first set foot on the mainland of America and gave his name to our beloved country? Was not the nation justified in giving a queen's welcome to this illustrious and beautiful lady?

It was. So thought the Senate of the United States. Likewise, so thought the House of Representatives. Statesmen of both houses of Congress set aside their political disputations to vie with each other in showering attentions on Miss America. Official Washington turned out in force, in best bib and tucker, to curtsy before her.

The lady was squired everywhere by the "greats" of Washington—to Boulanger's, to Carusi's, and Brown's Tavern, the best spots in the city. Her presence spread havocs of toasting.

In her honor Senator Daniel Webster spread a gay, festive party at his home on H Street. With masterly skill he blended a massive bowl of his famous "Daniel Webster punch," a potent mingling of Medford rum, brandy, champagne, arrack, maraschino, lemon juice, strong green tea, and sugar. Webster himself ladled out the first glass and raised it to the lady. The power of this potation, so the tale runs, approximated that of a Mickey Finn, but the guests quaffed off glass after glass of it, toasting the lovely lady until few of them could hardly mumble her name correctly.

For this distinguished visitor President Van Buren laid a magnificent, noble repast at the White House, even breaking out the famous gold plates and spoons for the extraordinary occasion. The President himself led the lady into dinner and seated her beside him. Around the gleaming table sat foreign diplomats glittering in gold lace, Cabinet officials, judges of the Supreme Court, high-ranking ladies in the social scale, leading members of the Senate and House of Representatives.

It is safe to say that the other 242 members of the House of Representatives envied Representative John Quincy Adams his delightful task of looking after the lady's affairs in the lower house.

Just before noon on this January 29th, 1839, Miss America had tripped light-heartedly into the Senate lobby. There waiting to greet her was the great Senator Thomas Hart Benton and Vice-President Richard "Tecumseh" Johnson, who immediately accorded her the privilege of sitting on the floor amidst the "most dignified body on earth" while Senator Benton, in stentorian voice, championed her appeal to Congress for citizenship and other perquisites which could hardly be denied a descendant of Amerigo Vespucci —and such a pretty descendant, at that.

Old Bullion was deeply inspired. Was not the lady sitting right beside him?

"Mr. President, I have read this lady's petition. She presents her case delicately and powerfully. Circumstances have thrown her upon our continent and brought her to solicit the aid of the Congress of the United States.

"Political reasons led her to withdraw from her own country—and in that respect she stands on a footing with others of noble intentions who have heretofore received aid from our government. She has not gone into the details of these political reasons. Delicacy of feelings prevents it."

Benton rambled on, getting more eloquent. "She is a descendant of one of those renowned navigators whose courage, skill and enterprise illustrated and illuminated the fifteenth century and, in the course of a few years, changed the face of the world."

The lady was thrilled. Was she not seated amid the nineteenth-century counterpart of the Roman Senate of old? Was not one of the most powerful voices in the Senate speaking in her behalf?

Benton went on. "She inherits the blood of that Amerigo Vespucci whose name has rested for three centuries and a half upon this quarter of the globe. She is a descendant and bears the name of that one of these patriarchal mariners who christened the new world with his own appellation and caused us to be called Americans.

"She is now without a country, without protection, without fortune; and she asks for a corner in that land which bears the name of her family, and for the right of citizenship among those who wear the title of Americans."

Now Benton moved that the lady's petition for a "corner of land" in America be referred to the Senate Public Lands Committee. It was all over quickly. It looked like an easy triumph. As Benton led the lady out of the chamber the Senate rose and bowed. At the door Senator Webster "cut in" and offered to guide the lady through the bewildering mazes of the rotunda and deliver her into the kindly hands of his old friend, Representative John Quincy Adams.

A few days later the "interesting exile" appeared before the Senate Public Lands Committee to plead her case and present her credentials. Chairman Senator Walker of Mississippi was gallantry itself. In broken English, flecked with lovely Italian nuances, Miss America appealed to the "honorable committee," presenting documents which traced her lineage and descent through generations of Vespuccis in Florence back to the original explorer himself.

Never was she more glamorous, more appealing. Her liquid eyes literally melted the hearts of the committee. Her exquisite manner was overwhelming. The committee was apparently swept off their feet.

As for credentials, Miss America had the best—letters from the King and Queen of France, who had wished her *bon voyage* and accorded her the honor of crossing the Atlantic on a French warship.

These and other testimonials, as well as "her own personal deportment, leave not a doubt of the identity of the memorialist and the truth of her representations." So said the committee officially.

But somehow the committee recovered its balance. On February 26th it struck a cruel blow—an adverse report on the lady's petition. This report is one of the curiosities of Congressional literature. No Congressional committee, before or since, has so eulogized a fair petitioner. The committee's babblings were delightful. With a wealth of regret, the committee said it simply could not give away a piece of the public domain. They would gladly do so if they could. Thus went the report:

"After the lapse, then, of more than three centuries a descendant of the celebrated Amerigo Vespucci is amongst us. This heroic navigator, before, and also after the close of the fifteenth century, landed upon the shores of the New World, among the most early and scientific of those who succeeded the great and preeminent Columbus in the discovery of this continent.

"A descriptive narrative of his several voyages was written and published by Amerigo, and Europe baptized with his name this mighty continent. This name can never now be abandoned. It is the name of our beloved country. It is associated with all the glories of the past and the still brighter hopes of the future. It is written upon our national Constitution, and engraved upon the heart of every true American. . . ."

"A descendant of Amerigo is now here; a young, interesting, dignified and accomplished lady, with a mind of the highest intellectual culture, and a heart beating with all our own enthusiasm in the cause of American and of human liberty. She feels that the name she bears is a prouder title than any that earthly monarchs can bestow, and she comes here asking of us a small corner of American soil where she may pass the remainder of her days in the land of her adoption.

"She comes here as an exile, separated forever from her family and friends, a stranger, without a country and without a home, expelled from her native Italy for the avowal and maintenance of opinions favorable to free institutions, and an ardent desire for the establishment of her country's freedom. That she is indeed worthy of the name of America; that her heart is indeed imbued with American principles and a fervent love of human liberty, is proved, in her case, by toils, perils and sacrifices, worthy of the proudest days of antiquity, when the Roman and Spartan matron were ever ready to surrender life itself in their country's service."

At this point the committee suggested a way out—a public subscription to raise funds to buy the lady "a corner of land" in America. In flattering words they commended Helena Maria Vespucci to the generosity of the American people:

"The petitioner desires the donation to her of a small tract of land by Congress. With every feeling of respect and kindness for the memorialist a majority of the committee deem it impossible for this Government to make·the grant. They think such a grant is without a precedent, and that it would violate the spirit of those compacts by which the public domain was ceded to this Government. It is the unanimous and anxious desire of the committee that the petitioner should receive all the benefits and recognition that this Government can bestow. What this Government cannot do is within the power of the American people. They feel, at least, an equal pride and glory with us in the name of America . . .

"This generous, patriotic and enlightened people will take into their own hands the case of America Vespucci. They will procure for her that home which she desires among us. They will do all that Congress is forbidden to do, and infinitely more than she asks or desires, and demonstrate to the world that the name of America, our country's name, is dear to us all, and shall be honored, respected and cherished in the person of the interesting exile from whose ancestor we derive the great and glorious title."

The lady wept copious Italian tears when the sad news was conveyed to her. Sympathy inundated her while at the same time subscriptions flowed in to Senate Sergeant-at-Arms Haight, whose heart beat so compassionately for the lady that he volunteered to launch the public subscription suggested by the committee.

First to put their names on the dotted line were Senator Daniel Webster and Representative John Quincy Adams. Beneath their distinguished signatures one might read the names of powerful Senators and imposing Representatives, judges, government officials, prominent citizens of Washington. It looked as if the lady would certainly get her cherished "corner of land."

What an ungrateful, hard-hearted Congress would not do for her, the American people would certainly do. At least, so it appeared for a while. In consequence, the lady bore up well under the Senate's rebuff, consoled by rounds of parties and receptions.

Spring breezed by and summer was coming on when a

chill wind blew across the Atlantic bearing unbelievable whispers from Florence and Paris. Statesmen listened and paled. Webster bowed his head over his desk. Old Eloquent wept openly. Could so fair a lady practice such deception? Could Helena Maria America Vespucci really be an adventuress? Fashionable Washington stood aghast, shocked into silence. There was a great shaking of heads on Capitol Hill, from the loftiest lawmaker down to the humblest page boy. Disillusionment shook the seats of the mighty like an earthquake.

Meanwhile Washington buzzed with the burning question: Had the Duke of Orleans paid off the lady, his long-time mistress, and hustled her to America and fresh fields of endeavor? Could such a thing be? It could, said the Prince of Joinville, the duke's brother, who reached Washington just as Miss America's dream burst into a thousand bright pieces. Hers, said the Duke, was an old, old profession on which she had embarked in her native Florence and plied in gay Paris. As to her lineage, the duke was enigmatic. She might be a Vespucci and she might not. There it rested.

Suddenly, the lady vanished! Where did she go? To the more friendly environs of New York where she poured out her heart to a gentleman, rich in sympathy and cash, who agreed to support her in the style and manner of a descendant of Amerigo Vespucci. But she never, it appears, obtained the "corner of land" she sought in the New World which was named for her presumed ancestor.

And the Congress of the United States, wiser in the ways of women, resumed its lawmaking!

11

THE LITTLE MAGICIAN SUCCUMBS TO OGLE'S MAGIC

"I put it to you, Mr. Speaker, and to the free citizens of this country, whose servant the President is, to say whether, in addition to the large sum of $100,000 which he is entitled to receive for a single term of four years, they are disposed to maintain for his private accommodation, a Royal Establishment at the cost of the nation! Will they longer feel inclined to support their chief servant in a Palace as splendid as that of the Caesars and as richly adorned as the proudest Asiatic mansion?"

With this outburst Representative Charles Ogle of Pennsylvania took off on one of the giddiest oratorical flights ever heard in Congress. For hours gales of laughter swept the House of Representatives as Ogle unfolded his mirthful, dazzling extravaganza on the fastidious personal habits and lavish tastes of President Martin Van Buren.

Had an applause-meter been available in the House on April 14th, 1840 it would have recorded that day as the most hilarious in the history of Congress. Decorum was almost nonexistent. Ever so often Speaker Robert Hunter of Virginia would wham his gavel when the statesmen grew too boisterous, but he himself was drawn into the maelstrom of mirth.

For the Whigs it was a field day. They sat entranced as spokesman Ogle spun out his claptrap fantasy of a President whose love of luxury and trappings of royalty were making a sham of the simple ways of American democracy.

Charles Ogle has never been given his political due. By

149

this one prodigious, masterful effort he achieved his fleeting fame. With Henry Clay he might be called President-maker, although conceivably Ogle would have preferred to be classified as President-breaker. Ogle was no ordinary Congressional windbag. He never dreamed his highly diverting, castigating burlesque of Van Buren would have such bombshell effect, yet in the fantastic election of 1840 Ogle's speech, which the Whigs printed by thousands, became their deadliest campaign document. Even the Whigs failed to give Ogle the credit he deserved, although this may be attributed to the fact that his death occurred when he was only 41, one month after that of William Henry Harrison for whose election Ogle did so much.

For the Democrats, Ogle's oratory was a major calamity. It literally blew Van Buren out of the White House. Charles Ogle's Gold Spoon Speech, for such it was called, was the most demolishing political utterance in the annals of Capitol Hill and certainly the most amusing. Waving his oratorical wand, Ogle transformed the Little Magician into a "lily-fingered," insufferable snob who perfumed his whiskers, wore corsets, kept cream-colored chambers under his French beds, rode in a gilded coach with outriders, and ate only French delicacies from golden plates with gold spoons and forks. If we are to believe Ogle, no oriental potentate ever wallowed in such bejeweled splendor or more decadent luxury than did President Van Buren, who at the moment was seeking a second term. Prestidigitator Ogle exorcised the White House into a regal palace the grounds of which were embellished with mounds, "clever-sized hills, designed to resemble and assume the form of an Amazon's bosom, with a miniature knoll or hillock at its apex, to denote the nipple."

How the Whigs roared! They all but rolled in the House aisles. Showman Ogle was in rare form as he took his audience on a personally conducted tour of Van Buren's "royal establishment" one mile from the Capitol.

"Let us," suggested Ogle to his 118 delighted Whig colleagues and the 125 depressed Democrats on the House floor, "survey its spacious courts, its gorgeous banqueting halls, its sumptuous drawing rooms, its glittering and dazzling salons, with all their magnificent and sumptuous array of gold and silver, crimson and orange, blue and violet, screens of Ionic columns, marble mantels . . . gold eagle cornices, rich cut glass and gilt chandeliers . . . French bronze gilt lamps, gilt framed mirrors of prodigious size . . . mahogany gilt-mounted and rosewood pianofortes . . . mahogany gilt-bronze-mounted secretaries, damask, satin and double silk window curtains . . . gilt and satin settees, sofas, bergères, divans, tabourets and French comfortables, elegant mahogany-gilt eagle-mounted French bedsteads, gilt plateaus, gaudy artificial flowers, rich blue and gold bonbons, tambours, compotiers, ice cream vases, splendid French china vases, olive boats, octagonal bowls, silver tureens, boats and baskets of every rich work, golden goblets, table spoons, knives and forks. . . ."

It sounded like an interior decorator's catalog, but Ogle dug deeper:

"And now, sir, having seen that this democratic President's house is furnished in a style of magnificence and regal splendor that might well satisfy a monarch, let us examine the manners, habits, conduct and political principles of the person who dwells in it and see if they correspond to the grandeur of the mansion."

Ogle's examination of the "manners, habits and conduct" was terrifying, at least for the Democrats.

General William Henry Harrison's election to the Presidency in 1840 has been generously ascribed to an orgy of log cabins, hard cider, coonskins, political doggerel, Tippecanoe and Tyler Too, and other rabble-rousing devices created by the Whig idea factory, but it would appear, at this distance, that Harrison was actually elected the day Ogle made his Gold Spoon Speech, although the formal vote-casting waited until November.

The editor of a Baltimore paper with Democratic leanings had already committed a massive political blunder by printing a slur on Harrison's supposed poverty: "Give him a barrel of hard cider, and settle a pension of two thousand a year on him, and my word for it, he will sit the remainder of his days in his log cabin."

The inference was clear. Harrison was not fit to be a President because he was a poor man, who lived in a log cabin, could afford only hard cider, and ate simple fare. Forthwith every plain, poor man in America felt insulted. It was a windfall for the Whigs. Harrison was not poor and he did not live in a log cabin, but it made no difference to the Whig publicity experts, among whom was Horace Greeley.

When the Whigs nominated Harrison in 1839 he was a simple, sixty-eight-year-old country gentleman who lived in a big, white house at North Bend, Ohio, which he called the Log Cabin and at which he served 365 hams a year to his many guests. This was his second try at the White House. His running mate was John Tyler. Harrison was no paragon as a general. At Tippecanoe the Indians surprised him. He survived by the skin of his teeth and the valor of numerous dead Kentuckians.

As a candidate Harrison was no campaigner. His most enlightening political utterance during the Whig hullabaloo of 1840 was to avow: "Should I be elected I will give my assent to all laws which may pass both houses of Congress, however much those laws may be against my own opinions and judgment."

It was a sweeping declaration. No presidential candidate ever before—or since—has uttered any such weak-kneed admission, or anything comparable to it. He apparently agreed with Nicholas Biddle, President of the Bank of the United States, who advised the Whigs, "If Harrison is taken up, let him not say one single word, or give his creed. Let no committee, no town meeting, extract from him a single word about what he thinks now or will do hereafter."

The Whig nomination had really belonged to Henry Clay who, during the convention, waited in Washington with a decanter to sustain him. When the news came that the Whig politicians had passed him up for Harrison, Clay exploded: "My friends are not worth the powder and shot it would take to kill them."

As for President Van Buren, he yearned for a second term. Handpicked by President Jackson, he had easily defeated Harrison in 1836. It was no sin that Van Buren was a *bon vivant*, but the American people were convinced that it was after the Whigs finished plastering the nation with Ogle's absurd travesty on the President's daily routine.

Of a sudden, hard cider became America's favorite beverage. Everybody wanted to live in log cabins. Daniel Webster, who supported Harrison, publicly apologized for not having been born in one. America was covered with pictures of Harrison standing before his log cabin offering a hospitable dipper of hard cider to all comers. Nailed to the door was the inevitable coonskin. Nearby stood the cider barrel.

Now, in April, 1840, came Representative Ogle to supply the devastating contrast to Harrison, the clodhopper, the plowman, the man who lived in a log cabin, drank only hard cider, the second Cincinnatus, by creating a farcical, fabulous figure of Martin Van Buren, scepter in hand, seated on a throne under a canopy of peacock's feathers, in a princely palace, where highborn ladies dripped with diamonds and priceless baubles available only to the very, very rich and the very, very aristocratic.

Strangest of all, the man in the street believed what Ogle had said. Spurred by Ogle's imaginings, Van Buren overnight became a symbol of dissolute royalty, a wastrel emperor, a mogul, and a sultan all packed in one. The average American even suspected Van Buren of keeping a harem tucked out of sight somewhere behind the White House walls.

If nothing else, Ogle dressed Van Buren up as a ridiculous fop who used exotic pomades on his hair and powdered his face, drenched his whiskers with French *Triple Distille Savon,* engirdled his chubby form in boned corsets while at the same time laying taxes on the farmers, mechanics, and laborers to pay for hemming his dishrags, keeping his foreign cut-glass wine coolers filled with choice vintages, and whiling away his official time "gallanting the Countess of Westmoreland" through the mazes of the waltz at Saratoga Springs.

When Ogle, hoarse from talking all day, finally yielded the floor to a Democratic wheel horse for a lame rebuttal, he had written the Whig campaign textbook. On this April day of 1840, the House was considering an appropriation for the civil and diplomatic expenses for the year 1840. Ogle took the floor to protest an item of $3665 for "alterations and repairs of the President's house and furniture, for purchasing trees, shrubs and compost, and for superintendence of the grounds."

Apparently he was loaded for bear, or rather for foxes, and in particular, for the Red Fox himself, the Whig's most important quarry. A strong Harrison man, Ogle moved to strike out this item on the ground that there was sufficient furniture already in the White House. To support his motion, Ogle produced facts, figures, bills, and vouchers out of which he wove his fanciful, deceptive portrayal of the iniquitous splendor in which President Van Buren lived.

Having launched his ridiculous lampoon by comparing Van Buren's life in the White House with that of an oriental potentate in the "proudest Oriental mansion," Ogle proceeded:

"Have the People chosen that servant to superintend the great and diversified interests of the nation; or will they consent that his time shall be occupied with the vanities, luxuries, and pleasures of life?

and abandon the care of the public service, to eat, drink, and be merry?

"I am constrained by a sense of duty to offer some remarks in relation to the incidental revenues—the annual profits and expenditures of the President of the United States—the magnificent splendor of his palace, and the pompous ceremonials that 'hold sway' at his republican court, and which are by many well-meaning people imagined to be equally indispensable 'to preserve the dignity' of a Democratic Chief Magistrate as of the despot on a throne."

First he turned his sarcasm on the elaborate and expensive plans Van Buren supposedly had for decorating the White House grounds after the manner of the "palace at Versailles" and the "rich and sumptuous parks and gardens of the Crown of England." He then went on to depict for his rapt listeners the "Amazon's bosom" mounds erected "to gratify the refined taste of an exquisite with sweet sandy whiskers." Next he led his delighted Whig listeners into the "palace" where President Van Buren lived amid oriental elegance. He began with the famous East Room.

"Who can deny that this room, intended for the comfort of our democratic Chief Magistrate, is adorned with regal splendor far above any of the grand saloons at Buckingham Palace, Carlton House, or Windsor Castle? I ask you, sir, whether in furnishing the East Room with all its gilded eagles, gilded stars, gilded rays, golden slabs, gorgeous drapery, and dazzling foreign ornaments, a due regard has been paid to the simplicity and purity of our institutions, or to the frugal, plain, unostentatious, and republican character of our people, who are represented in it? On the contrary, does not all this glittering display of costly finery, this blinding our eyes with the blaze of royal magnificence, approximate too closely the pride, pomp, and grandeur of those Governments in which stars and garters and shining coronets confer not only the means of luxurious enjoyment but of civil superiority?

"I cannot but admire and wonder at the great number of lamps, candles, and bracket lights, deemed necessary to illumine a single room in the President's palace. Here, Mr. Speaker, our democratic President shines with the overpowering lustre of one hundred and eighty lights. Had you the eyes of the fabled Argus, he would blind them all.

"Ay, Sir, every plain republican will now find a set of chairs in that splendid and royal saloon, which took the round sum of six hundred dollars of the people's cash to pay for. Is not that 'sitting down' with a vengeance? Martin Van Buren—plain, republican-hard-handed-democratic-locofoco Martin Van Buren—has it now garnished with gold framed mirrors as big as a barndoor, to behold his plain republican self in.

"What would the frugal and honest *Hoosiers* think were they to behold a *democratic peacock*, in full court costume, strutting by the hour before golden-framed mirrors, NINE FEET HIGH AND FOUR FEET AND A HALF WIDE?"

Ogle now injected the "Blue Elliptical Saloon" into the political campaign, describing it in the most intimate and elegant detail. He wondered audibly what an "honest republican sucker" from the Illinois prairies would think of the "silk-covered pillows, footstools, and tabourets" with which it was furnished, discussed the "natural history" of tabourets at exhaustive length, and dismissed the subject with this burst of eloquence:

"We shall now, Mr. Speaker, take our leave of the "Blue Elliptical Saloon"; but before we pass out of the door, turn your eyes, and take a moment's survey of the *tout ensemble*, not omitting the highly polished and beautiful marble mantel, with its superb but fantastic ornaments, and tell me whether this sumptuously garnished saloon bears the characteristics of an apartment intended for the accommodation of the CHIEF SERVANT of a plain, economical, hardy, and republican people? Or whether it does not more resemble the Audience Room of a Monarch, in which he receives his sleek and ribband-bedecked courtiers, as they present themselves with their humblest genuflexions and prostrations, crouching like fawning spaniels to the hand which has it in its power to throw them a bone?"

Van Buren's "court" drew Ogle's choicest sneers as he described the visitors who came in black and gilded coaches arrayed in "stars and ribands, jewels, . . . gold buttons and epaulets" to attend the "annual State levees." Ogle drew a telling contrast between the plain and homely fare of the average American and the luscious food which Van Buren served on furnishings which had cost exactly $11,191.32 of "the people's cash." At this point Ogle introduced the famous White House gold spoons from which his assault on Van Buren takes its name. He neglected to say that the White House gold service was purchased by President Monroe. Ogle charged Van Buren with procuring these iniquitous luxuries:

"Mr. Speaker, in my opinion, it is time the people of the United States should know that their money goes to buy for their plain hard-handed democratic President, knives, forks, and spoons of gold, that he may dine in the style of the monarchs of Europe.

". . . Oh! sir, how delightful it must be to a real genuine locofoco to eat his *paté de foie gras, dinde desosse,* and *salade à la volaile* from a SILVER PLATE with a GOLDEN KNIFE AND FORK. And how exquisite to sip with a GOLDEN SPOON his *soupe à la Reine* from a SILVER TUREEN. It almost makes my mouth water to talk about it."

The "Fanny Kemble Green Finger Cups" which were discussed over and over in the campaign were too much for Ogle. He waxed wroth over them:

"Mr. Speaker, don't you think that one of your plain republican 'Suckers' would feel 'kinder queer like' to be placed at the President's table . . . ? Why, sir, he would almost imagine that he had suddenly been translated to the *salle a festin en maison royale* of Louis Philippe, King of the French. I have no doubt that some of my constituents would much rather face the grizzly bear, on the Appalachian mountains, than sit down . . . for *five consecutive hours*—the period usually required by Kings and democratic Presidents to masticate a state dinner.

"Mr. Chairman, these three bills for table glass make, together, the clever sum of $2,596.50—an amount, I should suppose, sufficiently large to purchase the most democratic set of table glass in America. What, sir, will the honest locofoco say to Mr. Van Buren for spending the People's cash in FOREIGN FANNY KEMBLE GREEN FINGER CUPS, in which to wash his pretty tapering, soft, white, lily fingers, after dining on *fricandeau de veau and omelette soufflé?* How will the friends of temperance—the real teetotallers—relish the foreign 'CUT WINE COOLERS' and the 'BARREL-SHAPE FLUTE DECANTERS WITH CONE STOPPERS'?"

Ogle lashed himself into a frenzy over Van Buren requiring the people to pay for "hemming his dishrags." He rang the changes on this theme:

"I ask you whether it is just and equal for the President to charge the farmer, the mechanic, and the poor laborer with the cost of making his sheets, pillow-cases, and servants' aprons—with the pitiful price paid for HEMMING, yes, HEMMING his *kitchen rubbers*, or DISH CLOTHS—*straining cloths*, or STRAINER RAGS? The poor farmer has not only to purchase a *churn, milk-strainers*, and *skimmers* for his own family, but he is also taxed to pay for a *churn, milk-strainers*, and *skimmers* for the President of the United States, and for HEMMING HIS STRAINER RAGS into the bargain . . .

"Martin Van Buren must suppose, forsooth, that the farmers, mechanics, and laborers of the United States are so very stupid, or so very good-natured, that they will without a murmur consent to be taxed with the price of his LIQUOR STAND, and for SILVER and GOLD CHAINS to hang labels around the necks of his '*foreign barrel shape flute decanters, with cone stoppers,*' to apprize his sleek, prim court guests that he has introduced to the palace cellars '*Marcobruner Hock,*' '*Batailly Claret,*' '*Towers Port,*' '*Romance Burgundy,*' '*Ravini's Pale Gold Sherry,*' and *Red Seal, old, bottled E. I. Madeira.*"

Now Ogle began his devastating examination of Van Buren's personal "manners, habits and conduct." How he belabored the President's supposed use of pomades and perfumes!

"And if he is vain enough to spend his money in the purchase of rubies for his neck, diamond rings for his fingers, Brussels lace for his breast, filet gloves for his hands, and *fabrique de broderies de bougran a Nancy* handkerchiefs for his pocket—if he choose to lay out hundreds of dollars in supplying his toilet with 'Double Extract of Queen Victoria,' Eau de Cologne, *Triple Distillée Savon Davline Mons Sens,* Bouquet and Arabic, Corinthian Oil of Cream, *L'Huile de Rose,* Hedyosmia, Concentrated Persian Essence, and Extract of Eglantine, the latter the most charming perfume for the assembly or *boudoir,* imparting to the handkerchief an agreeable, refreshing, and lasting odor, and 'patronized by her most Gracious Majesty Queen Victoria, and her Royal Highness Dowager Queen Adelaide'—if, I say, Mr. Van Buren sees fit to spend his cash in buying these and other perfumes and cosmetics for his toilet, it can constitute no valid reason for charging the

farmers, laborers, and mechanics of the country, with bills for HEM-
MING HIS DISH RAGS . . ."

Now he turned to Van Buren's attentions to the Countess
of Westmoreland:

"Yes, sir, Mr. Van Buren has spent more than $70 for each and
every moment since he was sworn into the Presidential office. How
often has the clock ticked since that fatal hour? During the four
months of last year that he passed on his electioneering tour of the
State of New York, how many times did the clock tick then? The
President's hard dollars were going at the rate of $70 a minute while
he was dancing with the Countess of Westmoreland at Saratoga.
That was dancing to a pretty dear tune forsooth, but the President
paid the piper."

Here Ogle turned his fire on "Our Prince," Van Buren's
son John, who had been gallivanting about Europe like his
father before him:

"Our Prince! mind you. We must get familiar with these things, for
we must come to them. We have a President who was so great a
favorite with the English nobility that when his son goes there they
rank him above their titled noblemen. What has John Van Buren done
for his country to distinguish him? Nothing. But our Prince, I am
informed, is a very clever gentleman, and by the way, possesses a
great deal of drollery. I am told that one day he went to the palace
and seeing his father rather melancholy at the prospect of Old Tippecanoe coming in, he patted him on the back and said, 'Pa, you need
not despair, because, if you are beat, I will take you in to practice
with me.'
"Is not this all enough to sicken an old-fashioned Democrat? And
this is Van Buren democracy! This is bringing up the sons of a democratic President in fine style!"

Ogle's gibes even included the President's churchgoing.
He contrasted Van Buren's habit of riding the three hundred
yards between the White House and St. John's Episcopal
Church "in his Democratic Majesty's British Stagecoach"
with plain Henry Clay's "footing-it" from his lodgings to the
same place of worship. But Van Buren never mingled with

the people, according to Ogle. He invariably rode in his "gilded coach."

Ogle even charged that Van Buren was actually seeking a scepter and a throne in the White House. With these accusations he made his grand finale:

"It may with great propriety be alleged that, as we already have the palace, with its . . . regalia, palace grounds, palace gardens, grand levees, state banquets, Court ceremonials, Court costumes, stalls for the royal steeds, and royal revenues, we should not hesitate about a *throne*, which according to the definition of Napoleon Bonaparte, is '*six planchis de sapin et un tapis de velours*'—or SIX PINE PLANKS AND A VELVET CARPET. Why refuse a *crown*, which is merely a broad ring of gold, with diamonds and precious stones set in ouches, the ring being attached to a velvet-gold-embroidered cap, terminating on the top with a golden ball or cone? Why deny a *diadem*, or richly variegated riband, forming the border of a velvet cap garnished with gold tufts and tassels? Why reject a sceptre, or stick thirty inches in length, and lackered with golden varnish?

"Will not the pseudo-democracy be better pleased with a *President* who possesses not only the power, but is also covered with the trappings of royalty? Caesar was omnipotent at Rome with the plain title of *Consul;* Cromwell, with the simple name of *Protector*, controlled all the power of England; *Consul* Bonaparte was as absolute and despotic as the *Emperor* Napoleon.

"Sir, I am unwilling to grant the appropriation . . . because it will not be very inconvenient for *President* Van Buren to exchange his splendid Spanish cloak for a royal stole, and, having placed the crown upon his head, the diadem on his brow, and bedecked his person with the royal jewels, with the lackered sceptre in his hand, take his seat on that throne. And thus this democratic *President*, although deprived of the *title* of royalty, will be invested, not only with its *prerogatives*, but with its *trappings* also."

Ogle was done. So was the discomfited Van Buren. After reading Ogle's speech, Henry Clay epitomized the campaign: "The battle is now on between the log cabins and the palaces, between hard cider and champagne."

Ogle had injected many issues into the campaign, not the least of which were the "six cream-colored chambers" which the White House inventory disclosed. One thing was certain: he had expressed the feelings of the plain people. Washington laughed for a week. The nation never stopped laughing until November, when it voted Van Buren "out" and William Henry Harrison "in."

In the joyful Whig melée which followed Harrison's election, Charles Ogle was forgotten. He had nevertheless given a new political twist to White House extravagance. Although he drew largely on his imagination, it was the cleverest political trick ever played on the floor of the House of Representatives, for it killed off one President and virtually elected another.

12

GOLD IN CALIFORNIA AND WAR BELOW THE BORDER

The Fabulous Forties came in with a roar heard around the world. This decade would witness events and movements that would reshape American destiny. Before these ten momentous years would go down in history, steam would take over the main burden of transportation; the telegraph would be winging words through space; four new states would join the Union; the stagecoach would be heading toward oblivion; Elias Howe, a young Boston watchmaker, would be stoned for inventing a machine that could sew two hundred and fifty stitches a minute; the nation would complete its march to the Pacific by snatching California and a vast empire from Mexico; the North and South would be irretrievably split on the question of slavery.

In 1840 the national debt was $3,573,000. By 1850 it would rise to $63,450,000. Immigrants were pouring in through the portals of freedom: 84,000 in 1840; 379,000 in 1850. From 17,000,000 people in 1840, the nation's population would leap to 23,000,000 in 1850. Large cities were growing larger. New York had outstripped Philadelphia as the nation's leading metropolis. It was the nation's "great commercial emporium." The most scholarly city was Boston, the center of culture, the "hub." The leading Southern city was New Orleans.

Lushly appointed steamboats plied the Mississippi and other great arteries of trade and commerce. King Cotton was on his throne. Fabulous wealth was flowing into the pockets of planters of the fluffy white bolls. Throughout the Deep South, along the shores and bayous of the Mississippi, along the Gulf Coast, planters built palatial homes which they filled with treasures brought from the far corners of the world.

The leading spa in America was Saratoga. The American people were drinking floods of bitters, balsams, cordials, and elixirs. Brandreth's was the most popular pill. It brought the learned "Doctor" great wealth.

The New York waterfront bespoke the nation's growing opulence. Forests of shipmasts lined the shore. London packets docked beside fleets of China-bound ships. On Broadway an aspiring young showman, Phineas T. Barnum, established his American Museum and packed it with sideshow specialties. Wrote Captain Marryat, "In every place you will meet someone whom you have met walking on Broadway. Americans are such locomotives."

Beyond the Mississippi, on the vast plains of the West, countless herds of longhorn cattle were roaming and cowboys, with newfangled Colt revolvers at their belts, were singing, "Green grow the lilacs all sparkling with dew."

In 1845 a strange poetic figure, Edgar Allan Poe, wrote the poem by which posterity would best remember him, "The Raven." That same year the United States Naval Academy was established at Annapolis. In 1847 in a little Ohio town one cold night Thomas Alva Edison was born, who was destined to light up the world and invent a machine that could talk back. That year the Post Office Department issued the first adhesive postage stamps.

A new industrial era was setting in. The farm empire Jefferson had envisioned was giving way to an industrial democracy. The West caught the imagination of thousands of emigrants. Campfires gleamed along the Oregon Trail as long wagon trains moved on toward the boundless, untapped Northwest.

Climaxing this restless decade was the unbelievable Gold Rush to California. In 1848 a sawmill foreman, James Marshall, found yellow particles in a mill race on the American River near Sacramento. It was gold! And California became the· Eldorado men had dreamed of through the ages.

Old soldiers never die, they say. But one was dying, President William Henry Harrison. Sixty-eight years old, barely thirty days in office, Old Tippecanoe was fighting his last battle. Camped in the hallways outside his sickroom were job-hunters. They would not even let him die in peace. In his delirium he cried out against them, "These applications . . . will they never cease?" Outside his window at night an owl hooted dismally. The superstitious made much of it.

Riding bareheaded through a driving rain on his inaugural day, Harrison caught a cold that turned into pleurisy. Five doctors worked over him with every medicine and practice they knew. They bled him, blistered and cupped him (once a dark-ages torture routine). They plied him with innumerable pills, laudanum, calomel, rhubarb, Dover's powder, castor oil, serpentaria (snake root), opium, seneca (crude petroleum), camphor, wine, brandy,. and God knows what else. On April 4, 1841, no doubt glad to get away from the job-seekers and the drugs, he died with these last words, "Sir, I wish you to understand the true principles of the government—I wish them carried out—I ask nothing more." He was the first Chief Executive to die in office.

For years it was rumored about Washington that Harrison was done to death with poison. Eventually the legend disappeared. But Harrison was dead, and the Whigs, who had log-cabined and hard-cidered him into the White House, were aghast; the nation was stunned. Old Tip left two memorials of his presidency: an eight-thousand-word inaugural

address and a Bible he bought for the White House. Said he
to the bookseller, "The Bible ought to be a part of the furniture of the White House. I am going to buy the best copy
I can find and write in it 'The President of the United
States from the people of the United States.' "

After a hurried overnight trip from Washington, Chief
Clerk Fletcher Webster of the State Department found
Vice-President John Tyler at his Virginia home, Sherwood
Forest, down on his hands and knees playing marbles with
his boys. To Tyler, young Webster handed an urgent des-
patch from the Cabinet at Washington. Glancing through
it hurriedly, Tyler's face paled.
    "My God, the President is dead!"
    "And you, sir, are President."
    Short of funds, Tyler borrowed money and sped to Wash-
ington. The next day April 6th, at Brown's Hotel the erstwhile Vice-President took the presidential oath. He was the
first Vice-President death would elevate to the highest office.
Summoning Harrison's Cabinet, Tyler said he did not wish
to be dictated to, but he would be glad to have them remain
at their posts and cooperate with him. If they did not like
that, he would welcome their resignations. Within two years
Tyler's entire Cabinet had resigned save Secretary of State
Daniel Webster, and the Whigs who put him in office had
hanged him in effigy.
    What to call Tyler bothered many. Some suggested "Act-
ing President." To his diary John Quincy Adams confided, "I
paid a visit this morning to Mr. Tyler, who styles himself
President of the United States and not Vice-President,
which would be the correct style. It is a construction in
direct violation of the Constitution. . . ."
    Tyler's administration was a political roughhouse. In a
running fight with the Whig Congress, he vetoed pretty
much everything they did. They tried to impeach him and

drummed him out of the party though he was never in it. He changed his entire Cabinet four times. They dubbed him "President without a party."

After his first wife's death he courted lovely Julia Gardiner of New York who looked "like a Greek statue in her flowing gowns." Smitten, Tyler sent the marine band to New York to serenade her. He was fifty-four, she twenty-four. They married and lived happily. Already father of seven children, Tyler fathered seven more. As far as children were concerned, he was the most prolific of the presidents.

In the closing days of his administration Tyler seized the glory of annexing Texas by inducing Congress to pass a resolution authorizing the admission of the Lone Star Republic to the Union. Tyler signed the resolution on March 1st, 1845, three days before he went out of office. On the night of March 3rd, 1845, President Tyler gave a White House dinner in honor of James K. Polk who would be inaugurated next day. Queen of the evening was beauteous Mrs. Tyler wearing on a chain around her neck the small gold pen with which Tyler had signed the resolution admitting Texas to the Union.

Great figures were passing. At the Hermitage, near Nashville, on Sunday, June 8th, 1845, death came for Andrew Jackson. It was he who had first seen from afar the vision of Texas joining the American Union. Galloping furiously to reach the Hermitage before Jackson's heartbeat flickered out was the "greatest of Jackson's expeditionary captains," Sam Houston, President of the Texas Republic which he literally carried about in his vestpocket. Towards dusk Houston's coach rolled up to the Hermitage, but he was too late. Jackson's spirit had fled. With Houston came his small son. Taking the boy by the hand, he led him into the room where Jackson lay in his last sleep. To the lad Houston said, "My boy, try always to remember that you have looked on the face of Andrew Jackson."

In May, 1844, the first dark horse entered our political history at the Democratic convention at Baltimore. Martin Van Buren (still a powerful personage) apparently had the Democratic nomination sewed up, but he failed to win the necessary two-thirds' vote. Just then the "backroom boys" trotted out Young Hickory, protégé of Old Hickory, Tennessee's "Napoleon of the Stump," James K. Polk, whose name was not even mentioned until the eighth ballot. He got 44 votes. On the ninth he got 233 ballots and galloped off with the political bacon.

At this same moment in a room in the Capitol, forty miles away, inventor artist Samuel F. B. Morse sat over his "magnetic telegraph" taking messages transmitted direct from the Baltimore convention hall. Only five days before this, Morse's historic test message, "What hath God wrought?" had passed over the same wires. Crowded around Morse and his crude instrument were senators, representatives, and nondescript hangers-on. When the telegraph clicked off the news of Polk's nomination the politicians were dumfounded. "Who the hell is James K. Polk?" many asked.

On a platform of "Re-annexation of Texas and Re-occupation of Oregon" Polk defeated Whig candidate, Henry Clay, for the White House. He was the only former Speaker of the House of Representatives ever to reach the presidency. Greatest expansionist President (save perhaps Thomas Jefferson), Polk's creed was Manifest Destiny "to overspread and to possess the whole of the Continent which Providence has given us for the great experiment of liberty." First he forced a showdown with England on the red-hot Oregon boundary question. Polk's election slogan was "Fifty-four forty or fight," meaning he would enforce the American claim to the Pacific Northwest that far north. He compromised on the Forty-ninth Parallel, a good thousand miles southward.

In 1846 Polk ordered General Zachary Taylor and his small army to the Rio Grande for an inevitable clash with Mexico. Polk welcomed hostilities. In a hot message to Congress asking a declaration of war, Polk proclaimed, "Mexico has shed American blood upon the American soil. War exists, and notwithstanding all our efforts to avoid it, exists by the act of Mexico itself." Within two years Mexico was at our mercy and twelve thousand Americans lay dead on the battlefields.

Polk's peace terms carved from Mexico two-fifths of her territory, including California, New Mexico, and other vast stretches—a veritable empire. To lessen the pain, the United States agreed to pay Mexico $15,000,000 to compensate for the loss of her territory. The Treaty of Guadeloupe Hidalgo, signed February 2nd, 1848, brought peace between the two neighbors. Just five days before this James Marshall had discovered the first flakes of gold in his mill race near Sacramento, California. It meant untold millions in the nation's coffers and a new state within two years. In his last message to Congress, December, 1848, President Polk confirmed the finding of the precious yellow metal in California—and the Gold Rush was on.

13

THE MUSE OF HISTORY WRITES AS OLD
ELOQUENT DIES

"Mr. Speaker, what is the meaning of that beautiful statue over your clock at the entrance to this hall? Sir, it is the Muse of History in her car, looking down on the members of this House and reminding them that as the hour passes she is in the attitude of recording whatever they say or do on this floor."

As he addressed these words to Speaker Andrew Stevenson, the veteran ex-President and Representative John Quincy Adams pointed his palsied finger to Carlo Franzoni's Car of History Clock, the official timepiece of the House of Representatives in 1834.

This exquisite marble creation, perched above the north door of the Hall of Representatives, now Statuary Hall, shows the figure of a woman clad in flowing robes—the Muse of History—riding in a winged chariot across a globe on which are inscribed the signs of the zodiac. In her hands is a tablet on which, as she rides, she writes the history of the world. The wheel of her chariot is the dial of the clock.

On this day in 1834 Old Man Eloquent had risen to support a resolution for printing additional copies of the *Register of Debates,* the *Congressional Record* of its day.

"Mr. Speaker," continued the aged statesman, "the reporters at the sides and in rear of your chair are the scribes of that Muse of History; and this publication, for which the resolution before us proposes a subscription, is the real, I might say the living, record of this historic Muse."

The Muse of History, "looking down on the members of this House," had seen John Quincy Adams, on December 5th, 1831, take his seat in the House of Representatives and rise to new greatness as the envoy of the people of Quincy, Massachusetts. Sixty-four years old, fresh from the exalted station of First Citizen, he had deemed it an honor to serve in the lower House of Congress: "My election as President of the United States was not half so gratifying to my inmost soul."

During his brilliant, seventeen-year career in the House the Muse had often heard his shrill, eagle-scream voice rising above the roar of the tempestuous legislative breakers which at times verily inundated the House chamber. Punctual in attendance, he held his post through the longest, most grueling sessions. He regarded age as no excuse for desertion. While others far younger slumped in the chairs or staggered exhausted out of the chamber, he sat through the twenty-five-hour filibuster on the bill admitting Arkansas and Michigan to the Union. At five o'clock in the morning he rose to protest a clause in the proposed Arkansas constitution. It was of this occasion that torch-bearing Henry Wise of Virginia, said, "Sir, it was one of the most disgraceful scenes I ever witnessed; it was unbecoming barbarians and savages, much more the Representatives of a civilized nation! Sleepy, tired and drunk!"

But John Quincy Adams was neither sleepy, nor tired, nor drunk. He was alert to the last word of the debate.

Once he fasted for twenty-eight hours, through day and night, so that he could follow every word of a brawling, protracted session. Courageous, unwavering in what he believed was his duty, he opposed what he thought the wrong and fought like an archangel for what he considered the right.

John Quincy Adams, however, was no charmer. Back-
slapping was not one of his arts. Outwardly as cold as a
New England winter, he laid the foundations of American
foreign policy.

The loss of the Presidency in 1828 had embittered him.
His immediate election to Congress opened a new vista to
him. His squat, prim-lipped figure, clad in a well-worn,
swallow-tailed coat with brass buttons, was soon to become
the symbol of a principle for which he fought a running,
dogged fight for ten years. A versatile parliamentarian and
fearless patriot, he held his own with the best, with a never-
say-die doggedness which won the respect of his foes and
the esteem of countless admirers.

When Adams entered the House, abolition and slavery
were torturing the nation; Congress burned with bitter
sectionalism. North and South were slowly arraying themselves for the tragedy of the Sixties. Fiery, erratic William
Lloyd Garrison and his *Liberator* were broadcasting the
abolitionist propaganda of hate and blood.

Adams abhorred slavery, yet he was no abolitionist. However, believing wholeheartedly in the fundamental right of
petition, his first official act was to present fifteen petitions
from citizens of Pennsylvania for the abolition of slavery.
In his veins flowed the blood of the old revolutionist, his
father, to whom a king, to his sorrow, had denied the same
right. Congress was flooded with these incendiary petitions.
They were received, printed, and referred to a committee,
where they died.

On May 18th, 1836 the Muse of History must have hovered close by as John Quincy Adams opened his long, dramatic fight against the famous or infamous Gag Rule. It was
a milestone day in the nation's history. Almost three score
and ten, having served his country forty-two years, he drew
his sword and stood firm. Like the Old Guard, he would die
but never surrender. Southern leadership in the House had
decided that the time had come to still agitation against

bondage in the chamber by a resolution which would forbid the reception of anti-slavery petitions. It meant gag rule, but John Quincy Adams refused to be gagged while every Southern firebrand in the House leaped to support the proposal of his leaders.

On this issue, the right of petition, Adams waged his spectacular, ceaseless and, in time, triumphant battle, for which he was to receive the historic accolade, his sobriquet, Old Man Eloquent.

The first of the four resolutions presented by the Southern bloc ran: "Resolved, that Congress possesses no constitutional authority to interfere in any way with the institution of slavery in any of the States of this Confederacy."

Adams shot to his feet. "Mr. Speaker!" he pleaded, mopping the tears which ran from his rheumy eyes. "If the House will allow me just five minutes' time, I pledge myself to prove that resolution false and utterly untrue."

Through a bedlam of calls to order he took his seat, to be snowed under by 182 nays.

The gag on the right of petition was embodied in the third resolution, which, with its preamble, follows:

"Whereas, it is extremely important and desirable that the agitation on this subject should be finally arrested, for the purpose of restoring tranquillity to the public mind, your committee respectfully recommends the adoption of the following additional Resolution:

"Resolved, that all petitions, memorials, resolutions, propositions or papers, relating in any way, or to any extent whatever, to the subject of slavery, or the abolition of slavery, shall, without being either printed or referred, be laid upon the table, and that no further action whatever shall be had thereon."

The yeas and nays were called for. John Quincy Adams' name led all the rest. Disdaining calls to order and shouts from all over the floor, the ex-President shrilled, "I hold the resolution to be a direct violation of the Constitution of the United States, the rules of this House and the rights of conscience."

Refusing to vote, he sat sullenly and with burning glances watched the adoption of the first gag rule to pass the American Congress, 117 to 68. At that moment, on that spot, he began his indefatigable crusade to rescind it.

In February of 1837 the Muse of History saw him again embroiled.

Defiantly, he had continued to present petitions which were now coming to him in a flood. In December of 1836 he had forced Speaker James K. Polk to rule that the gag resolution had expired with the adjournment of the previous session. Yet, almost as fast as it could be written, a second gag was applied.

On February 6th Adams rose. His shaky hand held a fistful of petitions. Among them was one from nine ladies of Fredericksburg, Virginia, "praying Congress to put an end to the slave trade in the District of Columbia." Under the rule, it was tabled. As he was about to take his seat, he apparently remembered something else. Taking up a paper, he again addressed the chair.

"Mr. Speaker, I have in my possession a petition of a somewhat extraordinary character; I wish to inquire of the Chair if it is in order to present it."

"If the gentleman from Massachusetts," said the Speaker, "will inform the Chair what the character of the petition is, it will probably be able to decide on the subject."

"Sir," ejaculated Adams, with one of his rare smiles, "the petition is signed by eleven slaves of the town of Fredericksburg. It is signed partly by persons who cannot write, by making their marks, and partly by persons whose handwriting would manifest that they have received the education of slaves. The petition declares itself to be from slaves and I am requested to present it. I will send it to the chair."

Taken by surprise, Speaker Polk gave his chair a "hitch"

as he often did when excited or caught in a dilemma. A petition from slaves was a novelty. He needed time to consider it. In the meantime, he said he would consult the sense of the House.

For some moments the House sat in bewildered silence and then all at once fury enveloped the chamber. The enraged Southern bloc buzzed like a hive of angry, disturbed bees, excited and denunciatory. Cries of "Expel him!" "Expel the old scoundrel!" "Put him out!" resounded through the chamber.

A mountain of a man from Alabama, Representative Dixon Lewis, climbed over his desk and stood threateningly over Adams, shaking his huge fist.

"By God, sir," he sputtered, "this is not to be endured any longer!"

Up rose Waddy Thompson, brilliant South Carolina hothead, with a resolution demanding punishment of Adams for flagrantly violating the dignity of the House. Charging Adams with seeking the protection of age and respect for the high office he had once occupied, Thompson hurled a fiery tirade at him. He hoped to see Adams confined "within the walls of a penitentiary."

"The sanctuary of age is not to be lightly violated," thundered Thompson, "but when the sanctuary is used to throw poisoned arrows, it ceases to be sacred. Does the gentleman, even in the latitude which he gives to the right of petition, think it includes slaves? If he does not, he has wilfully violated the rules of the House and the feelings of its members."

Thompson finished. Adams got to his feet and stood his ground. Only five feet seven, he was nevertheless as immovable as the rock on which his rugged forebears had landed in America two centuries before him. The blood drained from his ruddy face. Calmly fingering a button on his blue coat, he let the storm break around him and then eloquently made answer to his assailant.

It was his duty, he said, to present any petition, respectfully written, "be its object what it may; be the prayer of it that in which I could concur, or that to which I was utterly opposed."

Then, to the discomfiture of his attackers, he revealed that the petition, strangely enough, was one opposing abolition, even though it came from slaves themselves. Fierily he fought back, flailing his foes with sarcasm, ridicule, and denunciation. "Where is your law which says that the mean and the low, and the degraded, shall be deprived of the right of petition, if their moral character is not good? Petition is supplication—it is entreaty—it is prayer. And where is the degree of vice or immorality which shall deprive the citizen of the right to supplicate for a boon, or to pray for mercy? Where is such a law to be found? And what does your law say? Does it say that, before presenting a petition, you shall look into it, and see whether it comes from the virtuous, and the great, and the mighty? No, sir, it says no such thing; the right of petition belongs ot all."

The pro-slavery forces were not to be denied. They pressed their attack on Adams for four days, but the old man met every onslaught. Finally, the resolution which would arraign Adams at the bar of the House, to be censured in the presence of its entire membership, reached a vote.

Valiantly, he made a last stand, refusing to ask for mercy or to surrender. "While I totally disclaim any intention of offending or provoking any of the members of this House, while I totally disclaim any contemptuous course or any violation of the rules or orders of the House, sir, at the same time I disclaim not a particle of what I have done; not a single word of what I have said do I unsay; nay, I am ready to do and say the same tomorrow."

The resolution failed, 137 nays to 21 yeas. Adams' flashing offensive-defensive was powerfully impressive. It was a spectacular victory for an intrepid veteran all but alone in a maelstrom of violence.

He never relaxed his attack. Slowly as the years went by,

unpopularity and isolation became his lot. His Whig colleagues forsook him. They wearied of the incessant battles into which he plunged, dragging them with him. Threats of expulsion, assassination, indictment left him unmoved. He was browbeaten, howled at, rebuked, assailed by the press which had once supported him. He fought back coolly, exasperatingly, persistently. The ranks of his enemies increased. He became a legendary figure, fighting a lone, valiant battle for the right of petition. Outside the chamber his long fight had drawn a greater audience, a legion of supporters who urged him on.

In 1841 he confessed pathetically to his diary: "The world, the flesh and all the devils in hell are arrayed against any man who now in this North American Union shall dare to join the standard of Almighty God to put down the African slave trade; and what can I, upon the verge of my seventy-fourth birthday, with a shaking hand, a darkening eye, a drowsy brain, and with all my faculties dropping from me one by one, as the teeth are dropping from my head, what can I do for the cause of God and man? Yet my conscience presses me on; let me but die upon the breach!"

The Muse of History bent even closer when, on January 25th, 1842, Old Man Eloquent rose to present a petition of forty-six citizens of Haverhill, Massachusetts "praying that Congress would immediately adopt measures peaceably, to dissolve the Union of these States."

This did Adams raise the curtain on a turbulent spectacle which drew suffocating crowds to the gallery of the House. The rank effrontery of presenting a petition to dissolve the Union, "to pull down the temple of Liberty," was monstrous to his enemies, who determined that now was the moment to crush him and his cause forever and so to humiliate him that he would gladly resign and go home. They would verily flay him alive with a resolution of censure which would damn him for all time.

Eloquent Thomas Marshall of Kentucky presented the

resolution, a vicious indictment sprinkled with "high treason," "deepest indignity," "utterly unworthy," "insult to the people," "overthrow of the Republic" and other stigmas aimed at Adams.

Encompassed by foes relentlessly determined on his destruction, he turned on his accusers. Palsy shook his frame; his watery eyes streamed, but not with tears. He was at bay and he knew it. His eyes burned back at the enemies who ringed him.

"I desire the Clerk to read the first paragraph of the Declaration of Independence!" His voice rose high and shrill. "The first paragraph of the Declaration of Independence! The first paragraph of the Declaration of Independence!"

Silence fell on the House. The tumult died instantly. The clerk hesitated, but Adams demanded, "Proceed, proceed, proceed! Read down to the 'right and duty'!"

Uncertain, hesitant, glancing at Speaker John White as if for permission, the clerk slowly obeyed the stern, keen voice. With shaky voice, the clerk read the opening passage of Jefferson's momentous document. When he finished Adams slowly repeated the last sentence: "But when a long train of abuses and usurpations, pursuing invariably the same object, evinces a design to reduce them under absolute Despotism, it is their right, it is their duty, to throw off such Government, and to provide new Guards for their future security."

With triumph in his eyes, Adams went on: "Now, sir, if there is a principle sacred on earth and established by the instrument just read, it is the right of people to alter, to change, to destroy, the Government, if it becomes oppressive to them. There would be no such right existing if the people in pursuance of that right had not the power to petition for it. . . . I rest that petition on the Declaration of Independence."

Staunchly he held on through two weeks of acrimony. The scenes were impressive. Every eye in the crowded galleries was fastened on an old, infirm man, tottering with age and trembling with palsy, delivering blows with terrible power. But great dramatic ability was still his. By a single word and the manner of uttering it he could devastate an enemy at one blow.

Henry Wise of Virginia made bold to cross swords with Adams. Amid profound silence Adams replied. Seldom in the history of the House of Representatives was there a more thrilling, sensational counter-attack.

"Four years ago," said Adams, flinging the words to every corner of the chamber, "there came into the House a man whose hands were dripping with the blood of a fellow-member. He had desired to be excused from voting on this case because I had then been instrumental in saving him from expulsion. I then did express my opinion against the right of the House to proceed in this manner, and it is likely that I saved that blood-stained man from being expelled."

He referred to Wise's part in the murderous Cilley Graves duel, in which Wise was Graves' second and for which the House considered Wise's expulsion.

Abuse ran riot. The Speaker hammered and hammered to no effect. Members shouted themselves hoarse at the aged ex-President. Adams held on defiantly.

"I am still in the power of the majority. If they say they will try me, they must try me. If they say they will punish me, they must punish me. If they say, that, in grace and mercy, they will spare me expulsion, I disdain and cast their mercy away; and I ask them if they will come to such a trial and expel me. I defy them. I have constituents to go to that will have something to say if this House expels me. Nor will it be long before gentlemen will see me here again."

On February 7th the resolution of expulsion was laid on the table, an action tantamount to defeat, by a vote of 106 to 93. Old Man Eloquent had triumphed again.

On December 3rd, 1844 the Muse of History saw the old warrior win his long fight. His motion to rescind the Gag

Rule—the now-famous Twenty-first Rule—was passed to carry it out of parliamentary existence.

His long career had reached its climax. He had come at last, through triumph and defeat, to the high point of a life crowded with colorful drama. He had held more high offices than any other man in the history of the American government: diplomat, scholar, legislator, patriot, statesman, ex-President—but this was the pinnacle. In his diary that night he recorded his gratitude for the triumphant issue of his ten-year struggle: "Blessed, forever blessed, be the name of God!"

February 21st, 1848. The Muse of History, still vigilant, saw an old man, buried by near eighty-one years, enfeebled by disease, weary of combat, writing quietly at his desk in the House chamber. He still served, faithful in his attendance, but his once-round cheeks were shrunken, his sturdy body bent. He had climbed the Capitol steps with apparent alacrity that morning. Cheerfully he had given autographs to two admirers who stopped him in the lobby.

Now, as was his hobby, he was composing a few stanzas of poetry for a friend. His left hand gripped his palsied right as he wrote. A few weeks before he had returned to the House after a long struggle with a stroke of paralysis. As he re-entered the chamber he received an ovation. He was escorted to his old seat on the west side of the chamber by Representative Andrew Johnson of Tennessee, who had occupied it during his absence and who now surrendered it gracefully.

In January of 1848 he took the floor for a last time to support a resolution calling on President Polk to state the objectives and peace proposals in the war with Mexico, which Old Man Eloquent had opposed with vigor.

Today, February 21st, 1848, the House was considering a resolution of thanks and the award of gold medals to the victorious generals of the Mexican War. The hands of the Car of History Clock pointed to one-thirty.

At that same moment, as fate would have it, a confidential message was en route from President Polk to Congress, transmitting the treaty of peace with Mexico.

Old Man Eloquent was slowly rising to his feet.

"Mr. Speaker!"

The salutation died in his throat. He toppled. There was a cry of "Stop! Stop! Look to Mr. Adams!"

But let the Muse of History, speaking in the dramatic, succinct, official words of the record, describe the scene:

"The Speaker then rose to put the question but he was interrupted by Mr. Hunt, who desired him to stop, and by several gentlemen who sprang from their seats to the assistance of the venerable John Quincy Adams, who was observed to be sinking in what appeared to be the agonies of death. Mr. Adams was immediately borne to the Rotunda for the benefit of purer air and afterwards to the Speaker's room assisted by many members of the House—and the House hastily adjourned."

Members crowded around the stricken, unconscious Adams. He was lifted into the area, the well of the House, immediately in front of the Speaker's rostrum. Quickly a sofa was brought and the insensible statesman carried out of the chamber into the rotunda. Here he rested while a physician-member worked over him. For fresher air he was moved near the door leading to the east portico of the Capitol. The day was cold, the air chilly. At Speaker Winthrop's suggestion, the dying patriarch was borne into the Speaker's room adjacent to the chamber.

Five physicians were soon at his bedside. He was cupped freely; mustard plasters were applied to his feet. About two-thirty he opened his eyes and asked for his wife, a sorrowful figure, an invalid herself, who was already at his side.

On an improvised bed in the Speaker's room Old Man Eloquent lingered for two days halfway between two worlds. Toward dusk of the twenty-third he roused himself to speak. "Thank the officers of the House," he murmured and then lay quiet again. The candles were lighted, shining down on the serene, motionless face of Old Man Eloquent.

Now he spoke again, so low as to be scarcely audible: "This is the last of earth." He paused. There was a long wait. His lips moved again: "I am content." Such were his last words in this world.

At seven-fifteen Representative John Quincy Adams presented himself to the Greatest Speaker of All in the highest House of Representatives. His prayer "to die upon the breach" had been answered. In his moving eulogy Senator Benton expressed the feeling of all: "Punctual to every duty, death found him at the post of duty; and where else could it have found him, at any stage of his career, for the fifty years of his illustrious public life?"

On February 24th the House of Representatives met long enough to pass this unprecedented resolution: "Resolved, that the seat in this hall just vacated by the death of the late John Quincy Adams be unoccupied for thirty days and that it, together with this hall, remain clothed with the symbol of mourning during that time."

On the marble floor of the Hall of Representatives, now Statuary Hall, a bronze tablet marks the spot where Old Man Eloquent fell. From her perch above the north door of the Hall the Muse of History still keeps watch and remembers.

14

OLD ROUGH AND READY MOVES IN WITH STORM

SIGNALS FLYING

1848. Election Year and the nation was dividing against itself. Abolition was in the saddle riding hell for leather. Sectional propaganda deluged the nation like a hot tide. The slavery issue literally forced itself down the country's throat. North and South were parting though for a dozen years longer they would keep up the travesty of a united people.

The Whigs were at it again, little dreaming their party would so soon vanish. Whiggery died hard yet it was to have one last fling at the Presidency. Military heroes had, on the whole, made excellent political candidates. Washington in 1789; Jackson, 1828; Harrison, 1840; bore out this conclusion. So the Whigs, after violently opposing the Mexican War about-faced and commandeered its most popular figure as their candidate, General Zachary Taylor, Old Rough and Ready. Taylor literally vaulted from the battlefield to the White House, no man ever rising so fast from political obscurity. His victories in Mexico thrust him so violently into the limelight that even the politicians were astounded at the spontaneous way his boom got started. His popularity zoomed overnight. They called it "Taylor Fever."

Sixty-three years old he had never voted in his life. He was so little concerned over the outcome that when the Whigs

mailed him official notice of his nomination he let it go to
the deadletter office rather than pay the ten cents postage
due on it. He just sat on the porch of his Baton Rouge plantation home, chewed tobacco and watched Old Man River
roll by. He owned three hundred slaves. This was a bitter
pill to the Whigs but they swallowed it gladly for the sake
of a candidate who could win the election for them. It was
to find an echo in the campaign in what the Democrats denounced as Taylor's Two Faces.

Taylor had spent most of his life in camp or on the frontier. He did not know the buzz of the presidential bee when
he heard it. There is a story that when a brother officer first
broached the idea Taylor growled, "Stop your nonsense
and drink your whiskey." His soldiers adored him. Blunt,
stocky, fearless, he always found his way to the thick of the
fight. The nation thrilled to his order to a battery at Buena
Vista: "Double-shot your guns and give 'em hell!" Some
claimed he really said, "A little more grape, Captain Bragg."
But it made no difference. It all became grist for the Whig
political mill.

Taylor's bandwagon began rolling of its own momentum
and both parties scrambled to get on. The Whigs went all
out. If he wasn't a Whig, they would make him one. The
Democrats looked on the general longingly but President
Polk's dislike of Taylor stood in their way.

Old Zack was not certain he even wanted the job. His
first reaction was indifference. Taylor's wife, Margaret, had
something to say about his candidacy, even if he did not.
She said it was a plot to deprive her of his company and
shorten his life. In the latter she was right, but nobody believed her, least of all, the Whigs.

He left Mexico in November 1847 and hurried home.
Every steamboat brought a politician to his door. One
April day in 1848 three big Whigs called on Taylor and
told him they had come to help him make up his mind.
With their help Taylor composed a declaration of his politi-

faithfully—I regret nothing, but am sorry that I am about to leave my friends."

At ten thirty-five Taylor died. Next day, before both houses of Congress, Millard Fillmore, last of the Whig dynasty, was sworn in as President.

15

THE GREAT TRIUMVIRATE AT ARMAGEDDON

It was the twilight of the demigods in the United States Senate. New, impulsive performers, a galaxy of fresh, younger talent awaiting their cues, stood in the wings, impatient for the aging actors to make their bows and depart. Yet, one last time would three of the greatest figures Congress has ever seen mount the stage. In a last throbbing scene this all-star cast would play out their stirring parts, though little could they imagine it was merely the prologue to the mightiest of American tragedies.

In 1850 crisis hovered over the land like a black cloud from which lightning would soon flash. The South was moving toward secession. John Calhoun was promoting a convention of the slaveholding states, the first long step on the highroad of dissolution. Agitators were flaying the North into a ferment. The nation was edging toward Henry Clay's "dreadful precipice." The breach had widened until it was a roaring gorge across which North and South hurled taunts and insults at each other. The great American fire dance was on and the dancers were whipping themselves into righteous fury.

The Thirty-first Congress which assembled early in December of 1849 was the last assembly of representatives of a really united nation before a shell flashed blood red over Fort Sumter in 1861. There were those who predicted it would be the last session of a Congress of the United States.

Like a two-edged sword, slavery slashed through the ranks of the House of Representatives, slicing party lines. Democrats and Whigs were so evenly matched that five Free Soilers held the balance of power. The House balloted tempestuously for seventeen days before choosing a Speaker. The Free Soilers were determined that the House must accept the Wilmot Proviso; otherwise there would be no Speaker. This pronouncement touched off pandemonium. The Democrats brought forward Howell Cobb of Georgia; the Whigs, Robert Winthrop of Massachusetts. Neither party could muster a majority as long as the Free Soilers tossed their votes to other candidates.

Wild-eyed, aristocratic Richard Meade of Virginia rose to announce angrily: "If the organization of this House is to be followed by the passage of these bills [abolition of slavery in the District of Columbia and in the Territories], if these outrages are to be committed on my people, I trust in God, sir, that my eyes have rested upon the last Speaker of the House of Representatives. If these be passed, there will be but one determination at the South—one solemn resolve to defend their homes and maintain their honor."

With measured coldness, William Duer, New York Whig, applied the spur: "You are a disunionist."

"You are a liar, sir!" retorted Meade.

The two men rushed at each other. The excited reporter for the *Congressional Globe* scrambled what he saw and heard in this official record of the scene:

"Indescribable confusion followed—threats, violent gesticulations, calls to order, and demands for adjournment were mingled together. The House was like a heaving billow.

The CLERK called to order, but there was none to heed him.

Some time elapsed.

The Sergeant-at-arms of the late House of Representatives now took the Mace in his hand and descending among the crowd of members held it on high.

Cries of "Take away the Mace! It has no authority here!"

favor with bows and a gallant salutation, "Lady, I salute you" or "Lady, let me give you my heart." His lips had phrased the Texas battle cry, "Remember the Alamo!" The glamor of San Jacinto still clustered about him.

To the second session of the Thirty-first Congress came a man with a strange rendezvous with destiny and a gutta-percha cane on the Senate floor one day in 1856, Charles Sumner of Massachusetts. Graceful of word and manner, impeccable, he was master of invective. Polished and re-polished were his speeches. Handsome, eloquent, his dark hair lay in wavy masses on his high forehead like a lion's mane. Hater of slavery, and of slaveholders, despiser of the South, no man could arraign her so stingingly as Sumner.

Came others: ambitious Free Soiler from Ohio, Salmon Portland Chase, bald on top, humorless and opinionated, who would one day be Chief Justice of the United States. With Chase from Ohio came bluff, hard-boiled Benjamin Franklin Wade, ruthless, able and radical. Into the House of Representatives limped a crippled, gaunt abolitionist dripping with hate and vengeance for the South, autocratic and so powerful that, in time, he could command the impeachment of a President. This was Thaddeus Stevens of Pennsylvania.

In the historic Senate chamber in 1850 coal gas burned in the great chandelier. Its bluish light was not so kindly to the faces beneath it as was the soft, amber candleglow, yet it deepened the color of the red draperies and carpets and polished mahogany desks. Sixty chairs and desks now almost filled the splendid semicircular chamber. The needs of an expanding nation would soon call for more room and a new Senate wing. The cords of Union holding thirty states together were frayed almost to the snapping point, but new states were in the offing and California was already knocking at the door.

California's application for admission in 1849 as a free state had precipitated the crisis. Gold, discovered in 1848, and the fevered rush to get rich had brought this region to the brink of statehood within twelve months. The Free Soilers were insisting that Congress pass the disputed and sidetracked Wilmot Proviso excluding slavery from the territory snatched from Mexico. Texas, by force of arms, was preparing to claim part of the territory of New Mexico. Congress was scourged by petitions for abolition of slavery in the District of Columbia. Northern agitators and statesmen demanded that the buying and selling of human flesh in the very shadow of the Capitol must cease. The South demanded drastic enforcement of the Fugitive Slave Act of 1793.

The South had blocked California's admission to the Union. Men would march, the South proclaimed, if the Wilmot Proviso passed. It was the deadliest attack on slavery since the Missouri Compromise. These and other bitter questions bred of slavery rent the nation. Free states and slave states blazed like prairie fires.

For Henry Clay, Great Compromiser, the hour had struck again. He had returned to the Senate with a single purpose: to save the Union. "Our country is in danger and if I can be the means of saving her, my health and my life is of little consequence." Twice before he had led the nation out of crisis by compromise, forbearance, and concessions. He would do it again. "Five bleeding wounds," he said, were draining the life of the Republic. If he could staunch the blood, he might hold the country together. He would wrap the bitter dissensions into a package—"a bundle of compromises" like the Constitution itself—which would soothe and settle the burning, pressing questions. It would be healing balm to the North and South alike.

Gone with the political winds were Clay's oft-crushed Presidential aspirations, gone his strength, his health, his light, springy step. Seventy-two years lay behind him. No longer was he the debonair Cock of Kentucky, wearing bright, flowered waistcoats which caught the ladies' eyes, as he wished it. Yet his flashing, brilliant words still made one think of the point of a rapier. His gestures lacked little of the finesse of yore. His verbal firepower was unquenched. His magnetic blue eyes could still charm, his ready wit still bubbled. "There is a peculiar power in his presence which makes you admire and love him." Age had not yet destroyed these qualities.

To the ladies he was still fascinating, profuse in his gallantries, an aged romancer, still unable to resist a pretty face, a trim waistline, and stolen kiss. At seventy-two his eye yet roved.

Of his sixty colleagues on the Senate floor, he alone was born in the throes of the American Revolution. He had seen bitter days as a boy. He could look back to a red-coated British dragoon thrusting a sabre into his father's fresh grave. That terrible day was never blotted from his memory.

In his room at the National Hotel Clay worked out his plan of compromise and trudged through the snow to ask and receive Webster's pledge to support it. Calhoun, implacable and dying on his feet, would have none of it.

On January 29th, 1850 a weary old man rose in the Senate to begin what he felt was his last great duty and service to his country: to save the Union.

"I hold in my hand," he said, "a series of Resolutions which I desire to submit for the consideration of this body. Taken together, in combination, they propose an amicable arrangement of all questions in controversy between the free and slave States, growing out of the subject of slavery." He continued:

"There are five bleeding wounds and they must be healed. Heat, passion and intemperance are being diffused throughout the land. But let us with the sacrifice of no great principle, arrange such a scheme of accommodation as will restore peace to our distracted country. In a few days now I shall lay aside all earthly ambition and honors for the habiliments of the tomb. Naught concerns me—for naught do I care, save a united country."

It was a massive, noble, eight-pronged piece of states-manship, a package of far-reaching panaceas which would put to rest the violent sectional disputes which were driv-ing the nation to the brink of dissolution. President Zachary Taylor christened it—with some derision—The Omnibus Bill. For each there was healing legislative balm.

His eight compromise proposals were:

1. California would be admitted as a free State.
2. The Territories of New Mexico and Utah were to have no restrictions as to slavery.
3. Texas and New Mexico would settle their boundary dispute by mutual concessions.
4. Texas would be compensated for extinction of her claims to part of New Mexico.
5. Slave trade in the District of Columbia would be abol-ished.
6. Slavery itself would be permitted in the District of Columbia as long as Maryland wished it.
7. Congress must pass a more stringent fugitive slave law.
8. Congress must recognize that it had no right to inter-fere with the domestic slave trade.

On February 5th, 1850 Henry Clay was coughing badly as he ascended the Capitol steps to plead for his resolutions. As he paused for breath halfway up the steps, the chaplain of the Senate came to him and, taking his arm, helped him to the top. For days the word had gone the rounds: "Mr. Clay is going to speak. Perhaps, for the last time."

The Senate galleries applauded as he entered. Handsome Vice-President Millard Fillmore made little effort to gavel for quiet. It was useless today. The floor was jammed with an "eager multitude" of hoop-skirted ladies and broad-clothed gentlemen. Foreign ministers, attachés in gold lace and spangles, privileged persons, sat on piles of papers in the aisles. The chamber was suffocating. Something had gone wrong with the heating system and the thermometer stood at one hundred degrees.

At his desk, waiting for Clay to speak, sat a figure who resembled "a- fugitive from the grave"—John Calhoun. Wrapped in a heavy shawl, he had come to listen grimly to every word of his ancient adversary. His eyes—such eyes!— smouldered with dark fires. Compromise was not Calhoun's price of peace. The South would not compromise the slavery issue as long as he had breath to fight it. Throwing sops on the burning issues could not quench them. He approved Clay's patriotic purpose, but the methods were distasteful.

Clay was still the drawing card of years gone by. When he rose the galleries burst into cheers. Standing there waiting for silence he looked centuries old. Ill and haggard, his cheeks were sunken. His head, now bald on top, was fringed with long white hair. Yet across his mouth played the same old bewitching smile, the Clay trademark, which had won so many hearts to him.

Few of those who fixed their eyes on him were unmoved by the erect, frail figure in a black frock coat which seemed a trifle too large for him. Above his high black satin stock rose a huge white collar which crept toward his ears.

He began falteringly: "I have witnessed many periods of great anxiety, of peril and of danger, but I have never before arisen to address any assembly so oppressed, so appalled, so anxious."

As he warmed to this theme age seemed to fall from his shoulders like a cloak. Deeply inspired by his message of salvation for his country, he was transformed all at once into a glowing, magnetic orator pleading with consummate skill and cogent, persuasive eloquence.

North and South must make concessions, he warned. It was the only way out, if the Union was to be saved. California had a right to come in as a free state. Had not Missouri been admitted as a slave state on the same grounds? Abandonment of the Wilmot Proviso meant nothing. Nature herself had prohibited slavery in the territory acquired from Mexico; the climate was not suited to slavery. "You have got what is worth a thousand Wilmot Provisos. You have got nature itself on your side."

One by one Clay defended his resolutions. Most controversial of all was the Fugitive Slave Law. Had not the Constitution itself imposed on the North the duty of returning escaped slaves to their owners?

The North must agree to the resolution not to abolish slavery in the District of Columbia while the South must agree that slave trade a stone's throw from the seat of government was inadmissible. "Why are the feelings of citizens here outraged by the cortèges which pass along our avenues, of manacled human beings? Who is there, that has a heart, that does not contemplate a spectacle of that kind with horror and indignation? Why should they not be outraged by a scene so inexcusable and detestable as this?"

For two days Clay pleaded. His voice wavered with emotion. Tears ran down cheeks. He closed with a personal plea to both North and South:

"Let me say to the North and to the South what husband and wife say to each other. We have mutual faults; neither of us is perfect; let us, then, be kind to each other, forbearing, forgiving each other's faults—and above all, let us live in happiness and peace together."

If not, he warned, secession would ensue, war which would end "in the extinction of this last and glorious light which is leading all mankind who are gazing upon it in the hope and anxious expectation that the liberty which prevails here will sooner or late be diffused throughout the whole of the civilized world."

Fellow Americans, he begged, "pause solemnly at the edge of the precipice before the fearful and dangerous leap be taken into the yawning abyss below, from which none who ever take it shall return in safety. I implore, as the best blessing which Heaven can bestow upon me upon earth, that if the direful and sad event of the dissolution of the Union shall happen, I may not survive to behold the sad and heartrending spectacle."

Hoarse, exhausted, the veteran patriot sat down. The tension broke with the sharp rap of the Vice-President's ivory gavel. As Clay made his way wearily out of the chamber he was smothered by the kisses and embraces of his feminine admirers. Men clamored to touch but the hem of his frock coat. It was a scene never before witnessed on Capitol Hill —and only once since.

Monday, March 4th, 1850. It was John Calhoun's last curtain call. News that the old nullifier would rise from his deathbed to sound his final warnings against a compromise which to him appeared as self-destruction of the Union brought a "brilliant and expectant audience." The New York *Tribune* reporter recorded that "a representative of the fairer portion of humanity" occupied almost every Senate seat, necessitating a vote to legalize their presence.

Leaning on the arm of a friend, Calhoun tottered into the forum where once with lordly power and scythelike logic he had sheared the very ground from under lesser men's feet. For him the Union could not be saved, at least not in Clay's way. A shock and gasp stirred the densely packed chamber as Calhoun appeared, literally feeling his way from desk to desk. In profound silence every eye watched his swaying, spectral figure, more like a ghost than a man, dragging to his chair. Over his emaciated shoulders hung a black cloak. His neck was swathed in flannel. A visitor noted his "deep cavernous black eyes and thick mass of snow-white hair." His face was pallid as marble; death had already locked step with him. As he reached his chair, Senator Jefferson Davis, his next desk-neighbor, rose and stood respectfully until Calhoun sank into his seat.

It was a spectacle solemn and impressive. A whisper might have been heard at the moment. Calhoun held his head erect at first, sullenly glaring around the chamber in which he had written so much history.

Presently he rose weakly. Regretting that infirmities had maimed him, he asked that his colleague, Senator Mason of Virginia, be permitted to read his carefully prepared speech.

As Mason began reading Calhoun's defiant, dying pronunciamento, the South Carolinian sat immobile, his feverish eyes roving from Senator to Senator, searching face after face for the effect of his words.

This was to be his last tragic warning to the nation and he filled it with dark forebodings. Eventually, he said, the South would be forced to choose between abolition and secession. His solution was to split the nation into two, with a President for the North and another for the South.

"I have, Senators," he began, speaking through Senator Mason, "believed from the first that the agitation on the subject of slavery would, if not prevented by some timely and effective measure, end in disunion . . . The agitation has been permitted to proceed, with almost no attempt to resist it, until it has reached a point when it can no longer be disguised that the Union is in danger.

"What is it that has endangered the Union? One of the causes is, undoubtedly, to be traced to the long continued agitation of the slave question on the part of the North . . .

"Unless something decisive is done, I again ask, what is to stop this agitation, before the final and great object at which it aims—the abolition of slavery—is consummated? It is certain then that the South will be forced to chose between abolition and secession.

"How, then, can the Union be saved? In no way but by removing the cause of the trouble; by satisfying the Southern States that they can remain in safety. The cry of 'Union, Union, the glorious Union!' can do nothing to help in the matter . . .

"It cannot, then, be saved by eulogies on the Union, however splendid or numerous. The cry of 'Union, Union, the glorious Union!' can no more prevent disunion than the cry of 'Health, Health—glorious Health!' on the part of the physician can save a patient lying dangerously ill.

"How can the Union be saved? There is but one way by which it can with any certainty; and that is, by a full and final settlement, on the principle of justice, of all the questions at issue between the two sections. The South asks for justice, simple justice, and less she ought not to take. She has no compromise to offer, but the Constitution; and no concessions or surrender to make.

"If you, who represent the stronger portion, cannot agree to settle them on the broad principle of justice and duty, say so; and let the States we represent both agree to separate and part in peace. If you are unwilling we should part in peace, tell us so, and we shall know what to do, when you reduce the question to submission or resistance.

"I have exerted myself, during the whole period [of slavery agitation], to arrest it, with the intention of saving the Union, if it could be done; and if it could not, to save the section where it has pleased Providence to cast my lot, and which I sincerely believe has justice and the Constitution on its side. Having faithfully done my duty to the best of my ability, to both the Union and my section, I shall have the consolation, let what will come, that I am free from all responsibility."

The long quiet broke. Lawmakers and senators came out of their trance. Webster went to Calhoun and took his hand. Now Henry Clay was beside him. Admirers thronged about the trio as the Great Triumvirate held their last reunion. Painfully, with a friend holding each arm, Calhoun left the chamber. The Senate and gallery rose and remained standing until he vanished. The end of Calhoun's long, tortured journey was not far off. In four weeks he was to die in the Old Brick Capitol, now a boarding house, and one day to be a prison in which Southern sympathizers would be incarcerated.

March 7th, 1850. The last of the Great Triumvirate donned his resplendent Revolutionary habiliments—blue coat with brass buttons, buff vest, and white tie. At noon he walked with firm, stately tread into the Senate chamber and took seat 29 just off the center aisle.

Still majestic was Daniel Webster. He "looked like a cathedral." To a visitor who saw him enter, his eyes resembled "catacombs of ancient wisdom." He had defied age better than Clay or Calhoun. He still stood erect like an Indian. His throat could still sound a trumpet call which reached into the very soul of his listeners. His booming voice made the very chandeliers vibrate. "Like tones of muttering thunder" his voice "reached everywhere, filled everywhere, and the effect upon the audience was to chain them to their seats."

Today he would speak in support of Henry Clay's great compromise. He would be damned for what he would say. Come what may, he would speak for the Constitution and the Union. The wreckage of his political career would be strewn at his feet when he finished, but he must take the risk. New England radicals would call him a "Benedict Arnold," a "Lucifer descending from heaven." He would be branded as a Judas Iscariot—but what of it?

To Webster, today, his theme was no less important than that of the January day in 1830 when he replied to Hayne. Pale and thin, Clay waited eagerly for Webster's supporting words. Calhoun's chair was empty. Long and often were Clay and Webster rivals. Many times had they crossed swords. Today they were fighting a common battle for the Union. Fifty-nine Senators were in their seats. The outpouring of people was an inspiration in itself.

From Varina Howell Davis, wife of the courtly Mississippi Senator, came a vivid portrayal of the occasion: "The Senate, before the morning hour, was crowded from gallery to the floor; outside of the railing was a parterre of brilliant palpitating color, a solid phalanx of ladies; on the steps of the Vice-President's seat every available inch was occupied, and even between the Senators, seated on the floor, the rosy faces and waving plumes of ladies made points of color against the Senators' black garments. The ladies kept as still as mice, feeling themselves present there on sufferance; and, besides, their interest was intense."

Promptly at noon Vice-President Fillmore set the stage by announcing that the floor belonged to Senator Walker of Wisconsin, who was speaking when the Senate adjourned. In a graceful gesture Senator Walker yielded the floor to Webster: "Mr. President, this vast audience has not come together to hear me, and there is but one man, in my opinion, who can assemble such an audience. They expect to hear him, and I feel it to be my duty, therefore, as it is my pleasure, to give the floor to the Senator from Massachusetts."

Calm, composed, and confident, Webster rose. "A thrill, as if from a noiseless electric shock, passed through the assemblage." Bowing to the Vice-President, thanking the Senator who had yielded to him, Webster began his classic Seventh-of-March Speech which will forever rank close beside his Reply to Hayne. His opening words sounded the keynote of his eloquent, patriotic address:

"Mr. President, I speak today, not as a Massachusetts man, nor as a Northern man, but as an American, and a member of the Senate of the United States. We live in midst of strong agitations, and are surrounded by very considerable dangers to our institutions of government. The imprisoned winds are let loose. The East, the West, the North and the stormy South, all combine to throw the whole ocean into commotion, to toss its billows to the skies, and to disclose its profoundest depths.

"I do not affect to regard myself, Mr. President, as holding or fit to hold, the helm in this combat of the political elements; but I have a duty to perform, and I mean to perform it with fidelity—not without a sense of surrounding dangers, but not without hope. I have a part to act, not for my own security or safety, for I am looking out for no fragment upon which to float away from the wreck, if wreck there must be, but for the good of the whole, and the preservation of the whole; and there is that which will keep me to my duty during this struggle, whether the sun or the stars shall appear, or shall not appear, for many days.

"I speak today for the preservation of the Union. Hear me for my cause!"

His deep, booming cadences resounded through the quiet chamber. He was still the master orator, a majestic, commanding figure. "There was only one Daniel Webster," thought an eyewitness; "there could never be another. His words become immortal the moment they fall from his lips."

A visitor seated in front of him noted that Webster, in delivering this powerful appeal for Union, never changed a single word or phrase. The entire address "flowed as the Mississippi rolls from its fountains."

As Webster pressed on, pouring his fire on the extremists of both North and South, he did not see "a tall, gaunt figure" enter the chamber and drag himself tremblingly to a chair. This apparition, for so he looked, was John Calhoun come back as it were from the grave. Dramatic was his entrance, equally dramatic its effect on the startled chamber.

Quickly, although not yet had he seen Calhoun, Webster turned his guns on Calhoun's proposal that the South and North separate and depart in peace:

"Peaceable secession! Peaceable secession! The concurrent agreement of all the members of this great Republic to separate! A voluntary separation, with alimony on one side and on the other! Why, what would be the result? Where is the line to be drawn? What States are to secede? What is to remain American? What am I to be? An American no longer? Where is the flag of the Republic to remain? Where is the eagle to tower? Or is he to cower, and shriek, and fall to the ground? Why, sir, our ancestors—our fathers and our grandfathers, those of them that are yet living amongst us with prolonged lives, would rebuke and reproach us; and our children and our grandchildren would cry out shame upon us . . .

"To break up—to break up this great government—to dismember this great country—to astonish Europe with an act of folly such as Europe for two centuries has never beheld in any government! No, sir; no sir! There will be no secession. Gentlemen are not serious when they talk of secession!"

Calhoun tried to rise, made a feeble motion to indicate his presence to Webster, who was still unaware of it. A few moments later Webster again referred to "the distinguished and venerable Senator from South Carolina who, I deeply regret, is prevented by serious illness from being in his seat today."

Summoning his last fleeting energy, Calhoun half rose. His cavernous black eyes flashed as his hollow, sepulchral voice proclaimed, not without pride, "The Senator from South Carolina is in his seat."

Webster was startled by the ghostly voice. Deeply touched, his eyes turned toward Calhoun. He bowed low to his ancient adversary who had risen from a death bed to come and hear him, but he exclaimed quickly, "Peaceable secession is an impossibility."

Webster closed with simple, genuine eloquence:

"Let us make our generation one of the strongest and brightest links in that golden chain which is destined, I fondly believe, to grapple the people of all the States to this Constitution for ages to come. No monarchial throne presses these States together; no iron chain of despotic power encircles them; they live and stand upon a government popular in its form, representative in its character, founded upon the principle of equality, and calculated, we hope, to last forever.

"In all its history it has been beneficent; it has trodden down no man's liberty; it has crushed no State. Its daily respiration is liberty and patriotism; its yet youthful veins are full of enterprise, courage and honorable love of glory and renown. Larger before, the country has now, by recent events, become vastly larger. This Republic now extends, with a vast breadth, across the whole Continent. The two great seas of the world wash the one and the other shore. We realize, on a mighty scale, the beautiful description of the ornamental edging of the buckler of Achilles:

'Now the broad shield complete the artist crown'd
With his last hand, and pour'd the ocean round;
In living silver seem'd the waves to roll,
And beat the buckler's verge, and bound the whole.' "

It was a masterpiece like his Reply to Hayne. Three hours and eleven minutes had he spoken, with seldom a reference to notes. There was a rush to his side to congratulate him; applause broke out in the galleries. He, like Clay, had really made an appeal to pure patriotism. It was, he felt, the most important effort of his career.

As the visitors began leaving they were suddenly riveted where they stood. John Calhoun had risen! Swaying uncertainly, he voiced his dissent:

"I cannot agree with the Senator from Massachusetts that this Union cannot be dissolved. Am I to understand him that no degree of oppression, no outrage, no broken faith, can produce the destruction of the Union?"

Webster replied in a kindly voice: "I know, sir, that this Union can be broken up—every government can be—and I admit that there may be such a degree of oppression as will warrant resistance and forcible severance. That is revolution. Of that ultimate right of revolution I have not been speaking. The honorable member and myself have broken lances sufficiently often before on that subject."

"I have no desire to do it now," commented Calhoun.

"I presume the gentleman has not," smiled Webster, "and I have quite as little."

Next day, March 8th, 1850, William W. Corcoran, Washington banker and art connoisseur, went to his strongbox and took out Webster's IOU for ten thousand dollars. Writing "Cancelled, paid in full" across the face of the paper, he sent it to Senator Webster on Capitol Hill. Accompanying it was a letter of congratulations on his speech and a check for a thousand dollars.

The curtain fell as slowly the lights went down on these dying political gods who had fought their Armageddon on the Senate floor. Now for Valhalla! First went Calhoun, still dreaming of a triumphant, sovereign South, still yearning at the last moment for the Senate where, "If I could have one more hour to speak, I could do more good than on any past occasion of my life." On March 31st, 1850 he joined the immortals. Clay and Webster stood by as pallbearers while the wasted frame of South Carolina's patron saint was lowered to its temporary rest in the Congressional Burying Ground.

Next Clay, believing that compromise had saved the Union from bloodshed. He had asked to be spared the "heart-rending spectacle" of secession; his prayer was answered. Two years later, on June 29th, 1852 he died in his room at the old National Hotel, in the very shadow of the Capitol, longing for the roses which bloomed around his Kentucky home.

Webster was the rearguard of the Great Triumvirate. "The marvel of his age," he passed from the scene on October 18, 1852, gazing on "the gorgeous ensign of the Republic."

Clay's compromise, hacked and disfigured, fought bitterly at every turn, but nevertheless a compromise, became law in September of 1850. Henry Clay had done his best, but compromise was not enough. So had warned Calhoun. No human power, no Congress, could slow up the ever-faster, downhill glide towards the "dreadful precipice" over which one million American lives would be poured before the chasm of disunion would be filled.

16

ENTER A NEW POLITICAL PARTY WHILE ABOLI-
TION RIDES THE WHIRLWIND

The Union was saved. The slavery question was disposed of forever. So thought many good Americans as the year 1850 drew to a close. Henry Clay's massive Compromise Bill, now law, had settled this troublesome issue once and for all and the ship of state could sail on to greater glories across an unsullied future.

The Great Commoner had reached the pinnacle of his career. It was the crowning triumph of a life soon to fade. Once more he was hailed as the savior of the nation. "I can sleep nights now," he said. "We have gone through the most important crisis that has occurred since the foundation of this government . . . the Union stands firm."

Jubilation broke out everywhere. In September, 1850, as the final clause of the Compromise staggered toward its adoption in Congress, Washington gave over to celebrating. Crowds gathered in the streets, in the corridors of the Capitol, to cheer the legislators. Rockets flared in the skies. Government buildings were illuminated. The nation exulted as city after city lit bonfires. Throughout the nation there was toasting the new compromise "look." The name of Henry Clay was on every lip.

And while the forts in New York Harbor roared out their one-hundred-gun salvos to celebrate the enactment of the

206

Compromise, the Swedish Nightingale, Jenny Lind, came sailing up the bay to charm the nation with her divine voice and to sing the praises of the great Henry Clay.

But the Compromise, after all, was merely a patchwork peace that postponed the final issue for a decade. The build-up toward war went on inexorably. Distasteful, reeking to high heaven in the nostrils of Northern abolitionists, was the Fugitive Slave Act, sixth of the measures in Clay's Compromise. Waves of indignation against the law rocked the North. Wrote Ralph Waldo Emerson, "This filthy enactment was made in the nineteenth century by people who could read and write. I will not obey it, by God." Thousands felt as did Emerson and said so in varying degrees of emotion.

Under the provisions of the stringent Fugitive Slave Act, runaway slaves who had escaped North could be seized by Federal officers, shackled and shipped back South to their masters. From pulpits the measure was denounced as a violation of the laws of God. Mouthpiece of the radicals on the floor of Congress was Senator William H. Seward of New York, who stated, "We deem the principle of the law for the recapture of fugitives, as thus expounded, unjust, unconstitutional and immoral." He it was who during the fight against the enactment of the Compromise solemnly declared, "There is a higher law than the Constitution."

Urged on by irreconcilables and radical abolitionists, Northern communities began resisting execution of the law. Disorders followed. Mobs snatched recaptured Negroes from their captors, whom they threatened with lynching. Posses of manhunters scoured the North, seizing Negroes who had lived in freedom for years and hustling them South. The abolition escape network along the Ohio River, the Underground Railroad, worked overtime, spiriting Negroes from slavery to partial freedom in the North.

"God wrote it. I was but an instrument in his hands." So said awestruck Harriet Beecher Stowe. She had but to put her pen to the paper and the words of *Uncle Tom's Cabin* or *Life Among the Lowly* gushed forth. This book, which first appeared serially in the *National Era* of Washington, D. C., in 1851, was an overnight sensation, the most powerful piece of propaganda the abolition crusade could have asked for. Letters from her relatives in Boston telling of the injustices of the Fugitive Slave Act sent Harriet weeping to a kitchen table to write (amid diaper-changing, cooking, and darning stockings) the most remarkable book of its kind in world history.

Mrs. Stowe's sentimental portrayals of slave life were exaggerated, bizarre, but they were moving and gripping and the Northern mind seized upon them as true pictures of what was happening in thousands of Southern plantations. No one who read the book ever forgot Eliza's dash for life and freedom across the Ohio River ice with a baby in her arms, or Little Eva's ascent to heaven, or Simon Legree, villain of the piece, with his bull whips and bloodhounds, who beat slaves to death (at $1,000 apiece) just for meanness or fun. It didn't make sense, but it whipped up popular agitation in the North against slavery better than all the words ever uttered by arch-abolitionist William Lloyd Garrison, who had long ago declared, "The United States Constitution is a covenant with death, and an agreement with hell."

Brought to the footlights, the book went on to incite greater animosity. Men crowded into Northern theatres merely to hurl curses at the black-mustached Simon Legree and not infrequently to take indignant potshots at the unfortunate actor playing the villainous role.

While the slavery caldron seethed, the nation kept expanding. California, admitted in 1850, was the thirty-first state. Congress had meanwhile outgrown the chambers it had occupied since 1819 and where so much of the nation's history had been written. Now two wings were to be added to the Capitol to accommodate the 237 members of the

House and the 62 Senators who were all but elbowing each other for room. On July 4th, 1851, with due ceremony, President Millard Fillmore laid the cornerstone of these additions. Orator of the day was Daniel Webster, then Secretary of State. Under the stone Webster deposited a paper on which he declared, "On this day the Union of the United States stands firm . . . the Constitution still exists unimpaired . . . growing every day stronger and stronger." Yet what was happening in the land hardly bore out Webster's glowing words of promise.

Next it was hands across the Pacific. Commerce and competition called for faster ships and America answered with her majestic, swanlike clipper ships. There was trade with Australia and China and even more remote places. During the Gold Rush long lines of men had stood at the docks in Boston and New York clamoring to board the clippers and speed to California. Down the Atlantic Coast the vessels slid, racing against time and each other, rounding the Horn and dashing up the Pacific to the Golden Gate. Masterbuilder of the clippers was Donald McKay. From his Boston yards came clippers each bigger, more beautiful and speedier than their predecessors. In McKay's sleek *Flying Cloud* Longfellow found inspiration for "The Building of the Ship." She set the all-time record for runs from New York to California, eighty-nine days and twenty-one hours.

In 1852 President Fillmore sent Commodore Matthew Galbraith Perry on a delicate mission to the hermit nation, Japan, Land of the Rising Sun. On July 8th, 1853, Perry's four "Black Ships," belching black smoke, steamed into beautiful Yeddo (Tokyo) Bay and dropped anchor. To startled Japanese officials, Perry let it be known that he and his ships had come ten thousand miles across the Pacific to bring a letter from the august President of the United States to the equally august Emperor of Japan. Perry's task was to pry open the oyster-tight Japanese Empire and persuade Nippon to become a friend and customer of the United

States. With rare diplomacy and veiled threats, Perry carried out his historic mission, opening Japan's closed doors to world trade and intercourse with all nations. Perry even suggested, in vain, to the President that the United States should annex the sizable strategic island of Formosa as an American bastion on the coast of China. He had his ships in this part of the world. Why not let him seize Formosa? But the President would have none of it.

In November, 1852, the Whig Party died at the polls. Once again, and for the last time, the Whigs picked a war-hero candidate. It was an old Whig custom. Twice it had turned the trick for them. This time they nominated gold-braided, six-foot-four General Winfield Scott, ablest commander since Andrew Jackson. "The Greatest Captain of the Age," the Whig electioneers called him. To oppose Scott, the Democrats selected Franklin Pierce of New Hampshire, who had commanded a regiment in the Mexican War, though his chief claim to military glory seemed to have been falling off his horse during the battle of Contreras. But Pierce had unfailing charm of manner and an ingratiating smile that won popularity, while soldier Scott was no politician. He had an unruly tongue and he radiated chilliness. Old Fuss and Feathers was also slightly on the pompous side. On issues there was little to choose between the two. Pierce made no campaign and Scott lacked the finesse to discuss the "issues." So the two parties fought it out on personalities. Scott carried only four states and the Whig Party, after failing so dismally, turned over on its back and died.

In the heat of the campaign the two greatest Whig figures passed from the scene. In June, 1852, Henry Clay, founder of the party, died at the National Hotel in Washington. The Great Commoner breathed his last within earshot of the Capitol where his genius in debate had given him the greatest following enjoyed by any man in American politics up to that time. Three times he had sought the presidency and failed. This coveted prize of his life had flickered before his eyes like a jack-o'-lantern. He had dreamed great dreams only to die in disappointment.

In October, 1852, up at Marshfield, his Massachusetts home, Daniel Webster closed out his accounts. He had hoped to get the Whig nomination that year. Failing to do so and believing the nomination rightfully belonged to him, he refused to support the Whig candidate, Winfield Scott. In his dying moments, a friend in Boston wrote urging Webster to change his stand and support Scott. Turning to his son, Webster said, "Write to this man and tell him to look over towards Charleston and see if Bunker Hill monument is still standing."

Near the end, Webster, who was far from a teetotaler, overheard the doctor tell an attendant, "Give him a spoonful of brandy in fifteen minutes, another in half an hour and another in three quarters of an hour, if he still lives." The dying Webster watched the clock. When it came time for the third spoonful those who were watching at his bedside were undecided about administering it. It seemed as if the statesman had passed on. While they deliberated, the dying Webster raised his head a little and feebly remarked, "I still live." He got the brandy, then sank into a deep sleep from which he never wakened.

The Whigs were dead, but in 1854 came their resurrection, at least in part. Joining up with the old Free Soilers and anti-Nebraska Democrats, the Northern Whigs christened their new amalgamation Republican, the name of Thomas Jefferson's original party. Adopting anti-slavery as the main plank of their creed, the Republican Party scaled the political ladder with such unbelievable speed that in six years it elected a president whose exalted name would ring down the ages.

But tension still mounted between the North and South—and three men who would play leading roles in the final flaming drama pursued the even tenor of their ways: Ex-Congressman Abraham Lincoln, none-too-good prairie lawyer, was eking out a living for his growing family at Springfield, Illinois; Ulysses Grant, bibulous lieutenant of infantry, was heading for California with his regiment; Robert E. Lee, captain of engineers, was at West Point training officers to lead opposing armies whose tread could already be heard coming over the horizon.

17

BLOOD ON THE SENATE FLOOR

Late afternoon, May 19th, 1856. In the Senate gallery, peering spellbound over the rail, sat a sensitive, frail Patent Office clerk, Clara Barton, watching the sullen drama below her. On the floor of this nation's "citadel of law, of order and of liberty" Senator Charles Sumner of Massachusetts was delivering "the most thorough Philippic ever uttered in a legislative body"—his withering, highly-chiseled, rhetorical masterpiece, "The Crime Against Kansas."

For Clara Barton, deeply stirred by Sumner's fierce arraignment of slavocracy, "That night war began. . . . It began not at Fort Sumter but with Sumner."

In the tense, tightly packed galleries sat also a robust veteran of the Mexican War, Preston S. Brooks, member of the House from South Carolina, representing John Calhoun's old Ninety-sixth District. He, too, was spellbound, but resentful of every lashing word which fell from Sumner's eloquent tongue. That night Preston went to his bed to toss feverishly, brooding over the gross insults Sumner had heaped on his kinsman, Senator Andrew Pickens Butler of South Carolina, the courtly, kindly, highly respected member of the upper House, who was absent from his seat.

On the Senate floor, barely twenty feet from Sumner, sat a trim, muscular figure, an alert, parliamentary pugilist, ready for combat at a moment's notice and now the target for Sumner's hot grenades. Clad in black broadcloth and gleaming linen he sat, not spellbound as were Clara Barton and Preston Brooks, but waiting for Sumner to finish. Well able to take care of himself was the five-foot-four Little Giant, Senator Stephen Douglas of Illinois.

Two thousand miles from the enthralled Senate chamber, blood was flowing on the plains of Kansas. For the prize of a vast new territory stretching from Missouri to the Rocky Mountains, Free Staters and Slave Staters were splashing the Kansas prairies with blood, rapine, and violence. Armed immigrants from the North and South were clashing along the frontiers. Northern churches were raising collections to send Sharp's Rifles—Beecher's Bibles, they called them—to the Free Staters in Kansas. Southern women sold their jewels to buy guns and bullets for the Missourians, who were moving into Kansas, carrying slavery with them.

The South had the advantage of proximity. The slave state of Missouri was next door and Missourians were rushing to settle the sparsely held territory. To counteract this advantage, the Massachusetts Emigrant Aid Society raised five million dollars to equip free-soil settlers with guns and plows to civilize Kansas.

On March 30th, 1855 the new territory held a Popular Sovereignty election. On that day five thousand slaveholders, called "Border Ruffians" by the Northern press, armed with rifles, bowie knives, and whiskey, crossed the border from Missouri, usurped the Kansas polls, and elected a pro-slavery legislature.

On May 21st, 1856, the day after Sumner's speech, guerrillas from Missouri sacked and burned the Free Soilers capital of Lawrence, Kansas. Blood flowed in the streets. Four days later a strange, hawklike man, who believed himself commissioned by God Almighty to avenge the Lawrence outrage, led his four sons to do the Lord's bidding. In cold blood they murdered five proslavery settlers at their cabin doors on Pottawatamie Creek. "Without the shedding of blood there is no remission of sins," avowed John Brown without blinking.

Headlines shrieked startling news at the nation, but the captions told conflicting stories: "FREEDOM BLOODILY SUBDUED" contrasted with "GLORIOUS TRIUMPH OF LAW AND ORDER PARTY OVER FANATICISM IN KANSAS." From afar an excited, disturbed nation watched the Kansas War, knowing it was the dress rehearsal for a mightier struggle.

To Senator Stephen Arnold Douglas and his Democratic colleagues in Congress—mostly Southerners—Senator Charles Sumner laid the blame for "The Crime Against Kansas."

Douglas had fathered the Kansas Nebraska Act of 1854, creating two new territories of Kansas and Nebraska and permitting the inhabitants to decide for themselves—Popular Sovereignty—the question of slavery.

Bucking a tidal wave of antagonism, scorn, and hate, Douglas had driven his bill through the Senate. Abolitionists and their press indulged in supercharged tantrums of abuse. Douglas epitomized the sentiment against him: "I could travel from Boston to Chicago by the light of my own effigy."

No act ever passed by Congress produced more momentous effects. A virtual repeal of the sacrosanct Missouri Compromise, it revived the heated animosities of the fight against slavery extension, which the Compromises of 1820 and 1850 had presumably buried forever. Slave power could now spread westward.

Douglas' "wicked" Nebraska bill exploded in one of the most desperately contested struggles ever witnessed in Congress.

Douglas, however, had something else in mind: he dreamed of empire-building in the Northwest. A project to build a railroad to the Pacific Coast tantalized him, but the plan was hampered by the absence of territorial government in the vast area west of Missouri and Iowa, the Nebraska Territory. Staking his business and political fortunes on the outcome, he introduced his celebrated Nebraska Bill which would split the territory into two pieces, Kansas and Nebraska, bring orderly government to both, and let the inhabitants make their own choice between slavery and non-slavery. Let Congress keep hands off and accept the decision of the people; thus, the slavery crisis would settle itself.

Out of the struggle against this bill emerged the Republican Party, a combination of Northern Whigs, Free Soilers, and anti-Nebraska Democrats.

Now in March of 1856 Douglas injected into the Thirty-fourth Congress a bill contemplating admission of the Territory of Kansas to the Union. Popular Sovereignty was written into the enabling act. A fiery, three-month filibuster ensued in consequence of the unyielding determination, voiced by Senators Seward of New York and Sumner of Massachusetts, that the bill should not come to a vote.

Tension heightened until on May 19th, 1856 Senator Charles Sumner rose in the full grace of his handsome, commanding presence to spew out "The Crime Against Kansas."

He was an impressive figure as he began the speech which was to canonize and martyrize him in the eyes and hearts of the North. To his beholders, those who idolized him and those who did not, he looked every inch a statesman. No more courtly figure ever stood in this august forum. Today he was immaculately clad. His wavy, lustrous hair was freshly curled as if just released from the hairdresser's hands. His silky sideburns glistened. Patrician to his finger tips, he looked more suited to the drawing room than to the sharp give-and-take of the Senate floor in 1856. A sardonic light flashed from his eyes as he stood where Clay, Calhoun, and Webster had so lately stood, and measured his enemies. In his five years in the Senate he had managed, by personal attacks, to alienate nearly one-half of his colleagues.

Intolerant, arrogant, egotistical, cruel at times, yet scholarly and supremely gifted, he was the best-hated man in the

Senate. Unbridled, polished aspersions rushed from his tongue in a maddening stream. His ability to wreathe unscrupulous vituperation with classical quotations from ancient history has never before nor since been matched in Congress. He was the acknowledged word-master of his time.

Obsessed with antislavery mania, he was nevertheless not unattractive to Southern ladies who were charmed by his exquisite renditions of classic bits of sentimentalism.

Sumner had written and rewritten this speech, committing it to memory with appropriate gestures, "clenched hands or rolling eyes," for almost every phrase. Compounding everything which might shock, horrify, and insult, Sumner searched out lewd Greek references to sharpen his barbed words. He sprinkled the speech with obscenities, lurid sentences, and vulgar similes. Friends before whom he rehearsed it warned him to be more moderate, yet even before its delivery a million copies had rolled from the press.

The Senate "grapevine" had whispered of its coming. Southern leaders knew what to expect. Senator Douglas waited quietly, knowing that perhaps he would bear the brunt of Sumner's attack. Whatever Sumner's foes may have anticipated was far surpassed by what they actually heard.

Threats of violence had already reached Sumner. He was armed, whether on his person or in his desk no one will ever know.

The day was well advanced when he took the floor, addressing the chair with outstanding elegance of manner. "The vigor and grace of his motions, the fervor of his oratory" caught up the crowded chamber and held it as in a vise.

He had a magnificent audience, deeply sympathetic toward every word he spoke. Delegates from a nearby abolition convention had rushed to Washington to pack the galleries. The afternoon was warm and the thermometer in the chamber stood at ninety. Over all pervaded a sense that violence and bloodshed were at this moment raging in far-away Kansas.

Sumner apparently believed he was delivering an oratorical masterpiece which would rank for all time with the best of Cicero and Demosthenes. "Mr. President," he began, "you are now called on to redress a great transgression." These opening words were a warning and a prophecy of what was to come:

"Take down your map, sir, and you will find that the Territory of Kansas, more than any other region, occupies the middle spot of North America. . . . Against this Territory, thus fortunate in position, a Crime has been committed which is without example in the records of the past."

With this start he put on his seven-league rhetorical boots to scale mountains of metaphors, similes, historical allusions, literary quotations, and plain scurrilities.

Condemning the treatment of Kansas as monstrous, tyrannical and depraved, he said:

"The wickedness which I now begin to expose is immeasurably aggravated by the motive which prompted it. Not in any common lust for power did this uncommon tragedy have its origin. It is the rape of a virgin Territory, compelling it to the hateful embrace of Slavery; and it may be clearly traced to a depraved desire for a new Slave State, hideous offspring of such a crime, in the hope of adding to the power of Slavery in the National Government."

Slave Power had corrupted every official of the government:

"Such is the Crime which you are to judge. The criminal also must be dragged into day, that you may see and measure the power by which all this wrong is sustained. In its perpetration was needed a control of Public Opinion through venal pens and a prostituted press; an ability to subsidize crowds in every vocation of life,—the politician with his local importance, the lawyer with his subtle tongue, and even the authority of the judge on the bench,—with a familiar use of men in places high and low, so that none, from the President to the lowest border postmaster, should decline to be its tool: all these things, and more, were needed, and they were found in the Slave Power of our Republic. There, Sir, stands the criminal, all unmasked before you, heartless, grasping, and tyrannical, with an audacity beyond that of Verres, a subtlety beyond that of Machiavel, a meanness beyond that of Bacon, and an ability beyond that of Hastings.

"Such is the Crime and such the criminal which it is my duty to expose; and, by the blessing of God, this duty shall be done completely to the end."

Having defined the crime and the criminal, he waxed personal, slashing his insults at Senator Douglas of Illinois and Senator Butler of South Carolina for aiding and abetting the offense against Kansas:

"The Senator from South Carolina has read many books of chivalry, and believes himself a chivalrous knight, with sentiments of honor and courage. Of course he has chosen a mistress to whom he has made his vows, and who, though ugly to others, is always lovely to him,—though polluted in the sight of the world, is chaste in his sight: I mean the harlot Slavery. For her his tongue is always profuse in words. The frenzy of Don Quixote in behalf of his wench Dulcinea del Toboso is all surpassed. If the Slave States cannot enjoy what, in mockery of the great fathers of the Republic, he misnames Equality under the Constitution,—in other words, the full power in the National Territories to compel fellow-men to unpaid toil, to separate husband and wife, and to sell little children at the auction-block,—then, Sir, the chivalric Senator will conduct the State of South Carolina out of the Union! Heroic knight! Exalted Senator! A second Moses come for a second exodus!

"As the Senator from South Carolina is the Don Quixote, so the Senator from Illinois (Mr. Douglas) is the squire of Slavery, its very Sancho Panza, ready to do all its humiliating offices. I will not stop to repel imputations which he cast upon myself; but I mention them to remind you of the "sweltered venom sleeping got," which, with other poisoned ingredients, he cast into the caldron of this debate.

"The Senator dreams that he can subdue the North. Against him are stronger battalions than any marshalled by mortal arm,—the inborn, ineradicable, invincible sentiments of the human heart; against him is Nature with all her subtle forces; against him is God. Let him try to subdue these."

He listed the four apologies for the crime against Kansas thus:

"The first is the Apology Tyrannical; the second, the Apology Imbecile; the third, the Apology Absurd; and the fourth, the Apology Infamous. This is all. Tyranny, imbecility, absurdity, and infamy all unite to dance, like the weird sisters, about this Crime."

The remedy for the crime, he concluded, was passage at once of a bill to admit Kansas to the Union as a free state. Heatedly he lashed in all directions. His sentences were studded with such terms as "assassins and thugs," "drunken spew and vomit," "murderous robbers," "human beings bred as cattle," "dance of death" (a favorite of his), and "complex completeness of wickedness."

Now he attacked the President for supporting the happenings in Kansas:

". . . As the gallant ship, voyaging on pleasant summer seas, is assailed by a pirate crew, and plundered of its doubloons and dollars, so is this beautiful Territory now assailed in peace and prosperity, and robbed of its political power for the sake of Slavery. Even now the black flag of the land pirates from Missouri waves at the masthead; in their laws you hear the pirate yell and see the flash of the pirate knife; while, incredible to relate, the President, gathering the Slave Power at his back, testifies a pirate sympathy."

Words by the thousand poured from Sumner's tongue. For three hours on May 19th and three hours more on the day following he continued, coming at last to: "Mr. President, an immense space has been traversed and I now stand at the goal." Here he should have paused. The extravagant, exaggerated denunciation which had fallen from his lips had outraged the feelings of two-thirds of his colleagues. During his tirade against Douglas, the Little Giant rose and walked out to the lobby where he confided to a newspaper man: "That damned fool will get himself killed by some other damned fool."

Sumner, however, did not know how to stop. Swept along

by his intemperate, hysterical ranting, he now proceeded to
further savage attacks on Senators Douglas and the venerable Butler, even adding Senator Mason of Virginia to his
targets. At the same time he shot vicious asides at the states
of South Carolina and Virginia:

"With regret I come again upon the Senator from South Carolina
[Mr. Butler], who omnipresent in this debate, overflows with rage at
the simple suggestion that Kansas has applied for admission as a
State, and, with incoherent phrase, discharges the loose expectoration
of his speech, now upon her representative, and then upon her people. But the Senator touches nothing which he does not disfigure—
with error. He cannot open his mouth, but out there flies a blunder.
    ". . . Were the whole history of South Carolina blotted out of
existence . . . civilization might lose—I do not say how little, but
surely less than it has already gained by the example of Kansas, in
that valiant struggle against oppression . . .
    "The Senator from Illinois [Mr. Douglas] naturally joins the Senator
from South Carolina, and gives to this warfare the superior intensity
of his nature. Sir, it is easy to call names; but I beg to tell the Senator,
that, if the word 'traitor' is in any way applicable to those who
reject a tyrannical Usurpation, whether in Kansas or elsewhere, then
must some new word, of deeper color, be invented to designate those
mad spirits who would endanger and degrade the Republic, while
they betray all the cherished sentiments of the Fathers and the spirit
of the Constitution, that Slavery may have new spread. Let the
Senator proceed. Not the first time in history will a scaffold become
the pedestal of honor.
    "Among these hostile Senators is yet another, with all the prejudices
of the Senator from South Carolina . . . I mean the Senator from
Virginia (Mr. Mason), who, as author of the Fugitive Slave Bill, has
associated himself with a special act of inhumanity and tyranny. He
represents that other Virginia, from which Washington and Jefferson
avert their faces, where human beings are bred as cattle for the
shambles, and a dungeon rewards the pious matron who teaches
little children to relieve their bondage by reading the Book of Life."

He was through. A sharp rap from the rostrum silenced
applause instantly. The hot-lipped sequel followed at once.
First to rise to rebuke Sumner was aged Senator Lewis Cass
of Michigan, Nestor of the Senate:

"I have listened with equal regret and surprise to the speech of the honorable Senator from Massachusetts. Such a speech—the most un-American and unpatriotic that ever grated on the ears of the members of this high body—I hope never to hear again here or elsewhere."

Into the lists came Senator Douglas with his forensic lance leveled. Behind him charged Senator Mason of Virginia. Now ensued one of the most virulent, unworthy exchange of personalities in the history of the United States Senate. This verbal swordplay is still hot with anger ninety-nine years after its delivery:

SENATOR DOUGLAS.   I shall not detain the Senate by a detailed reply to the speech of the Senator from Massachusetts. Indeed, I should not deem it necessary to say one word, but for the personalities in which he has indulged, evincing a depth of malignity that issued from every sentence, making it a matter of self-respect with me to repel the assaults which have been made.
    . . . He seems to get up a speech, as in Yankee land they get up a bed quilt. They take all the old calico dresses of various colors, that have been in the house from the days of their grandmothers, and invite the young ladies of the neighborhood in the afternoon, and the young men to meet them at a dance in the evening. They cut up these pieces of old dresses and make pretty figures, and boast of what beautiful ornamental work they have made, although there was not a new piece of material in the whole quilt.

Douglas then arraigned Sumner for his obscene and lascivious classical allusions, saying:

"It seems that his studies of the classics have all been in those haunts where ladies cannot go, and where gentlemen never read Latin."

Douglas then announced that

    . . . it happens to be well known, it has been the subject of conversation for weeks, that the Senator from Massachusetts had his speech written, printed, committed to memory, practiced every night before the glass with a negro boy to hold the candle and watch the gestures, and annoying the boarders in the adjoining rooms until they were forced to quit the House! [Laughter.] It was rumored that he read part of it to friends, and they repeated in all the saloons and places of amusement in the city what he was going to say. The libels, the gross insults which we have heard to-day have been conned over, written with cool, deliberate malignity, repeated from night to night in order to catch the appropriate grace, and then he came here to spit forth that malignity upon men who differ from him—for that is their offense.

Mr. President, I ask what right has that Senator to come here and arraign three-fourths of the body for a dereliction of duty? Is there anything to justify it in the fact that he came here with a deliberate avowal that he would never obey one clause of the Constitution of the United States, and yet put his hand upon the Holy Bible, in the presence of this body, and appealed to Almighty God to witness that he would be faithful to the Constitution with a pledge to perjure his soul by violating both that oath and the Constitution?

. . . Because I am faithful to the Constitution of my country, I am arraigned as a conspirator, as a traitor, as a man guilty of crime . . . I have been burned and hung in effigy under the advice and arrangement of these conspirators here, because of my fidelity to the Constitution of the country, and to the principles to which I stood pledged, and which my judgment approved.

The attack of the Senator from Massachusetts now is not on me alone. Even the courteous and the accomplished Senator from South Carolina [Mr. Butler] could not be passed by in his absence.

Senator Mason. Advantage was taken of it.

Senator Douglas. It is suggested that advantage is taken of his absence. I think that is a mistake. I think the speech was written and practiced, and the gestures fixed; and, if that part had been stricken out, the Senator would not have known how to repeat the speech. [Laughter.]

". . . Why these attacks on individuals by name, and two thirds of the Senate collectively? Is it the object to drive men here to dissolve social relations with political opponents? Is it to turn the Senate into a bear garden . . . ? These attacks are heaped upon me by man after man. When I repel them, it is intimated that I show some feeling on the subject. Sir, God grant that when I denounce an act of infamy I shall do it with feeling, and do it under the sudden impulses of feeling, instead of sitting up at night writing out my denunciation of a man whom I hate, copying it, having it printed, punctuating the proof-sheets, and repeating it before the glass, in order to give refinement to insult, which is only pardonable when it is the outburst of a just indignation.

SENATOR MASON. Mr. President, I did not intend to be betrayed into this debate. I am constrained to hear here depravity, vice in its most odious form uncoiled in this presence, exhibiting its loathsome deformities in accusation and vilification against the quarter of the country from which I come; and I must listen to it because it is a necessity of my position, under a common Government, to recognize as an equal, politically, one whom to see elsewhere is to shun and despise.

Mr. President, the first criminal known to the world, in the complaint which instigated him to crime, declared only that the offering of his brother was more acceptable than his. In the fortunes of those who are enlisted with the Senator from Massachusetts against this confederation now, let them go, as Cain did, with the curse upon their brow of fraternal homicide, but with the still deeper guilt that they instigate others to shed blood when they shed none themselves.

SENATOR SUMNER. To the Senator from Illinois I should willingly leave the privilege of the common scold—the last word; but I will not leave to him, in any discussion with me, the last argument, or the last semblance of it. He has crowned the audacity of this debate by venturing to rise here and calumniate me.

. . . Perhaps I had better leave that Senator without a word more; but this is not the first, or the second, or the third, or the fourth time, that he has launched against me his personalities . . . Since he has presumed to touch me, he will not complain if I administer to him a word of advice . . . Let the Senator remember hereafter that the bowie-knife and bludgeon are not the proper emblems of senatorial debate. Let him remember that the swagger of Bob Acres and the ferocity of the Malay cannot add dignity to this body. The Senator has gone on to infuse into his speech the venom which has been sweltering for months—ay, for years; and he has alleged facts that are entirely without foundation, in order to heap upon me some personal obloquy. I will not go into the details which have flowed out so naturally from his tongue. I only brand them to his face as false.

Sumner paused, gazed at his transfixed fellow Senators, then at the President *pro tempore* on the rostrum, finally raising his eyes to the packed, entranced galleries. With deadly meaning, intense deliberation, he uttered his next words.

I say, also, to that Senator, and I wish him to bear it in mind, that no person with the upright form of man can be allowed. . . .

Again Sumner hesitated only to be spurred on by Douglas' sharp, insistent, "Say it."

SENATOR SUMNER. I will say it—no person with the upright form of man can be allowed, without violation of all decency, to switch out from his tongue the perpetual stench of offensive personality. Sir, that is not a proper weapon of debate, at least, on this floor. The noisome, squat, and nameless animal, to which I now refer, is not a proper model for an American Senator. Will the Senator from Illinois take notice?

SENATOR DOUGLAS. I will; and therefore will not imitate you, sir.

SENATOR SUMNER. I did not hear the Senator.

SENATOR DOUGLAS. I said if that be the case I would certainly never imitate you in that capacity, recognizing the force of the illustration.

SENATOR SUMNER. Mr. President, again the Senator has switched his tongue, and again he fills the Senate with its offensive odor.

SENATOR DOUGLAS. I am not going to pursue this subject further. I will only say that a man who has been branded by me in the Senate, and convicted by the Senate of falsehood, cannot use language requiring reply, and therefore I have nothing more to say.

For Free Soilers, abolitionists, and the anti-slavery press, Sumner's speech was a "solemn, majestic anthem." Whatever it was, Sumner had reached a new high, or low, in personal slurs hurled by one Senator at another.

For handsome, upstanding Preston Brooks, nephew of Senator Butler, Sumner's stinging jabs at his kinsman were a call to action. Seated quietly at his desk in the House of Representatives, he brooded for two days, only to go to his bed at night and toss restlessly, unable to sleep.

In the forenoon of May 22nd, two days after Sumner's assault, Brooks entered the Senate chamber to call Sumner to an accounting. Having decided to take matters into his own hand, he planned to accost the Senator in a passageway of the Capitol and give him the choice of an apology or chastisement.

The Senate had met and adjourned at once out of respect for a deceased member of the House. The chamber was nearly empty when Brooks, carrying a stout gutta-percha cane, strode in with his bodyguards, Representatives Lawrence Keitt of South Carolina and Henry Edmundson of Virginia.

Sumner was at his desk busily writing. Before him was a pile of papers he was franking for mailing. He had denied himself to several visitors who had approached him. Fifteen or twenty Senators and friends stood loitering about the chamber. Senator Douglas was in the reception room. Senator Crittenden of Kentucky, who was Henry Clay's successor, was chatting with Senator Foote of Connecticut near the door. A reporter for the New York *Times* was conversing with two members of the House, Morgan and Murray of New York, at Senator Clayton's desk. Senator Toombs of Georgia was standing at the back of the chamber. It was such a scene as occurs over and over again directly after adjournment for the day.

Quietly, with no fanfare or excitement, Brooks entered, followed by Keitt and Edmundson. Walking directly up the aisle to Sumner's desk he paused. His manner was easy and businesslike. Absorbed in his writing Sumner had not observed the tall, youngish man who now addressed him twice in a restrained voice.

"Senator Sumner! Senator Sumner!"

Glancing up, pen still in hand, Sumner saw, standing directly over him a man whom he did not recognize. At the same time he heard the man ejaculate without bluster: "Senator Sumner, I have read your speech twice over, deliberately and dispassionately. You have libelled my state and slandered my white-haired old relative, Senator Butler, who is absent, and I have come to punish you for it."

Before the astonished Sumner could reply or get to his feet, Brooks dealt him a heavy blow with the gutta-percha cane on the top of his head. Sumner was stunned and momentarily deprived of his sight by the ferocity of the onset. Instinctively he tried to rise and grapple with his assailant, only to be beaten down by a rain of blows. Sumner was large and powerful, but wedged between his seat and desk so tightly that he could not rise quickly. Blood poured down his head and cheeks. Bowing his head he cried out, "I'm most dead! Oh, I'm most dead!" With a frenzied effort he struggled to his feet, wrenching his desk from the floor as he cried out again, "Oh, I'm almost dead—almost dead!" Covered with blood, staggering, he spun around and plunged forward to fall unconscious on the Senate floor ten feet away.

The cane broke in Brooks' hand, but he continued pummeling with the heavy half of it, striking Sumner's head with at least twenty rapid blows. Sumner's blood spattered his assailant.

Hearing a commotion, the New York *Times* reporter and Representative Morgan dashed across the chamber, only to be met threateningly by Representative Keitt, who brandished his own cane and warned them off: "Let them alone, God damn you!"

Senator Douglas, roused by the noise, glanced into the chamber but, seeing what was happening, withdrew at once lest he be accused of aiding and abetting an attack on the man who had addressed him so offensively two days before. Senator Toombs of Georgia looked on "approvingly." An eyewitness from New York who watched the exciting encounter from the gallery, said he heard Southerners shouting, "Don't interfere! Go to it, Brooks! Give the damned abolitionists hell!"

Senator Crittenden rushed up and seized Brooks, who immediately exclaimed, "I did not intend to hurt him much, but only to whip him." Brooks later said his first blow was but a tap intended to put Sumner on his guard.

Leaving Sumner bleeding and unconscious on the floor, Brooks and his companions leisurely walked out of the chamber, exchanged pleasantries with several Senators on the way out, and hurried out of the Capitol.

Around the prostrate Sumner's head circled a stream of bright blood contrasting sharply with the darker red of the Senate's carpet. It was all over in a minute. Senators dashed in from the lobby, while visitors drawn by the excitement of a brawl on the Senate floor made a cordon around the insensible Sumner. As soon as he regained consciousness, perhaps three minutes later, Sumner was assisted to a sofa in the Senate lobby, where a physician soon dressed his wounds and later carried him to his lodgings.

The assault on Sumner set the North on fire. Overnight his prestige soared, while "Bully" Brooks was assailed by the Northern press as a "villainous assassin." The Massachusetts legislature showed its gratitude and sympathy by re-electing Sumner to the Senate for a second term. Up to now his popularity had been waning and his chances to succeed himself had been lessening. Now he became a symbol of the fight on slavery; he was literally apotheosized. Martyrdom was his crown. Indignation meetings, pulpits, and platforms of the North and West flared with denunciation of Brooks and Southern barbarity.

To the South Brooks became a hero. Southern newspapers exulted in his "chivalrous" attack on Sumner. In an editorial rich with onomatopoeia, the Richmond *Examiner* said: "Sumner was a poltroon who when caned for cowardly vituperation falls to the floor in an inanimate lump of incarnate cowardice."

"Violence reigns in the streets of Washington . . . violence has now found its way into the Senate chamber," wrote William Cullen Bryant, editor of the New York *Evening Post*, while a banner in a Democratic victory parade along Pennsylvania Avenue proclaimed: "SUMNER AND KANSAS— LET THEM BLEED."

How grave were Sumner's wounds is still a mystery. His cuts were deep, he lost considerable blood, his nervous system was badly shocked, but several months later, in his letter of acceptance to the Massachusetts legislature, he spoke of his "complete restoration to health." To a friend at this time, who asked what he intended to do when he returned to the Senate, Sumner replied: "I will make a speech upon slavery which those who heard what I said before will say is as first-proof brandy to molasses and water." Yet, however serious or slight was Sumner's incapacitation, he did not return to the Senate for over three years.

Handsome canes, appropriately engraved to commemorate the assault on the calumniator of the South, poured in on Brooks by the score. His admirers in the Senate and House gave him a roaring banquet at Willard's Hotel and presented him with a cane bearing the inscription: "Use knockdown arguments." Citizens of Charleston, South Carolina, sent him a cane engraved with the words: "Hit him again!" The students of the University of Virginia raised funds to purchase a heavy gold-headed cane on which was carved Sumner's badly cracked and broken head.

On Capitol Hill Republicans moved to avenge the assault on Sumner, but the Senate Select Committee, which investigated the fracas, reported that "the Senate, for a breach of its privileges, cannot arrest a member of the House of Representatives, and, *a fortiori,* cannot try and punish him." Bludgeoning an unpopular Senator was regrettable, but the Senate had no jurisdiction in the matter.

In the House matters stood otherwise. The Republican majority rushed through a resolution of expulsion against Brooks and one of censure for his two confederates. But expulsion failed, 123 yeas to 95 nays, lacking the necessary two-thirds. When the vote was announced, Brooks was on his feet instantly. In dramatic silence he addressed the chamber:

"Mr. Speaker, I cannot, on my own account, assume the responsibility, in the face of the American people, of commencing a line of conduct which in my heart of hearts I believe would result in subverting the foundations of this government and in drenching this Hall in blood. No act of mine, and on my personal account, shall inaugurate revolution; but when you, Mr. Speaker, return to your own home, and hear the people of the North—and they are a great people —speak of me as a bad man, you will do me the justice to say that a blow struck by me at this time would be followed by revolution—and this I know. [Applause and hisses in the gallery.]

"I went to work very deliberately, as I am charged—and this is admitted—and speculated somewhat as to whether I should employ a horsewhip or a cowhide; but, knowing, that the Senator was my superior in strength, it occurred to me that he might wrest it from my hand, and then—for I never attempt anything I do not perform—I might have been compelled to do that which I would have regretted the balance of my natural life."

From the House came a voice: "He would have killed him!"

"And now, Mr. Speaker, I announce to you, and to this House, that I am no longer a member of the Thirty-fourth Congress."

So saying, Brooks turned and walked out of the chamber, only to be surrounded by a bevy of Southern belles in the hall and "smothered with kisses."

His resignation was already in the hands of the Governor of South Carolina, but hardly was it received before he was triumphantly re-elected. On August 1st, 1856 he "came forward and the Speaker administered to him the oath to support the Constitution of the United States." Haled into the District Circuit Court, Brooks was fined three hundred dollars and the case ended there.

Six months later the country was startled by the sudden death of Preston Brooks at his Washington hotel. In another three months Senator Butler, for whom Brooks was knighterrant, was dead. Representative Lawrence Keitt, who fended off those who would rescue Sumner from Brooks' blows, fell charging Grant's lines in the Wilderness of Virginia in 1864.

In 1857 old "Captain" John Brown of Ossawatomie, sat chatting with Senator Sumner in the latter's fine home on

Hancock Street in Boston. Sumner was describing the attack on him by Brooks the year before.

"The coat I had on at that time is hanging in that closet," said Sumner. "Its collar is stiff with blood. You can see it, if you please, Captain."

John Brown rose, went to the closet and took out the coat. Stroking his long, scraggly beard, he gazed reverently on the coat as if it were the relic of a saint. Two years after touching the dried blood on Sumner's coat, John Brown lay bleeding on the floor of the firehouse at Harper's Ferry after his abortive, murderous raid.

During those same two years Sumner sojourned at European spas, enjoying his martyrdom while his seat in the Senate remained eloquently vacant. Northern visitors gazed on it with religious awe.

On December 2nd, 1859 Senator Sumner arrived at Washington to resume his membership in the "most exclusive club in the world." At that same hour at Charleston, Virginia, they were cutting down the body of John Brown from the end of a hemp rope.

18

THUNDER OVER WASHINGTON

In its half-century or more of history the nation's capital had never mirrored public sentiment so clearly as in the mid-eighteen fifties. Here more than anywhere else it was apparent that the "irrepressible conflict" was indeed irrepressible. Here, in the halls of Congress, North and South first collided.

In an angry clash on Capitol Hill a hotspur Southern senator had already suggested that the city might remain the capital, but of the "Southern Confederacy"-to-be. Break-up of the Union might well make Washington a deserted city, shunned by North and South alike, its significance gone, its very existence threatened. Overrun by Southerners, Washington was really a sprawling Southern town, overwhelmingly Southern in its sympathies.

Yet even while the fuse sputtered toward the inevitable explosion, the social world in Washington kept up appearances. It was a pleasure-bent, hard-drinking, heavy-eating community. The bars of the hotels along Pennsylvania Avenue were busy from seven in the morning until all hours of the night. The most famous hostelry in the city was Willard's whose rococo, multi-mirrored bar was lined day and night with drawling, argumentative planter-gentlemen in broad-brimmed hats from the deep South whose thirst for bourbons and juleps was unquenchable. In convivial groups one could hear them discussing taking over Washington as calmly as they did the price of cotton or a new recipe for Southern punch. Willard's was the rendezvous for politicians of all persuasions, celebrities, diplomats, gay blades and local tipplers, who could stand all day at the bar absorbing incredible quantities of whiskey. Social affairs in Washington were never more gay or brilliant as in these days when the nation was cracking up. In an atmosphere of eat-drink-and-be-merry-for-tomorrow-we-part, ladies and gentlemen herded to parties, ate prodigious feasts, swallowed quantities of potables.

Showplace of the nation was, of course, the legislative coliseum on Capitol Hill where crackling sectional disputes drew crowds like a prizefight ring. Spectators flocked to the galleries to see the fireworks and cheer on their respective champions. The two shiny new marble wings of the Capitol, begun in 1851, were almost finished. In 1857 the House wing was ready for occupancy. Centerpiece of this imposing architectural pile was Thomas Walter's immense central dome whose castiron framework was slowly rising in a skeletal fashion above the rotunda. Strewn about the Capitol grounds were marble columns, capitals and blocks, lumber, castiron girders, waiting their turns to be set in place.

Seated on the east plaza, solemnly presiding over this disarray and facing the east front of the Capitol, was Greenough's nude marble atrocity—a statue of George Washington—for which Congress had appropriated $40,000 only to have the sculptor vanish into his Roman studio for nine years and emerge with a "statue" of the Father of His Country which resembled "a sunbathing Roman Senator," naked from the waist up, the loins draped, but the big marble toes peering out. Shocked spectators gazed and wondered how on earth anyone could ever have created such a monstrous visualization of the great and simple patriot.

Just a mile from the Capitol where the slavery issue boiled hot and bitter—and only a block from the White House—those inclined could buy black ivory at the weekly flesh auctions held in the courtyard of Stephen Decatur's famous mansion on Lafayette Square. This took place in 1856 when the new Republican Party was making its initial bid for the presidency on the moral issue of human slavery.

With "Bleeding Kansas" as the war cry, the Republicans rushed to their first political battle with an evangelistic fervor never before seen in America. Their candidate was forty-three-year-old John Charles Fremont, Pathfinder of the West, a dashing, glamorous figure who had explored the Rockies and helped wrest California from Mexico. Into the campaign the Republicans introduced the novel attraction of sex appeal in the person of gifted, lovely thirty-two-year-old Jessie Benton Fremont, wife of their nominee.

In 1856 the Democrats comprised the party of slavery. They had fathered the Kansas Nebraska legislation repealing the Missouri Compromise and sprinkling the Kansas plains with blood. A plank in their platform endorsed this unfortunate legislation. Their candidate was aging James Buchanan of Lancaster, Pennsylvania, who at least was tolerant of slavery. A dignified statesman-politician, he had held so many government posts he nicknamed himself "Old Public Functionary."

Bellowing that America's Armageddon was at hand, the Republicans called for moral war on slavery. The idea caught on like prairie fire. Poets, authors, preachers, college presidents, professors flocked to the Republican standards. Longfellow, Emerson, Bryant, Walt Whitman, Bayard Taylor struck their poetic lyres with pleas to the voters. Chanted John Greenleaf Whittier:

> "Rise up Fremont and go before,
> The hour must have its man,
> Put on the hunting shirt once more
> And lead in freedom's van."

But the Democrats, old hands at this business, had ten dollars to spend for every Republican one. Alarmed by

Democratic talk of secession, Wall Street poured money into their coffers. August Belmont of New York reputedly gave them $50,000.

As the campaign progressed the Republican anti-slavery blast seemed overpowering, but it fell short on election day. Buchanan carried nineteen states, with 174 electoral votes. Fremont got eleven states, 114 electoral votes. Forgotten in the mounting fervor was a segment of the defunct Whig Party which merged with the so-called Native Americans and nominated Millard Fillmore, who siphoned off 900,000 popular votes, just enough to elect Buchanan, a minority president.

In his inaugural address on March 4th, 1857, incoming President Buchanan did a singular thing. He told the nation that the "long agitation" over slavery and the Constitutional questions involved would soon be stilled by a decision pending in the Supreme Court. He then advised the nation to bow to the decision "whatever it may be." He referred to the famous Dred Scott case then before the high tribunal. Indeed, two of the associate justices of the court had already secretly "leaked" the decision to President-elect Buchanan nine days before the inauguration.

Two days later on March 6th, 1857, Chief Justice Roger B. Taney handed down the cataclysmic decision, which declared slaves were not citizens and had no "rights which the white man was bound to respect." Slaves were merely chattels, said the court, and "the right of property in a slave is distinctly and expressly affirmed in the Constitution." The Chief Justice then went out of his way to declare the Ordinance of 1787, the Missouri Compromise, and all other federal geographical restrictions on slavery, void and unconstitutional. Dred Scott, about whom the political furor whirled, was a Missouri slave who claimed he was free because of his temporary residence on free soil.

Dazed by this fateful decision, abolitionists and anti-slavery forces reeled about in the political arena. There would be no more free states. In the North secession was openly discussed. This decision actually tore the Democratic Party apart and hastened the Civil War.

Into the sullen, agitated slavery picture now stepped Abraham Lincoln, an inconspicuous, gangling Illinois lawyer who on June 17th, 1858, accepted the Republican nomination for senator to oppose the Democratic incumbent, Stephen Arnold Douglas, father of the Kansas Nebraska Act. It became the most famous race for a senatorial seat in American history.

In his acceptance speech. Lincoln struck a new note that was headlined across the nation:

"A house divided against itself cannot stand. I believe this government cannot endure permanently half slave and half free. I do not expect the house to fall; but I do expect it will cease to be divided. It will become all one thing or all the other."

This political contest produced the joint stumping tour of Illinois, the Lincoln-Douglas Debates which captured the imagination of the nation and made Lincoln a national figure. Lincoln was defeated, but Douglas' re-election actually cost him the presidency in 1860.

At Freeport, Illinois, Lincoln ingeniously and with uncanny skill trapped Douglas into quibbling on the Dred Scott case. Douglas' blacksliding reply to Lincoln's loaded slavery question is known as the Freeport Doctrine, or Freeport Heresy as the Southern Democrats preferred to call it. Asked Lincoln, "Can the people of a United States Territory, against the wish of any citizen of the United States, exclude slavery from its limits prior to the formation of a State Constitution?"

Douglas answered in the affirmative, admitting that the voters could, if they desired, invalidate the Dred Scott decision by "unfriendly legislation" and thus exclude slavery from a territory. Northern Democrats cheered Douglas' reply, but the Little Giant alienated Southern radicals who controlled that wing of the party. Thus Lincoln drove a wedge between the Democrats of the South and North, split the party and, unconsciously perhaps, insured a Republican victory, his own, in the election of 1860.

While Lincoln and Douglas were debating and Senator William H. Seward was telling an audience at Rochester, New York, that the conflict between slavery and freedom was "an irrepressible conflict between opposing and enduring forces," other militant personalities were at work in the nation. It was time for action. There had been words enough.

So thought a strange, wild-eyed, scraggly-bearded old man, arch-abolitionist John Brown, who conceived of himself as God's agent to avenge the evils of slavery in the South. Ever since his massacre of the pro-slavers on Pottawattamie Creek in Kansas in 1856, John Brown's sinister shadow had haunted the slavery drama. Now he would invade the South and foment slave insurrection. "When I strike the bees will swarm," he said, his mad brain deluded into believing the slaves would rise, murder their masters and flock to his standard.

Certain that God had appointed him to deliver 3,000,000 serviles from bondage, Brown led his forlorn "army" of eighteen fanatics into action on the night of October 16th, 1859. Armed with pikes, Sharps rifles and revolvers, Brown and his men suddenly "invaded" Harpers Ferry, Virginia, fifty miles up the Potomac from Washington, and began slaying innocent citizens in cold blood in the streets. But no slaves answered his call to revolt. Most of them had never heard of John Brown whose raid was crushed so soon. Seizing the Federal arsenal, Brown and his men barricaded themselves in the engine house within the arsenal enclosure. Here, besieged by hastily mobilized Virginia militia and United States marines commanded by then Colonel Robert E. Lee, Brown and his little band were shot down one by one. At daybreak of October 18th marines stormed the engine house, smashed in the doors and beat out the last spark of resistance. Brown's raid was over and he was badly cut up by a marine lieutenant's sword. Amid the dead and dying on the engine-house floor lay Brown's two sons, lifeless.

Overnight North and South were convulsed. Shuddering at the horrors latent in Brown's wild scheme, the South demanded his execution while the North acclaimed him as a second "savior." Emerson anointed Brown as a "new saint, than whom none purer or more brave was ever led by love of men into conflict and death."

Death indeed came to John Brown who, tried and convicted of treason and murder, died at the end of a rope at Charlestown, Virginia, December 2nd, 1859, leaving behind a name soon to become the theme of a song a million men would sing as they marched to battle to finish his task.

On the morning of his execution as he left the jail to ride on his own coffin to the near-by gallows, Brown handed his guard a piece of paper on which he had written his famous last-moment prophecy:

"I, John Brown, am now quite certain that the crimes of this guilty land will never be purged away but with blood. I had, as I now think vainly, flattered myself that without very much bloodshed it might be done."

No prophet was ever more right.

19

THE CRISIS OVER JOHN SHERMAN, WOULD-BE
SPEAKER

"Oh, Thou great protector, Thou Pilot, Our Father at the helm, guide us through this storm into a haven of safety and peace. Give to thy servants assembled in this Hall of Legislation the spirit of conciliation, of kindness, of peace, of patriotism, of piety; and, if it be Thy will, may they be guided this day in their choice of a Presiding Officer. May brighter, better prospects open before us. May the sun never see these States divided, discordant, belligerent, but may we always be a happy, united people, and become an increasingly happy and prosperous people."

Thus did Chaplain Stephen Hill, on December 26th, 1859, earnestly beseech Almighty God to take a hand in electing a Speaker of the House of Representatives. Three weeks had gone by—three weeks of acrimony and confusion, rankling debate and emotions run amuck as the House balloted vainly to choose a man to occupy the coveted chair on the rostrum. Well might the chaplain ask divine intercession, for only a kind, overruling Providence could have averted bloodshed on the beautiful, new carpet of the House Chamber now turned into a cockpit.

Save for the undertone of deadly animosity, the scenes in the House reeled off like oldtime melodrama, with hisses and applause, boos and threats, gunplay and gleaming knives. Statesmen walked the aisles with weapons buckled under their coats. "Every man on the floor of both Houses is armed with a revolver—some with two revolvers and a

Bowie knife," declared Senator Hammond of South Caro-lina, who knew what he was talking about. The Palmetto State's delegation bulged with ill-concealed pistols. In the Senate Ben Wade of Ohio put a sawed-off shotgun ostenta-tiously in his desk, making sure that it was observed by all.

Only a spark—a shot—a blow—would have started a bloody brawl to shock the world. The din of the uproar in the House could be heard all over the Capitol. "The members of both sides are mostly armed with deadly weapons," wrote Sena-tor Grimes of Iowa, "and the friends of both are armed in the galleries. The Capitol resounds with the cry of dissolu-tion and the cry is echoed through the city."

The Thirty-sixth Congress had assembled in a stern, highly-charged atmosphere. John Brown's body was still unburied when, on December 5th, 1859, the two hundred and thirty-seven members of the House strode in to their benches. First on their agenda was the election of a Speaker—a con-test which brought on a saturnalia of vituperation and near-violence, deadlocking the House for eight weeks. There was little banter between the gentlemen of the North and South. Absent was the geniality and badinage which in for-mer days marked the opening of the national legislature.

For, even as Congress assembled, John Brown's body, hailed from city to city by emotional multitudes, was slowly journeying towards North Elba, New York, its last resting place. The guns which fired and the bells which tolled in the North at the hour of his execution were hardly stilled before abolitionist hysteria had enshrouded Old Pottowat-tamie in a haze of sainthood. While Northern hallelujahs glorified Brown as a Christ-like martyr, waves of anger, fear, and resentment came surging up from the South to break with resounding fury against the very portals of the Capitol. The South was appalled. Brown had sought to incite a slave insurrection with all its attendant atrocious horrors. Had John Brown's body been brought from nearby Charlestown and laid in state in the rotunda of the Capitol, it could not have had a more explosive effect on the Thirty-sixth Congress.

Actually, the North and South were clearing for action. The Union was breaking up, and the first shots of Civil War, it seemed, were to be fired in the very halls of Congress. Yet, before the dissolution, Congress would keep going through the motions of being united. Already men were drilling and drums were beating on village greens north and south of the Potomac. Momentous and fateful, this would be the last Congress in which the South would participate until half a million men had fallen on fiery battlefields and armies had devastated homes, cities, and commerce of one-third of the country. Out of this Congress walked the men who cradled the Southern Confederacy and brought dead John Calhoun's long dream to life, if only for a little while.

Glancing through the turmoiled ranks of the House, one saw striking figures, men who would be heard from now or later. Some were newcomers; others were assuming vaster rôles in the tragedy on which the curtain was fast rising.

Down front on the Republican side sat two future Speakers of the House: Schuyler Colfax of Indiana and Galusha Grow of Pennsylvania. For Colfax the Vice-Presidency also loomed. Grow was to win renown as one of the ablest, sincerest men ever to wield the House gavel.

Here was Elihu Washburne of Illinois, the man who was to "find" a man named Grant. That turkey-cock of a man, strutting so proudly down the aisle was Roscoe Conkling of New York, vain, party-zealous and an orator of great capacity. Yonder was John A. Logan, a Douglas Democrat from Illinois, raven-haired, handsome, who at this distance little dreamed of commanding a division of Sherman's army on its march to the sea.

Spoiling for a fight was South Carolina's Milledge Bonham, veteran of the Seminole and Mexican wars. He would soon command a brigade at Bull Run and help turn the tide for the Confederacy in that first clash of the war.

Sitting quietly with the Ohio delegation was slender John Sherman, able and moderate, who is best remembered today for the anti-trust law which bears his name. His red-headed brother, then a military schoolmaster in Louisiana, would one day overrun Georgia with his torchbearing myrmidons.

Pre-eminent among his Republican fellows was stern Thaddeus Stevens, clubfooted and athirst for battle. In the next seven years this man was to amass such power as to make him king on Capitol Hill. Grim, imperious, and intolerant, unpopular but feared, he could envisage but one issue: slavery. Slave-hater though he was, he was to become the slave-driver of his party and crack the whip over his fellows as stingingly as ever a Southern overseer applied the lash to manacled Negroes.

From Mississippi came a talented parliamentarian and eloquent master of words adorned with three Roman names, Lucius Quintus Cincinnatus Lamar. He was to shoulder a Confederate rifle, return to Capitol Hill as Senator when his state rejoined the Union and, finally, don the robes of the Supreme bench.

Handsome beyond words was a spirited politician from New York, Daniel Sickles. He wore the distinction of his late acquittal of the charge of slaying Philip Barton Key, son of the author of "The Star Spangled Banner," for intimacy with his flirtatious, Spanish-born wife. A seer might have told Sickles he would command the Federal Third Corps at Gettysburg and lose a leg in a blundering maneuver.

From a famous New England family came its third statesman, Charles Francis Adams of Massachusetts, son of John Quincy Adams. He would soon be its third diplomat. Like his father and grandfather, he was to represent the nation at the Court of St. James.

The House had occupied its spacious hall in the new South Wing of the Capitol since 1857. Richly ornamented in red and gold, the chamber had a ceiling of glass panels decorated with the coats of arms of the thirty-three states which then composed the Union. Fifteen hundred gas jets behind this ceiling illuminated the embattled night sessions. The Speaker presided at a high marble table on the rostrum. To the right of the Speaker, on its marble pedestal, rested the mace, time-honored symbol of the Speaker's authority, which in the session just opening was to be flouted like useless stage property and trotted out to no avail to quell tumults which refused to be stilled.

It was a House closely divided; no party had a controlling majority. Great political upheavals loomed on the horizon. The Democrats had lost their long-time superiority in the House. Party lines were now a matter of latitude and longitude involving the North and the South. The stripling five-year-old Republican Party boasted 109 members on the floor; the Democrats mustered 101. The American Party, the so-called "South Americans," leftovers from the Whigs and Know Nothings and mostly Southerners, had 27. In the Senate the Democrats still held the upper hand with 38 out of its 66 seats.

Hardly had the session opened before Northern and Southern extremists leaped into the saddle to ride challengingly through the House lists. Presiding over the pandemonium was "Mr. Clerk." There was no Speaker; there were no rules. Neither was there a member of the House so forceful that, like John Quincy Adams in the wild impasse of 1839, he could mount the rostrum, take control by sheer power of words and personality, restore discipline and lead the House into orderly organization. Events had progressed too far; so had the nation.

Heaving, disorderly debate was not new in the House. Seventy years of parliamentary existence had produced turbulent scenes, but never before was the House convulsed by such deep, outspoken hatred.

The House had even its own Mason and Dixon's line, the center aisle separating the benches of the Republicans and Democrats. Venturing to the wrong side was sometimes dangerous business. Imperiling the proceedings and intensifying the bitterness was a psychological factor—a new seating arrangement—which the previous Congress had overlooked when it ordered all desks removed and benches substituted, thus bringing Southern hotspurs into close proximity with their Northern counterparts. It was like tossing all the wild animals of the zoo into the same cage. The benches were bunched in the middle of the then seemingly vast chamber. As tempers rose and rancor and recrimination hurtled across the floor, the new layout made for easier violence.

When Roger Pryor of Virginia appeared on the floor wearing a suit of "Confederate gray," a Northern member hurled a prophetic challenge at him: "Virginia, instead of clothing herself in sheep's wool, had better don her appropriate garb of sackcloth and ashes."

If the nerves of the lawmakers were jangled and edgy, so were those of an excited, worried nation. The fanfare of Northern dreamers, idealists, and extremists was matched by the flaming furor of the South. Despite this, few Americans knew how close to bloodshed the nation came in the tense weeks of the battle to elect a Speaker of the House of Representatives of the Thirty-sixth Congress.

As the battle for the Speakership got under way, the galleries seethed with disorder. Sharp fights broke out. Packed with a melée of clerks, politicians, and hangers-on there was no stopping the angry, raucous applause and the hisses which greeted bitter passages on the floor. Thunderous handclapping and foot-stamping rolled through the Capitol. Scowling ruffians and Secession Rowdies milled in the lobbies. Men with pistols bulging under their coats stood and glared at each other. The turmoil on Capitol Hill spread through the nation like racing infection. The women of official Washington, deeply alarmed, thronged the galleries. From morning to the hour of adjournment they would sit, spellbound and frightened, as one lawmaker after another painted lurid pictures of disunion and war. Their bright bonnets and flowered dresses conflicted sharply with the dark forebodings in their hearts.

Contrasting with the violent scenes on the floor and in the galleries were the rosy, cherubic little pages, in white blouses and cambric collars, flitting to and fro, "bearing, with smiling faces, dynamic notes and messages from one Representative to another. They represented the future which these gentlemen were engaged in wrecking. Many of these boys were sons of Southern widows, who even now, under the most genial skies, led lives of anxiety and struggle." Mrs. Roger Pryor might have added that before long many even of these striplings would don blue or gray and charge gunfire with the same youthful ardor they tripped hither and yon through the angry ranks of the lower House.

At noon on December 5th, 1859 the House came to momentary order, only to plunge at once into the Speakership struggle around which the black incubus of the slavery wrapped its rancorous coils. Presiding over the touchy scene was the clerk of the previous House, James C. Allen, a frightened, helpless, indecisive fellow, ill-equipped to handle the mob spirit which quickly overran the House.

The Republicans, still a loose coalition, had agreed on John Sherman of Ohio as their candidate for Speaker, although they could not elect him without support from either the Democrats or the Americans. The Democratic caucus had picked Thomas S. Bocock of Virginia. The first ballot was orderly enough. Sixteen candidates divided 230 ballots. Bocock led with 86, Sherman ran second with 66. 43 went to Galusha Grow who immediately withdrew from the race.

Confident that they could realign their ranks, pick up outside support, and rush Sherman through to a majority on the morrow the Republicans moved at once for adjournment. Up to this moment the proceedings remained orderly enough; the fires were merely banked.

Mark well the name of the man who now rose: Representative John B. Clark of Missouri. He was a slaveowner whose pronounced views led to his expulsion from the House on July 13th, 1861 despite the fact that his state had not seceded. In his hand he held a firebrand, a piece of paper on which he had written these words that would embroil the House for eight weeks:

"Whereas certain members of this House now in nomination for Speaker, did endorse and recommend the book hereinafter mentioned,

Resolved, that the doctrines and sentiments of a certain book called *The Impending Crisis of the South—How to Meet It*, purporting to have been written by one Hinton R. Helper, are insurrectionary and hostile to the domestic peace and tranquillity of the country, and that no member of this House who has endorsed and recommended it, or the compend from it, is fit to be chosen to be Speaker of the House."

The House exploded instantly in an uproar while Clark was still on his feet. Men rushed about the floor like madmen, clamoring wildly for or against the resolution. From the galleries came "applause mingled with hisses," says the official record.

Thus did a book, unknown to a large percentage of Americans then and to most Americans today, precipitate the most desperate parliamentary battle in American history— a book whose impact on the affairs of the nation was far more resounding than the exaggerated, emotional picture drawn by *Uncle Tom's Cabin*.

Appearing in 1857, *The Impending Crisis* was the economic equivalent of Harriet Beecher Stowe's novel. Its author was an obscure North Carolina "poor-white," Hinton Rowan Helper, who, in passionate, hysterical style, depicted the wrongs slavery had inflicted on the poverty-stricken non-slaveholders of the South. It was not a new viewpoint, nor did it appeal to slaves but, garbed in threat and invective, it contained much that was enraging to the slaveholding South. Helper urged direct warfare on slavery, "be the consequences what they may." Behind his lines loomed the ghastly picture of slave insurrection, burning homes, throat cutting and devastation.

Fortified by facts and statistics, Helper boldly asserted that slavery had plunged the South into the state of "comparative imbecility." He drew a picture of a minority of Southern whites living in splendor, luxury, and culture while the greater mass of their brethren lived in hovels, poor and illiterate, all because of the slavery system. Convincingly he preached a crusade by the Southern proletariat against King Cotton and the few who shared the wealth of his court. Eight states, including Helper's native North Carolina, had banned the sale of the book.

With John Brown so lately hanged and his body still an object of fanatic veneration, the very mention of the book was—to Southerners—like putting match to gunpowder. Thus, all at once, the book attained fame far beyond its merit.

To make matters worse, Northern politicians, in the recent congressional campaign, had made use of this ill-written and violent assault by a Southerner on the most cherished of Southern economic institutions. During the campaign sixty-eight representatives, mostly Republicans, had signed an endorsement of a condensed version of the book and, by the same token, of Helper's insurrectionary principles. They had even gone further and appealed for funds to broadcast one hundred thousand free copies of the compendium. This compendium, like *The Impending Crisis* itself, contained harsh, violent, offensive strictures on the South. One chapter flaunted this heading, "Revolution Must Free Slaves."

Prominent among the endorsers of the compendium of Helper's book was Ohio's John Sherman, around whom the Republicans now rallied for Speaker. To have endorsed Helper's incendiary doctrines was—to Southerners—unpardonable, even criminal; to offer endorser John Sherman for Speaker was adding insult to injury. Then and there the Southern contingent determined to block his election; if need be, to obstruct the processes of government until a new House took seats on March 4th, 1861; to use every weapon in the parliamentary arsenal, and some which were not, to prevent the election of a Speaker whose principles would be inimical to the South.

Fifty-eight Democrats, all from slaveholding states, secretly pledged themselves to resist the organization of the House and the election of a Speaker until they were sure no Republican could be elected. It was revolutionary, but it gained its ends. Actually, it was a secret filibuster. If the Republicans sought to adopt a plurality, instead of majority rule, in the election, the fifty-seven still controlled. Thus was Congress paralyzed. This group permitted only three votes in the first week of the contest.

The Speakership was always—and still is—the top prize in the House. Then, as now, it was the second most powerful office in the government. If the Republicans succeeded in placing John Sherman in the chair, it would mean committees unsympathetic to the South and continued agitation against slavery, with investigations of the Kansas débacle, the slave trade, and other projects dear to the South. It would mean all the vast influence of the Speakership marshaled against the South.

Caught off balance by Clark's resolution, the Republican leaders moved for delay. If there was to be a conflict, they must prepare for it, but the South would have no delay and pressed the Clark resolution. Political panic seized the Republican ranks as one after another of the sixty-eight endorsers of Helper's book rose to deny their sympathy with radicalism and bloodshed. However, the fat was in the fire and John Sherman was drenched with it.

Having lit that fire, Representative Clark proceeded to pour oil on it. In raking, scathing denuciation Clark fanned the flames of sectional animosity with hot words and inflammatory quotations from Helper's book:

"Mr. Clerk, have we fallen upon such evil times that when this House wishes to select a presiding officer, there is no party here which can present a candidate who is loyal to the Union and the Constitution; and we must take one who has thrown a firebrand into our midst, and whose advice, if taken, would drench one half of this Union in blood?

"Surely, we have not so fallen. Surely we have not come down to the level that we are to select a man who had signed a paper advising rebellion and treason; advising steps that will result in insurrection; advising a portion of our constituencies to declare non-fellowship with the others, who would divide us asunder and destroy an institution secured to us by the Constitution. . . ."

Into the verbal fray plunged John Millson of Virginia. The light of battle gleamed in his eyes as he ranted:

"One who consciously, deliberately, and of purpose, lent his name and influence to the propagation of such writings is not only not fit to be Speaker, but is not fit to live!"
[*Applause and hisses from gallery, says the official record.*]
"Sir, I will not attempt to penetrate the hidden sanctions which, in the relations between himself and his Maker, regulate human conduct, by saying he is not fit to die!"

Thus challenged, the man around whose head the Southern lightning was crackling got to his feet. John Sherman was a man of courage. He met the onslaught head-on, although his colleagues were wavering under the sudden, fiery attack. He walked slowly down the center aisle to the front of the rostrum before he spoke a word. There was a momentary silence; the chamber held it breath and its fire.

"Mr. Clerk, I have, until this moment, disregarded this debate because I presumed it was simply thrown at the House at this time to prevent an organization. But the manner of the gentleman from Virginia and the serious impression which this matter seems to have made on his mind induce me to say what I have to say.

"I do not recollect signing the paper referred to; but I presume, from my name appearing in the printed list, that I did sign it. I therefore make no excuse at all."

A storm of boos and catcalls greeted his words. To have signed a paper endorsing Helper's violent doctrines and not to recollect it and then to expect to be elected Speaker! It was as atrocious as the signing itself!

Amid shouts and jeers and hisses from the Republican benches Virginia's Shelton Leake leaped to his feet. Virginians were touchy; the Old Dominion had borne the brunt of John Brown's raid. She wanted no more of the same thing and her representatives were hot for battle. John Brown's ghost could be seen by every man on the floor. There he was, an evil-looking wraith, preaching terror, insurrection, rivers of blood, and setting men's minds on fire.

Shaking his fists at the Republican benches, Leake unleashed his salvo:

"I desire to make a remark in reply to the observations that have fallen from the lips of the Abolition candidate for the Speakership of this House.

[*Hisses from the Republican benches, says the official record.*]

"I beg gentlemen when they hiss to remember that Rome was saved when the geese cackled. I understand the Abolition candidate for the Speakership to admit that he signed that recommendation, and puts in a special plea of *non est factum*—that he signed it without knowing its contents.

"We, on this side, are entitled to know who it is that we are to elect Speaker, whether we are to elect a man, who, while I am here in the discharge of my public duties, is stimulating my negroes at home to apply the torch to my dwelling and the knife to the throats of my wife and helpless children. He has not disavowed it; nor has anybody in this House disavowed the sentiment yet."

"Mr. Clerk, upon the 9th day of March last, this publication in relation to Helper's book, was written with that gentleman's signature affixed to it, in which he is pledged to revolution in the South, to throttle slavery, and to abolish the institution—peaceably if he can, forcibly if he must. That was his pledge.

"We hold that a man who endorses the sentiments of that Helper pamphlet is unfit to be Speaker, unfit to hold any office, unfit to hold a seat upon this floor, because he comes here sworn to destroy the Constitution and everything we hold dear."

Cheers rose from the Democrat benches; the galleries joined in. Bad blood was rising and it was all too evident. Hoodlums were stamping their feet. The rumble of it could be heard in the Senate chamber on the other side of the Capitol.

There was little semblance of order as the floor grew stormier. The clerk was powerless, amazed, and horror-stricken at his own inability to control a situation which was obviously out of hand. He turned his eyes appealingly from one member to another.

Here came impetuous, lovable Lawrence Keitt of South Carolina. Storming down into the well of the House, he shouted wrathfully,

"The South here asks nothing but its rights. As one of its Representatives I would have no more; but as God is my judge, as one of its Representatives, I would shatter this Republic from turret to foundation stone before I would take one tittle less.

"Let the government pass into the hands of the Abolition party of this country; let us know that, and it is all we wish to know. We of the South are on the defensive and we shrink from meeting no act of aggression which may be committed against us from any field. We mean now to defend ourselves."

The chamber was now supercharged. There was an instant of quiet. To his feet came Thaddeus Stevens, looking like the god of bitterness. Hate boiled in his eyes as he returned Keitt's fire:

"I do not blame the gentlemen from the South for taking the course they do, although I deem it untimely and irregular . . . Nor do I blame them for the language of intimidation, for using this threat of rending God's creation from turret to foundation. All this is right in them, for they have tried it fifty times, and fifty times they have found weak and recreant tremblers in the North who have been affected by it and who have acted from those intimidations. They are right, therefore, and I give them credit for repeating with grave countenances that which they have so often found to be effective when operating upon timid men."

Incandescent with rage, Martin Crawford of Georgia broke in upon Stevens:

"Will you keep down your Union meetings in the North, and not deceive the South by pretending to respect our rights whilst you never intend to give us peace?"

Members began reaching into their coats or feeling at their waists for their holsters as Crawford's voice rose to high, penetrating pitch:

"My object is only to make a single remark and it is, that I hope that the Black Republican Party will not undertake to deceive the South by a pretended friendship for our constitutional rights now and when our apprehensions are gone, then renew their warfare upon slavery."

At this Stevens snarled back:

"That is the way they frightened us before. Now you see exactly what it is and what it has always been."

All at once there was a mad rush for the well of the House: "Members from both benches crowded down into the area and there was, for a time, great confusion and excitement in the Hall." In later times Thaddeus Stevens was to refer to this occasion as the time "when bowie knives were drawn."

Frantically, the clerk called out above the tempest: "The clerk has no power to enforce order. He is powerless and therefore throws himself upon the generosity of the gentlemen upon both sides to assist him in enforcing order." But the gentlemen were not generous. Through the melée moved the Sergeant-at-Arms bearing aloft the revered mace. "Take away the mace! Take away the mace!" shouted several members.

Slowly order was restored. Exchanging bitter glances, Northern and Southern lawmakers sullenly returned to their seats. Up rose sedate Isaac Morris of Illinois:

"Mr. Clerk, there is a good deal of ill-blood in the House.

"Sir, it may be, if these exciting discussions are to be continued, that unpleasant if not fatal consequences will ensue. A few more such scenes as we had on the floor will hear the crack of the revolver and see the gleam of the brandished blade."

Ill-blood, indeed! Soon it might be spilled blood. As he spoke, an Alabama representative could be seen industriously sharpening his Bowie knife on the sole of his shoe! Nearby, holding a long, glittering dagger, stood William Barksdale of Mississippi, who, with the courage of his convictions, was destined to fall, a Confederate brigadier, one thunderous afternoon in 1863 at Gettysburg.

Lucius Quintus Cincinnattus Lamar of Mississippi took the floor and with words of blowtorch intensity dragged John Brown's body all over the floor of the House:

"These gentlemen have assured us that when they signed that document inciting to insurrection, they did not know what was in it; and that they had no intention of indorsing its sentiments.

"You may get up now and say you did not know what you were signing, but it will not reach the dull, cold ear of John Brown and his associates, who now fill felons' graves. You cannot, by that disclaimer, call back into life the men who were shot down like wild beasts in the streets of Harper's Ferry; and I call upon you, gentlemen, now to rise and answer, in the name of God, are you guiltless of the blood of John Brown and his co-conspirators, and the innocent men the victims of his ruthless vengeance? No, sir, you cannot."

The Southerners were unquenchable. Came Roger Pryor of Virginia, inveighing against the possibility of a Black Republican President. In polished eloquence Pryor discharged his sack of venom at Senator William H. Seward of New York and his "Black Republican Party." Seward's, said Pryor, was a program of "treason, rapine and murder."

On December 7th the House took a second ballot. John Sherman, endorser of Helper's book, took the lead with 107 votes. He lacked 9 of the 116 necessary to a choice. The battle must go on. Legislation must wait.

Sherman, the Republican standard bearer, badgered by Southerners for every word he uttered, found his position increasingly more difficult as the day went by. He could not disavow his signature endorsing the Helper book and its compendium. To do so would repudiate the leaders of his party who had also affixed their signatures to the same document. To admit that he endorsed Helper's sentiments would insure defeat. He and his Republican supporters decided to wait out the Southern storm. It became a mad riot of crimination and recrimination, with the Republicans defending their candidate only when pressed to the wall to do so. Southerners carried the burden of wrath, bespattering the Republicans and their leaders, Senator Seward in particular, with blazing, odious epithets. The House rocked with insult and defiance.

Nor were sideshows lacking. John Logan, Democrat, and William Kellogg, Republican, both of Illinois, rushed at each other's throats in an exchange of personalities over the merits of Senator Stephen Douglas.

Logan charged Kellogg with shrinking responsibility and cowering "like a spaniel."

He got no further. Kellogg came towards him threateningly, "Does the gentleman call me a spaniel coward?"

"Here," says the official record, "Mr. Kellogg advanced in a menacing attitude towards Mr. Logan. They were with some difficulty kept apart by members surrounding them, in the midst of the utmost confusion and disorder."

The poor "Mr. Clerk!" No one paid attention to him, but there he was calling out: "The Clerk does not know whether the Sergeant-at-Arms is or is not in the Hall or whether the Clerk has the power to call him if he was."

But the Sergeant-at-Arms snatched the mace from its pedestal and went shouting "Order! Order!" through the statesmen packed below the rostrum. The galleries shouted and hallooed: "Beat him up!" "Let 'em fight!" "Kill the abolitionists!" There was no restraint. King Mob was taking over.

On December 14th a fourth ballot was taken amid much confusion. John Sherman held his lead with 108 votes, though 114 were necessary to elect.

Clement Vallandigham of Ohio, arch-Copperhead of the coming Civil War, rose and tossed onto the flaming pyre of debate words which sent Southerners into a frenzy. Quoting from another pamphlet inspired by Helper's book, Vallandigham read these words, "Teach the slaves to burn their masters' buildings, to kill their cattle and horses, to abandon labor in seedtime and harvest and let crops perish. To make slaveholders objects of derision and contempt by flogging them. . . ."

The House went into a tantrum. Crawford of Georgia got into the fight again shouting, "I repeat, sir; that no Democratic Representative from Georgia will ever submit to the inauguration of a Black Republican President."

Militant and defiant, Milledge Bonham of South Carolina shot to his feet, hurling his words directly at John Sherman:

"The honorable member from Pennsylvania, Mr. Hickman, speaks of the numerical power of the North being sufficient to compel us to remain in the Union. Sir, whenever force is found necessary or expedient the Union no longer exists; and as to disunion, upon the election of a Black Republican, I can speak for no one but myself and those I have the honor to represent, I am in favor of an immediate dissolution of the Union.

"And when you come to excite servile insurrection or to force us back into the Union, these non-slaveholders in common with their brethren, will welcome your myrmidons with bloody hands to hospitable graves."

Thomas Davidson of Louisiana rose to sound warnings to his own colleagues:

"I tell you that if you elect a man who has endorsed doctrines of the Helper book when we go home, our brethren there, the fire-eaters, will go before the people and they will whip us like dogs.

"I will stand here until the 4th of March 1861 if, by so doing, I can avert the calamity which might befall us by the election of a Black Republican."

On Christmas Eve the House balloted for the twenty-first time. Sherman lacked only four votes to achieve the Speakership. Little wonder that on December 26th the Chaplain sought the aid of Providence in quieting passions and bringing about an election.

Outside the Chamber panic spread and the nation held its breath. Any moment might bring news of bloody scenes on the floor of the House. Governor Wise of Virginia notified his state's delegation that, if fighting broke out, Virginia militia would march on the capital. South Carolina's governor pledged that if the issue was to be settled by force, he would have a regiment in Washington overnight. The sparks were flying closer and closer to the powderpile in the House. Every breeze which blew carried these alarming prospects to the corners of the nation.

Taking her pen in hand, a sensitive, lovely South Carolina girl, wife of fire-breathing Representative Lawrence Keitt—he who would render the nation from "turret to foundation stone"—wrote to her brother, voicing the fear and the dread which filled the hearts of the women who could only stand and watch and urge their men on:

"We are having frightful times here—war any moment and no knowing who may fall. Southerners are resolved a black Republican shall not take the chair. They are armed and determined to fight to the knife there on the floor of Congress. Governor Wise has ten thousand men, drilled and armed, that would march to the Capitol at the first sound of war. Oh, Alex, I am so uneasy . . ."

While the House fight raged, while the dividing line was slowly drawn, Washington echoed to sounds of revelry by night, with rounds of dinners, balls, levees, and feasts. Southerners and Northerners began passing each other in the street without speaking or with frigid bows. At White House receptions gentlemen of the Congress met, exchanged frosty glances and passed on with ceremonious nods. At mixed social affairs politics was taboo, but there was no keeping it out. Neutral subjects were hard to find. The bitter dissension on Capitol Hill beclouded everything. When Mrs. Charles Francis Adams, wife of the distinguished Massachusetts representative, spoke out in favor of John Brown, her Southern hostess cut her down without mercy.

As the tension mounted, so apparently did social gaiety. Senator William Seward, the "Black Republican" candidate for the nomination in 1860, gave a seventeen-course dinner. His guests included his bitterest opponents on the Senate floor. At his palatial home on H Street, William W. Corcoran, banker and art collector whose Southern leanings were pronounced, still dispensed his fabulous hospitality. He served the finest Rhine wine in Washington. His canvasback and terrapin were matchless. At quadrilles and germans, Southern gentlemen promenaded with Northern ladies, and vice-versa, although a new formality marked their light-footed capers and their sweeping bows.

January 7th, 1860 brought the twenty-ninth ballot. John Sherman held on, but he needed three votes to elect him. January 17th was a climactic day. If blood was to be shed on the floor, this was the moment. Personalities were flying thick and fast. John Haskin of New York and John McRae of Mississippi were trading hot abuse. Gesticulating at McRae, Haskin walked slowly to the foot of the center aisle. The clerk vainly attempted to cajole the two gentlemen back to their seats. Suddenly a revolver popped out of Haskin's breast pocket and struck the floor, bouncing down the aisle.

"Take your seats! Sit down!" yelled the frightened clerk, but the galleries mocked him.

The uproar was immediate. Scores of members leaped to rally about their respective champions, believing that Haskin had drawn his revolver to do murder in the very halls of Congress. Members rushed pell-mell to be in on the "killing."

Haskin pounced on his revolver with a dozen Southerners piling on top of him. Slaughter seemed imminent. Pistols appeared as if by magic. The wildest confusion ensued as curses and threats poured from raging members. The Sergeant-at-Arms dashed in with the mace, which he shoved into the confused scramble.

Slowly order appeared. Presently Haskin rose to make a lame explanation that he lived in a lonely part of the city "where many outrages have been committed" and the night before, having been out late, he felt it best to carry a revolver. But, he said, others were armed. Why should he not be likewise?

Davidson of Louisiana rose up to remark gravely: "I desire to say that if these things are to continue in the future I must bring a double-barrelled shotgun into the House with me."

On January 27th the thirty-ninth ballot projected William N. H. Smith, a North Carolina Know-Nothing into the lead, with 112 votes to Sherman's 106. Smith lacked only three votes of election. In a surprise deal the Democrats had joined up with the "South Americans."

Behind the scenes events were shaping up. During the seven weeks his name was before the House, John Sherman had not voted. He had relied on his colleagues to bear the brunt of Southern assaults. But Sherman had run his race. That was apparent to the Republicans who had stood by him through the long battle. Up to now the Republicans had prevented a vote on the Clark resolution, but they had elected no Speaker. Faced by the ceaseless fire of Southern sharpshooters, Sherman had but one choice, if he was to rescue the Speakership for his party.

On January 30th John Sherman got to his feet. His colleagues watched him with dismay, but they knew what was coming. Thaddeus Stevens had sworn to stand by Sherman to the crack of doom. Tom Corwin had vowed to hold on till Gabriel blew his trumpet, but the bitter practicalities said John Sherman could not be elected Speaker. In the meantime government was paralyzed.

It seemed as if the next vote would push William Smith into the Speaker's chair. Southerners were jubilant; the long fight would end in victory. Already they were crowding the telegraph office to send news home of Smith's impending election.

At a turbulent night caucus the Republicans determined to play a last card by bringing forward a Whig, William Pennington, former Governor of New Jersey, to whom Sherman's support would be thrown.

It was at this crisis that on January 30th, 1860 John Sherman rose. William Smith stood on the threshold of the Speakership. In a calm, clear voice Sherman began:

"Mr. Clerk: Eight weeks ago I was honored by the votes of a large plurality of my fellow members for the high office of Speaker of this House. They had stood undismayed amidst threats of disunion and disorganization. On the other hand they have seen their ancient adversary, and their only natural adversary, reviving anew the first of sectional discord and broken into fragments.

"Mr. Clerk, I should regret exceedingly, and believe it would be a national calamity, to have anyone who is a supporter directly or indirectly of this Administration, or who owed it any allegiance, favor or affection occupying a position of importance in this House.

"Therefore, Mr. Clerk, I respectfully withdraw my name as a candidate. And if I can ask one more favor of my political friends it would be that in an unbroken column, with an unfaltering front, and unwavering line, each of them will cast his vote in favor of anyone of our number who can command the highest vote, or who can be elected Speaker of this House."

There was a stunning silence, then a burst of Southern victory cheers. John Sherman, "Black Republican," was out of the race. Quickly the fortieth ballot was taken. William Pennington led with 115 votes, William Smith ran second with 113. But Pennington still lacked three votes to elect him. Ballots came faster now.

On February 2nd, John Clark of Missouri, the man who

had started it all with his anti-John Sherman Resolution, rose to his feet. He was apparently well-satisfied with his eight-weeks' work: "Sir, that Resolution of mine has worked its effect, so far, at least, that it has smoked out before the American people the fact that an endorser of the Helper book cannot be Speaker of this House."

On February 1st, 1860 the House took its last and forty-fourth ballot. William Pennington of New Jersey went into the Speakership with 117 votes out of 233 cast. He had one extra vote necessary to elect him. The House of Representatives had elected perhaps the most mediocre, incompetent Speaker in its history, a man who, incidentally, shared with the greatest Speaker, Henry Clay, the distinction of being elevated to the Speakership upon his entrance into Congress. He had little to commend him otherwise.

The nation breathed freer. At least blood was not shed on the floor of the Capitol.

At the peak of the Southern furor over the Speakership battle, John Sherman had received a letter from his brother, William Tecumseh Sherman in Louisiana. The man, who was in 1864 to sweep the deep South with fire and sword, wanted to know something:

"I have watched the despatches and hoped your election would occur without the usual excitement, and believe such would have been the case had it not been for your signing for that Helper's book. Of it I know nothing, but extracts made copiously in Southern papers show it to be not only abolition, but assailing.

"Now I hoped you would be theoretical and not practical; for practical abolition is disunion, civil war, and universal anarchy on this continent, and I do not believe you want that.

"Write me how you came to sign for that book."

When this letter reached John Sherman it seemed as if he still had a chance of becoming Speaker, but he waited until Christmas Eve, 1859 before replying. By then his prospects had faded considerably, so he wrote:

"You ask why I signed the recommendation for the Helper book. It was a thoughtless, foolish, and unfortunate act. Everybody knows that the ultra sentiments in the book are as obnoxious to me as they can be to any one; in the proper circumstances I would distinctly say so, but under the threat of the Clark Resolution, I could not, with self-respect, say more than I have."

With the Speakership at stake he could only sit and bear the brunt of the Southern attack. To deny his sympathy with Helper's doctrines would have wrecked the Republican chances of electing the chief officer of the House!

On January 16, 1860 brother William Tecumseh replied prophetically: "Disunion would be civil war, and you politicians would lose all charm. Military men would then step on the tapis, and you would have to retire." These brotherly letters did not come to light for fifty years after. Apparently, John Sherman took no stock in his brother's warning. The country was safe, he said, now that the Republicans had elected a Speaker. Stocks had risen, cotton was selling for eleven cents a pound, slave prices were near the top, and the nation was calm. God's in his heaven, all's well with the world, and a recently-converted Republican in the Speaker's chair. So thought John Sherman, the man who would be Speaker.

Mrs. Roger Pryor, however, thought otherwise. As the darkening clouds spread this winter of 1860 she wrote: "I am afraid the evening is at hand when we must bid adieu to the bright days—to the balls, the merry hairdresser, the rounds of visits, the levees and the charming 'at homes.'"

20

STATE OF THE UNION, 1861

History has overlooked a simple poignant scene which occurred on Capitol Hill, Washington, on January 4th, 1859. On that wintry day the Senate assembled for the last time in the historic chamber it had occupied since the restoration of 1819. Then, girding up their togas and led by Vice-President John Cabell Breckenridge, the conscript fathers soberly walked two by two through the long corridor to their new, roomier quarters in the new north wing of the Capitol. Few light hearts marched in that little procession.

Deep solemnity, tender reminiscence, and moving eloquence marked this last session in the chamber where once sat Clay, Webster, Calhoun, Benton, and a host of immortals "whose fame," proclaimed Senator John Crittenden, "is not surpassed, and whose power and ability and patriotism are not surpassed, by anything of Grecian or of Roman name."

Fittingly chosen to express the Senate's regret on leaving its long-time home were two Kentucky statesmen: venerable Senator Crittenden, foremost Unionist in the Southern states, and youthful, polished Vice-President Breckinridge, who uttered the last senatorial words of sheer eloquence ever heard in the old chamber. Thus did he close the scene:

"We leave this memorable Chamber, bearing with us unimpaired, the Constitution we received from our forefathers. Let us cherish it with grateful acknowledgements to the Divine Power who controls the destinies of empires and whose goodness we adore. The structures reared by men yield to the corroding tooth of time. These marble walls must moulder into ruin; but the principles of constitutional liberty, guarded by wisdom and virtue, unlike material elements, do not decay. Let us devoutly trust that another Senate, in another age, shall bear to a new and larger Chamber, this Constitution vigorous and inviolate, and that the last generation of posterity shall witness the deliberation of the Representatives of the American States still united, prosperous and free."

Now, two years later, in January, 1861, the "more perfect Union" was breaking up. Reason and compromise had failed. Civil war was a certainty. The bonfire the politicians had spent forty years kindling was about to burst into a great blaze. All the political compromises achieved with finespun words and lofty sentiments were soon to go up in the smoke of a thousand battles. On December 20th, 1860, South Carolina had carried out John Calhoun's threat of thirty years ago by seceding from the Union. Now, one by one, the Southern States of America were seceding to set up a rival republic, The Confederate States of America, stretching from the Potomac to the Rio Grande, and to adopt a remodeled version of "the Constitution we received from our forefathers." In January, 1861, it seemed as if "these marble walls" of which Vice-President Breckinridge had spoken so eloquently would not "moulder into ruin," but would soon be demolished in civil fury.

Symbolic of the wreck of the Union was the half-finished dome of the Capitol on which work had all but stopped. It would be for a new president with a determination to preserve the Union to decree that work on the dome should not cease because of civil strife. "If the people see the Capitol going on, it will be a sign to them that we intend the Union to go on."

But in January, 1861, the very foundations of the Union were quaking.

21

THE SOUTH WALKS OUT . . . MAY GOD SAVE
THE RIGHT!

For her, he was always the man of her dreams, her beau ideal. Today her dark, liquid eyes caught his every gesture; her heart drank in his eloquent, fervent words.

Varina Howell Davis loved this man passionately, loved him far more deeply today than sixteen years ago when she married him at Natchez under a bower of roses with the shining river as a distant backdrop.

Flaming against the dark waves of her hair was a scarlet camellia, love-symbol of their life together. It had just come up from Mississippi, and she wore it for him, a reminder, no doubt, that whate'er betide, even disintegration of the Union, *their* union was eternal, as fixed as the positions of the planets. She remained ever inflexibly loyal to him; his life was hers and in that she gloried. He was her lodestar.

She was immeasurably proud of being Mrs. Jefferson Davis, ever so proud of the erect, West Point figure of the man on whom every eye in the American House of Lords was fixed. Yet, beneath the flush which tinted her soft, olive cheeks there lurked a fear of what might happen to him now that the nation was rushing at express speed toward dissolution.

Around her in the Senate gallery were others who, like herself, deeply concerned with the future, were drawn daily and irresistibly by what might be the closing scenes of the

American drama. "The season which was always ushered in
on New Year's Day," said Mrs. Roger Pryor, "resolved itself
literally this year into a residence in the galleries of the
Senate Chamber and House of Representatives."

Varina Davis knew them all: Mrs. Slidell, youthful Créole
wife of the aging Senator from Louisiana; Mrs. Clement
Clay of Alabama, "one of the brightest ornaments" of Washington; tall, stately Adele Cutts Douglas, belle of Washington and adored of the Little Giant of Illinois; Mrs. George
Pugh, wife of the senior Senator from Ohio and most beautiful of Congressional wives; Mrs. John Crittenden, wittiest of
them all and wife of Kentucky's venerable Senator. Going
the rounds was her most famous saying: "I have married
three times and in each alliance I got just what I wanted.
My first marriage was for love, and it was mine as fully as
I could wish; my second was for money and Heaven was
good to me in this instance. My third for position and that
too is mine. What more could I ask?"

It was January 10th, 1861. With fast-beating heart Varina
Davis watched *her* Senator rise and with courtly grace bow
to Vice-President John C. Breckenridge. The chamber was
hushed and tense. Yesterday Senator Davis' own state, Mississippi, had dissolved the bonds which held her to the
union. Overnight the news was flashed to Washington and
today an awestruck Senate had assembled in an atmosphere
of bewilderment, gloom, and alarm.

Deepening the drama was the knowledge that, at this
very moment, Alabama stood poised on the threshold of secession. By night she would take the fatal leap.

South Carolina had already left the Union. On December
20th, 1860, with roaring cannon, ringing bells, bonfires, parades, cheers, and shrilling bugles, she had sailed off into
political space with the Palmetto Flag nailed to her masthead. The jubilee was at hand.

Throughout the state the Stars and Stripes were lowered.
Seizing arsenals, navy yards, the mint, custom houses, and

post offices, South Carolina hoisted the States Rights flag, a single red star on a white ground. Old Glory still flew from a lone outpost, Fort Sumter in Charlestown Harbor, where Major Robert Anderson and seventy-five men defied the demands of South Carolina's governor to surrender the fortress.

In the White House sat President James Buchanan, irresolute and wavering, counseling the nation that peace and conciliation were better than war, holding that neither he nor Congress had the power to compel a state to remain in the Union. South Carolina's secession was a blow to the white-haired, bachelor President, who divided his time "between praying and crying."

The news of South Carolina's withdrawal reached Washington the night it occurred. It found President Buchanan at a fashionable wedding reception. Hearing excitement in the hall, he turned to a Congressman's wife: "Madam, do you suppose the house is on fire? I hear an unusual commotion in the hall." Hurrying out, the lady met South Carolina's Representative Lawrence Keitt waving a telegram and exulting, "Thank God! Oh, thank God! South Carolina has seceded!" Returning to the President the lady said quietly, "It appears, Mr. President, that South Carolina has seceded from the Union." Stunned and speechless, Buchanan summoned his carriage and returned to the White House.

Yet Buchanan did little to halt the onrush. He insisted that even if the government possessed the right to use force against a state, it would be unwise to exert it. Blood would be spilled and treasure squandered. "Our Union rests on public opinion," said he, "and can never be cemented by the blood of its citizens shed in civil war. If it cannot live in the affections of the people, it must one day perish." To a friend he confided he would be the last President of the United States.

Out in Springfield, awaiting his turn at the helm of the nation, was a gangling Illinois lawyer, besporting a new, sprouting beard. He failed to share Buchanan's yielding, hesitant sentiments. On November 6th, 1860 the American people had elected Abraham Lincoln as Buchanan's successor. As Republican standard bearer, Lincoln was pledged by his own feelings and his party to block the intrusion of slavery into the territories, whereas Buchanan was now asking Congress to meet the crisis by guaranteeing slavery in the Territories until they became states. As to enforcing Federal laws and protecting Federal property in seceded South Carolina, Buchanan said he had no power to do so. Lincoln felt otherwise, but first he must be inaugurated and that must wait until March 4th. Anything might happen in the meantime.

Yes, the lightning might strike at any moment. Crisis hung over Charleston Harbor and the nation. Ringed by South Carolina batteries, squat, sullen Fort Sumter was a powder-pile ready to be flashed off by a single, vagrant spark.

Grim was the atmosphere of Washington. A nameless dread hung over the city. The very flags on the Capitol seemed to droop. The hurricane was gathering fast; old ties and moorings would be swept away. New Year's Day had dawned on the blackest year in American history. Already in Washington secessionist blue cockades were blossoming like early spring violets. It was John Calhoun's old talisman. Treason and treachery were in the air.

On Capitol Hill statesmen knew that the verbal hand-to-hand fighting was nearly done. Thirty years of political strife, wrangling, and compromise had come to the final arbitrament of the sword. The thing against which Webster had thundered, which Clay had waived off by compromise, which Calhoun had foretold, was coming to pass: break-up of the Union—and the words of sixty-four Senators were powerless to avert it. On the Senate floor already two desks were unoccupied—South Carolina's. Now, with Mississippi gone and Alabama going, there would be four more vacancies.

Today, as Congress assembled, there came from the President a confidential message which sent a second tremor through Capitol Hill. The news was whispered from senator to senator. Yesterday, while Mississippi was seceding, South Carolina had fired on the flag of the Union! Palmetto batteries had driven off the *Star of the West* which was carrying needed food, reinforcements, and munitions to beleaguered Fort Sumter.

Against this stirring background elegant, aristocratic Senator Jefferson Davis took the floor. He was a gentleman above and in all things, great and small. Soldier, planter, and politician, about him still clustered the glamor of the charge of his Mississippi Rifles at Buena Vista. As his bluish-gray eyes swept the floor, he saw old familiar faces, men with whom he had tilted many a day, but the jousting was over. Now it was for blood.

There, a few feet from him, sat Senator Zach Chandler of Ohio, proclaiming from the housetops: "Without a little blood-letting this Union will not, in my opinion, be worth a rush." Scowling their blackest, Senators Wade and Sumner waited for the man from Mississippi to speak. In a privileged chair beside Wade sat Thaddeus Stevens, come over from the House and brimming with hate.

It was the next to the last time Davis would ever address the Senate. He was no ebullient orator, but his words and ideas had finish and polish and came easily. Often they were glinted and powered with logic as if, in catching Calhoun's falling mantle, he had shared the legacy of Calhoun's keen art of reasoning. Davis was the ultra-Southerner. Like Calhoun, the South and Southern Rights were his political creed.

He knew, and his colleagues knew, that leadership of the South in her ill-starred flight toward independence would fall on him who had championed her battles on the Senate floor for a decade, who had dreamed of a Southern empire.

On the Senate tapis, this January 10th, 1861, was President Buchanan's despairing State of the Union Message admitting that "the prospect of a bloodless settlement fades away." Washing his own hands of the crisis, Buchanan tossed the explosive enigma into the lap of a divided Congress.

Senator Davis would speak for the South. He was still Senator, still its spokesman. Mississippi had not yet officially notified him of her action of yesterday.

For the North Senator William Seward of New York would speak. Each would give the state of the union as he and his followers saw it; each would offer a solution. Of the many oratorical gems hidden in Congressional tomes no two shine brighter against the dark confines of yellowing pages than these by Senators Davis and Seward.

These were the words Senator Jefferson Davis wished posterity to accept as his *apologia* for the South, his state, and himself. It was not a momentous manifesto of revolution. It was a motif of what was to come which he opened eloquently:

"Events, with a current hurrying on as it progresses, have borne me past the point where it would be useful for me to argue the question of rights. Today, therefore, it is my purpose to deal with events.

"What, Senators, today is the condition of the country? From every quarter of it comes the wailing cry of patriotism pleading for the preservation of the great inheritance we derived from our fathers.

"Tears are now trickling down the stern face of man; and those who have bled for the flag of their country, and are willing now to die for it, stand powerless before the plea that the party about to come into power laid down a platform, and that come what will, though ruin stare us in the face, consistency must be adhered to, even though the Government be lost."

Why should not the garrison at Fort Sumter be withdrawn, if it would ease the tension and save bloodshed? And as for the flag:

"Is there any point of pride which prevents us from withdrawing that garrison? I have heard it said by a gallant gentleman that the great objection was an unwillingness to lower the flag. To lower the flag!

"Can there, then, be a point of pride upon so sacred a soil as this, where the blood of the fathers cries to Heaven against civil war? Can there be a point of pride against laying upon that sacred soil today the flag for which our fathers died? My pride, Senators, is different. My pride is that that flag shall not set between contending brothers; and that, when it shall no longer be the common flag of the country, it shall be folded up and laid away like a vesture no longer used; that it shall be kept as a sacred memento of the past, to which each of us can make a pilgrimage, and remember the glorious days in which we were born."

Now he offered a plea and a threat: state sovereignty or war. He had no desire to dissolve the Union if the Union could be held together without interfering with the South's most cherished institution. Peace he wanted; if not peace, war.

"My friend from Louisiana referred to the disastrous scenes which might be occasioned by the invasion of the South. There is, however, another side of the picture . . .

"In a country of populous cities, of manufacturing towns, where population is gathered from the country into towns and villages, the torch and the sword can do their work with dreadful havoc, and starving millions would weep at the stupidity of those who had precipitated them into so sad a policy.

"We do not desire these things. We seek not the injury of anyone. We seek not to disturb your prosperity. If we must part, I say we can put our relations upon that basis which will give you the advantage of a favored trade and still make the intercourse mutually beneficial to each other. If you will not, then it is an issue from which we will not shrink; for, between oppression and freedom, between the maintenance of right and submission to power, we will invoke the God of battles, and meet our fate, whatever it may be.

"When you talk about having your heel on the slave power and grinding it into dust; when you talk about the final triumph; when you talk about the extinction of slavery, an institution with which you have nothing to do and of which you know nothing, is this the fraternity, is this the Union, to which we were invited?

"It is needful that we should understand each other. With all this warning you paused not. The quarrel was not of our making. Our hands are stainless; you aggressed upon our rights and our homes, and, under the will of God, we will defend them."

He closed with all the fire of his soul poured out in his words:

"I have striven to avert that catastrophe which now impends over the country, unsuccessfully; and I regret it. If you desire at this last moment to avert civil war, so be it; it is better so. If you will but allow us to separate from you peaceably, since we cannot live peaceably together, then there are relations which may still subsist between us.

"If you will not have it thus; if in the pride of power, if in contempt of reason and reliance upon force, you say we shall not go, but shall remain as subjects to you, then, gentlemen of the North, a war is to be inaugurated the like of which men have not seen.

"Is there wisdom, is there patriotism in the land? If so, easy must be the solution of this question. If not, then Mississippi's gallant sons will stand like a wall of fire around their State . . ."

No glamorous halo enveloped the head of Senator William H. Seward, Republican leader in the upper House. Nature had not endowed him with magnetic eloquence and dramatic power. He lacked the grace of manner which became Jefferson Davis as if it were tailored for him. Nevertheless, there were those who at this moment believed he had but to speak the word and the Union would be saved.

Today—January 12th, 1861—the Senate was overrun by friends of the Union come to hear Seward pronounce the magic formula which would dispel the gloom and resolve the crisis. He had already promised that within sixty days the storm would blow over and the sun of peace and prosperity shine again.

Runner-up for the Republican nomination in 1860, he was slated for a place in Lincoln's Cabinet. Seward presumably knew the inner secrets of the incoming administration. Yet, if the pale, slight figure in the ill-cut, ill-fitting gray frock coat had the golden key to the safety of the Union, there was nothing to indicate it save his calm self-assurance as he rose and bowed to the chair.

William Seward and Jefferson Davis were intimate friends, although they stood at opposite political poles. Often had they broken lances, yet often were the Davises honor guests at Senator Seward's many-coursed dinners. He had accepted an invitation from Jefferson and Varina Davis to visit them at "Brierfield" on the Mississippi. "Come when the roses are in bloom," urged Varina, but Seward never went.

Able, sagacious, and slight in person, Seward was in many quarters regarded as the nation's greatest statesman. The former Governor of New York's anti-slavery views carried great weight with the public. In the Senate he refused to engage in heated polemics with his Southern colleagues. He had the habit of smoking cigars by the box, acquired after using snuff for a quarter of a century. Youthful Henry Adams depicted Seward as "unorderly hair and clothes; hoarse voice; offhand manner; free talk and perpetual cigar."

Once, after Louisiana's Senator Benjamin had flayed Seward for what he felt was bad faith, the New Yorker walked over to his accuser to say affably: "Benjamin, give me a cigar and when your speech is printed send me a copy."

Lincoln and Seward were to differ on many things, but Lincoln was to support him through thick and thin and to defy the most powerful figures on Capitol Hill who sought to decapitate the slouchy, free-and-easy Secretary of State.

Republican radicals and hot-headed secessionists alike hooted at Seward's conciliatory words. Secession, said Seward, was a bad dream which would vanish like mist before the sun. "I am the only hopeful, calm, conciliatory person here."

Eager, expectant, unprecedented crowds came early to Capitol Hill on January 12th, to play their part as unconscious actors in the nation's legislative drama! Today powerful Senator Cameron of Pennsylvania made a special plea that the ladies be permitted to sit on the floor, but defiant Senator Toombs of Georgia would have none of it.

Like an earthquake, news was coming in a series of shocks.

The nation's capital was dazed. This morning Alabama's secession flooded the telegraph wires. Today Florida was making her exit. The pattern was fast emerging. One by one the Southern states were arraying themselves solidly from the Potomac to the Rio Grande. Georgia's secession call had gone out. Louisiana stood at the brink. Texas, with old, yet defiant, Sam Houston trying to hold her steady for the Union, careened dizzily in the secession hurricane. Pivotal Virginia would soon be tugging at her sheet anchors.

Today Seward came not to bury the Union, but to glorify it. With chaos and confusion raging about him, his was the voice of a peacemaker crying in a wilderness of dissension. Two great anti-slavery speeches—"Irresponsible Conflict" and "There is a Higher Law than the Constitution"—had brought him fame. These were political appeals, attuned to the white-hot slavery issue. His "Appeal for the Union" speech went echoing out of the Capitol to fall on barren ground. Still, it was his finest, most felicitous literary production. It was certainly the noblest patriotic call he ever uttered, yet it was no call to arms. His watchwords were moderation, conciliation, and compromise.

Rising, Seward smiled at his colleagues, smiled at the galleries, smiled at Vice-President Breckenridge. Apparently all was well with the United States and the world:

"Mr. President: I dread, as in my innermost soul I abhor, civil war. I do not know what the Union would be worth if saved by the use of the sword. Yet, for all this, I do not agree with those who, with a desire to avert that great calamity, advise a conventional or unopposed separation, with a view to what they call a reconstruction. It is enough for me, first, that in this plan, destruction goes before reconstruction; and secondly, that the strength of the vase in which the hopes of the nation are held consists chiefly in its remaining unbroken.

"We are a homogeneous people; we have only one language, one religion, one system of government, and manners and customs common to all. Why, then, shall we not remain henceforth, as hitherto, one people?"

Seward deplored dissolution. To Southern demands he would offer concessions; to Southern violence he would offer peace; to Southern prejudice he would answer with conciliation:

"Dissolution would not only arrest, but extinguish the greatness ot our country. If the constellation is to be broken up, the stars, whether scattered widely apart or grouped in smaller clusters, will henceforth shed forth feeble, glimmering and lurid lights.

"Dissolution would signalize its triumph by acts of wantonness which would shock and astound the world. It would provincialize Mount Vernon and give this Capitol over to desolation at the very moment when the dome is rising above our heads that was to be crowned with the statue of Liberty.

"No petty confederacy that shall follow the United States can prolong, or even renew, the majestic drama of national progress. Perhaps it is to be arrested because its sublimity is incapable of continuance. Let it be so, if we have indeed become degenerate. After Washington, and the inflexible Adams, Henry, and the peerless Hamilton, Jefferson and the majestic Clay, Webster, and the acute Calhoun, Jackson, the modest Taylor, and Scott, who rises in greatness under the burden of years, and Franklin, and Fulton, and Whitney, and Morse, have all performed their parts, let the curtain fall!

"While listening to these debates I have sometimes forgotten myself in marking their contrasted effects upon the page who customarily stands on the dais before me, and the venerable Secretary who sits behind him. The youth exhibits but pleased emotion in the excitement while at every irreverent word that is uttered against the Union the eyes of the aged man are suffused with tears. Let him weep no more. Rather rejoice, for yours has been a lot of rare felicity. You have seen and been a part of all the greatness of your country, the towering national greatness of all the world. Weep only you, and weep with all the bitterness of anguish, who are just stepping on the threshold of life; for that greatness perishes prematurely and exists not for you, nor for me, nor for any that shall come after us."

Never was he more effective, more appealing, than in his memorable, eloquent picture of an American warship entering a foreign port after the break-up of the Union. Senator Crittenden wept openly as Seward said:

"The American man-of-war is a noble spectacle. I have seen it enter an ancient port in the Mediterranean. All the world wondered at it, and talked of it. Salvos of artillery, from forts and shipping in the harbor saluted its flag. Princes and princesses and merchants paid it homage, and all the people blessed it as a harbinger of hope for their own ultimate freedom. I imagine now the same noble vessel again entering the same haven. The flag of thirty-three stars and thirteen stripes has been hauled down, and in its place a signal is run up, which flaunts the device of a lone star or a palmetto tree. Men ask, 'Who is the stranger who thus steals into our waters?' The answer contemptuously given is, 'She comes from one of the obscure republics of North America. Let her pass on.'"

Seward suggested a convention to hew out of all the vexing constitutional questions a settlement which would stand till the end of time. And he closed with a simple reiteration of his faith in the destiny of America:

"And now, Mr. President, what are the auspices of the country? We already have disorder; and violence has begun. Still my faith in the Constitution and in the Union abides because my faith in the wisdom and virtue of the American people remains unshaken.

"Whatever dangers there shall be, there will be the determination to meet them; whatever sacrifices private or public, shall be needful for the Union, they will be made. I feel sure that the hour has not come for this great nation to fall.

"This Union has not yet accomplished what good for mankind was manifestly designed by Him who appoints the seasons and prescribes the duties of States and empires. No, sir; if it were cast down by faction today, it would rise again and reappear in all its majestic proportions tomorrow. It is the only government that can stand here. Woe! Woe! to the man that madly lifts his hand against it. It shall continue and endure; and men, in after times, shall declare that this generation, which saved the Union from such sudden and unlooked for dangers, surpassed in magnanimity even that one which laid its foundations in the eternal principles of liberty, justice and humanity."

It was for Thaddeus Stevens, as he left the Chamber, to snarl out these biting words at Seward's plea: "I listened to every word and by the living God I have heard nothing."

Yet, there were those who wept, and Senator Crittenden of Kentucky was one of them.

January 21st, 1861. The battlements of the nation were about to topple—and Mrs. Jefferson Davis sent her maid at seven o'clock in the morning to hold two seats in the Senate gallery for her.

Today, in a dramatic, tearful, never-to-be-repeated scene five Senators from Florida, Alabama, and Mississippi would bid farewell to the distinguished assembly in which they served and hurry South for weal or woe. It was really Jefferson Davis' day. He would speak last. His words would echo longest. They could even be the requiem of the Union.

The stage was set, not in the historic old Senate chamber where so much of the grandeur of America's legislative drama had been enacted, but in the more spacious hall in the new north wing of the Capitol. Unlike the outmoded, outgrown drawing-room—for to such it was often compared —with its plain walls, low-vaulted dome, and cramped gallery, the new chamber had galleries on all four sides where over seven hundred spectators could view the greatest lawmaking show in the world—and today every seat was filled.

Ornamenting the Senate rostrum was brilliant, handsome Vice-President John Cabell Breckenridge of Kentucky, one of three who had competed with Abraham Lincoln for the Presidency in 1860. A statesman of consummate grace and dignity, he was to play a weird rôle in the Senate before the bright mirage of secession lured him away.

Varina Davis has set the scene:

"Mr. Davis had been ill for more than a week, and our medical attendant thought him physically unable to make his farewell to the Senate. On the morning of the day he was to address his colleagues, the crowd began to move toward the Senate Chamber as early as seven o'clock. By nine there was hardly standing room within the galleries or in the passway behind the forum. The Senators' cloakroom was crowded to excess, and the bright faces of the ladies were assembled together like a mosaic of flowers in the doorway. The sofas and the passway were full, and ladies sat on the floor against the wall where they could not find seats. There brooded over this immense crowd a palpitating, expectant silence which was afterward remarked as very unusual. The gallery of the reporters was occupied by the Diplomatic Corps and their respective families.

"Curiosity and the expectation of an intellectual feast seemed to be the prevailing feeling, and I, who had come from a sleepless night, all through the watches of which war and its attendants, famine and bloodshed had been predicted in despairing accents, looked on this festive crowd and wondered if they saw beyond the cold exterior of the orator—his deep depression, his desire for reconciliation and his overweening love for the Union in whose cause he had bled and to maintain which he was ready to sacrifice all but liberty and equality. We felt blood in the air, and mourned in secret over the severance of ties both of relationship and friendship; but a cloud covered all the rest and our hearts were 'exceedingly sorrowful even unto death'; we could even guess at the end."

Not a Senator was absent when the Vice-President's gavel fell at midday. First came prayer. In funereal quiet Chaplain Phineas Gurley approached the throne of grace. To some his words resounded like prayers for the dying. Strange that this man should one day speak the last solemn words over dead Abraham Lincoln!

First business before the Senate today was the admission of Kansas to the Union, but the crowds were not storming Capitol Hill for this. Nobody cared about Kansas. She had waited six years; let her wait an hour longer. Still, the move was well-timed. Senator Jefferson Davis and his Southern colleagues had long stood in the breach, fending her off. Kansas would have her hour, but only after they had sheathed their swords.

Jerkily, uncertainly, the Senate went through its parliamentary paces. The crowds were patient, silent, waiting only to hear one man, Jefferson Davis. What was coming was no secret, but Senator Ben Wade of Ohio—he with the sawed-off shotgun in his desk—pretended he did not know. It was a play to the galleries which fell flat.

First Southerner to rise was Senator David Levy Yulee of Florida, a man of gestures. Planter and railroad promoter, he was a warm secessionist. The withdrawal of his state, he said, left him no other course than to bow out with good grace, yet, for the record and posterity, he defended his state and reproached the North.

Next Senator Stephen Mallory, also of Florida, Chairman of the powerful Senate Naval Affairs Committee and soon to fill a similar post with the Confederacy. From him came fire-and-thunder warnings. Perhaps, he had already conceived his brain child, the *Merrimac,* which was to send a thrill of terror through the North. He admonished his listeners:

> "In turning from the Union to the veiled and unknown future we are neither ignorant nor reckless of the lions in our path. But, sir, be our difficulties what they may we stand forth a united people to grapple with and to conquer them; for the people of the South, as one man, declare that, sink or swim, live or die, they will not, as freemen, submit to the degradation of a constrained existence under a violated Constitution.
>
> "We seek not to war upon, or to conquer you; and we know that you cannot conquer us. Imbrue your hands in our blood and the rains of a century will not wash from them the stain, while coming generations will weep for your wickedness and folly."

Nevertheless, he made his exit with "profound regret" and appreciation of the "kindness and courtesy from the gentlemen of the opposition."

Came distinguished Senator Clement Clay of Alabama, arch-secessionist. From him poured a bitter indictment of the North for "enmity, injustice and injury to the South." It was his Parthian arrow before his flight into oblivion. Yet, he, too, regretted breaking with old friends.

For only forty seconds did Senator Benjamin Fitzpatrick of Alabama hold the floor, to express his hearty concurrence in his state's secession. He offered no farewell.

As each of the retiring Senators sat down, Southern ladies

in the galleries and lobbies fluttered their handkerchiefs in
outbursts of applause.

Now came Senator Davis' valedictory. This was his hour.
All eyes turned to him as, graceful, grave, and deliberate,
he rose amid dramatic silence to play his part in the saddest
drama ever witnessed on Capitol Hill. Already ladies were
dabbing their tears. Pale and drawn from recent illness, he
was a pathetic figure as he stood glancing about the Senate
"with the reluctant look the dying cast on those upon whom
they gaze for the last time." He had no rancor to voice, no
bravado, no threats. He was still the aristocrat and the gentleman. Perhaps, at this last moment, he was counting the
cost. Perhaps, face to face with finality, he saw his bright,
bold dream of a Southern empire shattered into a thousand
pieces and men's blood reddening the land he loved.

In a low, faltering voice, strained with emotion, he began:

"I rise, Mr. President, for the purpose of announcing that I have
satisfactory evidence that the State of Mississippi, by a solemn ordinance of her people, in convention assembled, has declared her separation from the United States. Under these circumstances, of course,
my functions are terminated here."

With eyes blurred, Varina Davis listened. His voice
seemed so distant, yet, for her, "soon it rang out melodiously
clear, like a silver trumpet, to the extremest verge of the
assembly. Unshed tears were in it, and a plea for peace
permeated every tone. Every graceful gesture seemed to
invite brotherly love. His manner suggested that of one who
parts from his family because even death were better than
estrangement. He was listened to in profound silence":

"It has seemed to me proper, however, that I should appear in the
Senate to announce that fact to my associates, and I will say but very
little more.

"It is known to Senators who have served with me here that I have
for many years advocated, as an essential attribute of State sovereignty, the right of a State to secede from the Union. Therefore, if

I had not believed there was a justifiable provocation, or without an existing necessity, I should still, under my theory of government, because of my allegiance to the State of which I am a citizen, have been bound by her action.

"I hope none who hear me will confound this expression of mine with advocacy of the right of a State to remain in the Union, and to disregard its constitutional obligations by the nullification of the law.

"Secession belongs to a different class of remedies. It is to be justified upon the basis that the States are sovereign.

"I, therefore, say I concur in the action of the people of Mississippi, believing it to be necessary and proper, and should have been bound by their action if my belief had been otherwise; and this brings me to the important point which I wish, on this last occasion, to present to the Senate. It is by this confounding of nullification and secession that the name of a great man whose ashes now mingle with his mother earth has been invoked to justify coercion against a seceded State.

"It has been a conviction of pressing necessity, it has been a belief that we are to be deprived in the Union of the rights which our fathers bequeathed us, which has brought Mississippi to her present decision. . . .

"Then, Senators, we recur to the principles upon which our Government was founded; and when you deny them, and when you deny to us the right to withdraw from a Government, which, thus perverted threatens to be destructive to our rights, we but tread in the path of our fathers when we proclaim our independence and take the hazard."

Plaudits broke in repeatedly. Tears shone in his eyes. There was no question, even in the minds of his enemies upon the floor, that this man was grief-stricken. Like another great man's speech on a solemn occasion, Davis' words would be long remembered—at least, by the South, where they still echo. "Had he been bending over his bleeding father, needlessly slain by his countrymen, he could not have been more pathetic or inconsolable. Not his wife alone, but all who sat spellbound before him knew how genuine was his grief."

Still, there was no retreat from that for which he had stood and fought so long. He wanted peace, but if there was no peace to be had, then the dogs of war must be unleashed:

"I am sure I feel no hostility toward you, Senators from the North. I am sure there is not one of you, whatever sharp discussion there may have been between us, to whom I cannot now say, in the presence of my God, I wish you well; and such, I am sure, is the feeling of the people whom I represent toward those whom you represent.

"I, therefore, feel that I but express their desire when I say I hope and they hope for peaceable relations with you, though we must part. They may be mutually beneficial to us in the future, as they have been in the past, if you so will it.

"The reverse may bring disaster on every portion of the country, and if you will have it thus, we will invoke the God of our fathers, who delivered them from the power of the lion, to protect us from the ravages of the bear; and, thus putting our trust in God and in our firm hearts and strong arms, we will vindicate the right as best we may."

Davis paused. Was there more to say? Far off to the South bugles were blowing and the sun lay warm and fair on the land. Yes, there was more. Good will he could leave behind. Again he spoke:

"In the course of my service here, associated at different times with a great variety of Senators, I see now around me some with whom I have served long; there have been points of collision, but, whatever of offense there has been to me, I leave here. I carry with me no hostile remembrance. Whatever offence I have given which has not been redressed, or for which satisfaction has not been demanded, I have, Senators, in this hour of parting, to offer you my apology for any pain which, in the heat of the discussion, I have inflicted. I go hence unencumbered by the remembrance of any injury received and having discharged the duty of making the only reparation in my power for any injury offered.

"Mr. President and Senators, having made the announcement which the occasion seemed to me to require, it only remains for me to bid you a final adieu."

He was finished. The long suspense was over; the South was free! Long live the Southern Confederacy! A red rose fell from the gallery, scattering petals as it fluttered down.

For a time no one moved. Senators and spectators sat transfixed. Through the silence could be heard women's sobs while men strove mightily to hold back their tears. Ex-Senator Jefferson Davis gazed about him, as if suddenly he had become a stranger in a land where once everybody knew him. Looking inexpressibly sad, he sat down. From his Northern colleagues came not a word, not a gesture of good-bye. Raising his eyes to the east gallery, he saw a woman with a bright handkerchief to her eyes rise and hurry to the exit.

The moments dragged awkwardly. Then Davis rose. Erect and proud, he walked up the center aisle toward the door; his four Southern colleagues fell in behind him. Vice- President Breckinridge came to his feet; fifty-eight Senators obeyed the same impulse. Already the crowds were standing respectfully. Slowly, five Southern senators walked out of the chamber, forever, without looking behind, without a wave of the hand. In the corridor Jefferson Davis found a woman's arms waiting for him and a hundred hands seeking to touch the hem of his coat.

With unseemly haste, as the doors closed, Senator Seward pressed the bill admitting Kansas, the thirty-fourth State. It was passed that same day, 36 to 16.

That night Varina Davis heard her husband wrestling in prayer: "May God have us in his holy keeping, and grant that before it is too late peaceful counsels may prevail."

Spring came early in 1861 and the soft February sunshine found Jefferson and Varina Davis pruning Cherokee roses in the garden at "Brierfield." Hither galloped a messenger with a telegram from the convention of the seceded States at Montgomery. Jefferson Davis opened and read it slowly. He reeled as if struck a blow. Grief spread over his face as he turned mutely to Varina. "After a few minutes' painful silence he told me, as a man might speak of a sentence of death—he had been elected President of the Confederate States of America!"

22

LINCOLN OFFERS PEACE, SECESSION MARCHES ON

"I hold that, in contemplation of universal law, and of the Constitution, the Union of these States is perpetual."

Abraham Lincoln's voice rang out across the Capitol plaza, across the divided nation. Even as he spoke the windows of the Capitol bristled with hawk-eyed riflemen. Gunners stood by parked batteries ready to rake every avenue leading to the Capitol. A cordon of soldiers with fixed bayonets ringed the inaugural platform where the incoming President stood, bareheaded, declaring his intention of holding the Union together whatever the cost.

In calm, conciliatory words Lincoln appealed directly to the Southern people.

"In your hands, my dissatisfied fellow-countrymen, and not in mine, are the momentous issues of civil war. The government will not assail you. You can have no conflict without being yourselves the aggressors. You have no oath registered in heaven to destroy the government while I shall have the most solemn one to 'preserve, protect and defend' it. . . . We are not enemies, but friends. We must not be enemies. Though passion may have strained, it must not break, our bonds of affection. . . ."

The day was March 4th, 1861. The land of the free and the home of the brave stood on the brink of bloody, fratricidal war.

Already Jefferson Davis, President-elect of the newly formed Confederate States of America, had proclaimed, "England will recognize us and a glorious future is before us. The grass will grow in Northern cities where the pavements have been worn off by the trade of commerce. We will carry war where it is easy to advance—where food for the sword and torch await our armies in the densely populated cities."

On March 6th, 1861, two days after Lincoln held out the olive branch, the Confederate Congress at Montgomery, Alabama, empowered President Davis to call for 100,000 volunteers to sustain the new Southern Republic by force of arms. Wildfire martial excitement swept the South. Regiments marched off as gaily as if on holiday parade. Bands played on street corners night and day. The South literally rushed to arms. Few dreamed of the awfulness of the struggle ahead.

On Friday, April 12th, 1861, the four-month war of nerves at Fort Sumter in Charleston Harbor, South Carolina, blazed into a shooting war. Just at daybreak a shell from a Confederate mortar exploded with a red thundering flash directly above the fort. It was the opening roar of the American Civil War. The die was cast.

The cannon that battered Fort Sumter into submission blasted hesitant Virginia out of the Union into the waiting arms of the Confederacy. Trailing the Old Dominion came North Carolina, Arkansas, and Tennessee. The eleven-state arc of the Southern Confederacy was complete. The border states of Maryland, Missouri, Kentucky, and Delaware still clung to the Union by an eyelash. Now eleven states with a population of 9,000,000, of whom 3,500,000 were slaves, were arrayed against twenty-three states with 20,000,000 people.

On April 15th President Lincoln called on the North for 75,000 volunteers for three months. Force would be met with force. From village, town, and city men rushed to arms to fight for the Union. The North was aroused in the twinkle of an eye. Drums beat and flags waved. The clerk left his desk and the farmer his plow. Near Waterloo, New York, a farmboy heard the drums beating. Hanging his scythe in the crotch of a poplar tree, this boy, James Johnson, told his father, "Let it hang there till I get back." But he never came back. He was killed at Gettysburg, but the scythe still hangs there though the tree has grown round the blade. At Chicago the man who had debated slavery so intensely with Lincoln in 1858, Stephen Douglas, struck the keynote of the North: "There can be no neutrals in this war; only patriots, or traitors."

Washington reeked with confusion, treachery, and treason. It was openly predicted the Stars and Bars of the new Confederacy would soon fly over the Capitol. Certainly it looked that way. The capital swarmed with disunionists. No one knew who was loyal to the Union and who was not. In the chambers of the House and Senate whole rows of vacant desks gaped at the spectators. Southern legislators had flown. Defection and exodus of Southern officials and clerks virtually paralyzed government departments.

Save for the District of Columbia militia which President Lincoln had hurriedly mobilized, the city of Washington was for six weeks virtually helpless and defenseless. Of fortifications it had only obsolete Fort Washington, a dozen miles down the Potomac on the Maryland side, facing Mount Vernon. Garrisoned by an old Irish pensioner, General Scott said it could easily be captured with a bottle of whiskey.

The nation's treasury was empty. Officials friendly to the South had stripped Northern arsenals of muskets and rifles. Transferred to Southern depots and already commandeered by Confederate officers, these weapons were now being rushed into the eager hands of Southern volunteers. General-in-Chief of the regular army was Winfield Scott, once the mighty conqueror of Mexico, but now aged, corpulent, and argumentative. The army itself, about 16,000 men, was scattered throughout the West guarding frontiers against the Indians. What little navy there was, was dispersed over seven seas.

While Lincoln and his Cabinet waited anxiously from day to day for the troops he had called for to arrive, Maryland secessionists tore up railroad tracks leading to the capital, cut telegraph communications and virtually isolated Washington from the rest of the country. Regiments supposedly on the way to Washington from Rhode Island, Massachusetts, and New York seemingly vanished without word of their whereabouts. "Why don't they come?" cried out Lincoln in despair. As the Sixth Massachusetts Regiment marched through Baltimore it was hooted and stoned by a secessionist mob. Leaving four dead and many wounded, the regiment went on to Washington where Lincoln himself greeted them with bitter words, "I begin to believe there is no North. The Seventh Regiment [of New York] is a myth. Rhode Island is another. You are the only real thing."

There came a delegation of Baltimore citizens protesting against Federal troops marching through the city to relieve Washington. But Lincoln chided them with sharp words:

"You, gentlemen, come here to me and ask for peace on any terms, and yet have no word of condemnation for those who are making war on us. You express great horror of bloodshed, and yet would not lay a straw in the way of those who are organizing in Virginia and elsewhere to capture this city. The rebels attack Fort Sumter, and your citizens attack troops sent to the defense of the government, and the lives and property in Washington, and yet you would have me break my oath and surrender the government without a blow. There is no Washington in that—no Jackson in that—no manhood nor honor in that. I have no desire to invade the South; but I must have troops to defend the capital. Geographically it lies surrounded by the soil of Maryland; and mathematically the necessity exists that they should come over her territory. Our men are not moles, and can't dig under the earth; they are not birds, and can't fly through the air. There is no way but to march across, and that they must do."

Meanwhile martial law was declared in the city. Patriotic citizens joined the weak soldiery to help convert government buildings into citadels for last stands against the Confederates who might come storming across the Potomac any moment. There were 15,000 Virginia militia at Alexandria poised for a blow at the capital, waiting, so it was said, only for their artillery. Symbol of the nation's power and glory, Washington was to be defended to the last will and ditch. But relief came at last. Men began pouring into the city and the long alarm was over, temporarily at least. If New York, Massachusetts, and Rhode Island had not rushed regiments to Washington, the city would probably have been in Confederate hands soon after Virginia seceded on April 17th.

Vital information meantime flowed in a steady underground stream across the Potomac. The capital was filled with people who reported every government move to the Confederate authorities. The most dangerous source of treachery were the higher social circles of the city where Southern charm worked treasonable miracles. Still seated in Congress, however, were a few men whose hearts were with the Confederacy—men who listened in on the nation's defense secrets and lost no time in relaying them South.

23

TREASON IN THE SENATE, OR NINE WORDS
TO BULL RUN

"I propose to ratify whatever needs ratification. I propose to render my clear and distinct approval not only of the measure but of the motive which prompted it. I propose to lend the whole power of the country, arms, men, money, and place them in his hands with authority almost unlimited until the conclusion of this struggle.

"He has asked for $400,000,000. We propose to give him $500,-000,000. He has asked for four hundred thousand men. We propose to give him half a million; and for my part I would cheerfully add a cipher to either of these figures."

"I want sudden, bold, forward, determined war; and I do not think anybody can conduct war of that kind as well as a dictator.

"I do know that the determined, aggregated power of the whole people of this country—all its treasure, all its arms, all its blood, all its enthusiasm, kindled, concentrated, poured out in one mass of living valor upon any foe—will conquer!"

Ned Baker's voice rang out like martial music and the Senate surged with stormy applause. One may search in vain through the whole panorama of Congress for more electrifying words than Senator Edward Dickinson Baker's magnificent call to arms on July 10th, 1861.

"All its blood," he said. His own blood! For hardly had his words ceased echoing before he lay dead, riddled by Confederate bullets, on a bluff overlooking the Potomac barely twenty-five miles from the Senate chamber.

In this burst of dramatic eloquence Senator Baker of

Oregon gave *his* answer to President Lincoln's request for men, munitions, and money to meet the onslaught of civil war. Silver-tongued, silver-haired, he was a superb orator, a striking figure on the Senate floor. Such was his long-time intimacy with Lincoln that the President's second son, Eddie, dead back in Illinois, was named for him. Lincoln often told how Ned Baker, English-born boy, used to cry because he could never become President of the United States.

Refusing a brigadier's commission because it would necessitate his resignation from the Senate, Baker had accepted a colonelcy and raised the "California Regiment." Baker meantime performed the double duty of commanding his regiment and representnig Oregon in the Senate. Veteran of the Mexican War, he had said: "If a man whose hair is gray, who is well-nigh worn out in the battle and toil of life, may pledge himself, so again, if Providence shall will it, this feeble hand shall draw a sword."

On this July 10th, 1861—a red-letter date—President Lincoln's war program was speeding through the Senate, paced by Senator Baker's driving eloquence. Shepherding this war legislation was Senator Henry Wilson, all-powerful chairman of the Senate Military Affairs Committee.

Conspicuous as chief obstructer of war preparations was Senator John Cabell Breckinridge of Kentucky, late Vice-President and master of forensics. His tongue was keen-edged; his mind penetrating. Charges of treason flashed about his handsome head, but he was no mean foeman, not one to cringe or draw back under fire. He stood virtually alone, ringed and baited by Senators bent on his destruction, determined to lead him—or let him lead himself—before a firing squad. One after another rose and told him to leave the Senate and take his treason South with him but, cornered, he fought back, reminding them sharply that he was still the Senator from Kentucky—and Kentucky was still in the Union!

"I stand alone, but I will speak," he asserted as he demanded for Kentucky the right to refuse not only men but money, for so he interpreted his state's policy.

Listening eagerly in the gallery as the scenes unfolded was a smartly dressed woman on whose ears Ned Baker's inspiring words fell with little effect. She was not there to listen, but to glean. Daily she watched and waited. Her immediate interest was in a man now playing a leading rôle in the Senate. He was not a romantic looking figure, to be sure, but under the guidance of this man, Senator Henry Wilson of Massachusetts, the massive war program was being steered past the parliamentary pitfalls of the Senate. Deep in the confidence of the administration, he was privy to military secrets she wished to know. Rose O'Neal Greenhow plied her clandestine business under the very dome of the Capitol and, for the present, at least, unmolested.

Across the Virginia countryside at Manassas, barely twenty miles away, at this moment an army of thirty thousand Confederates was poised ready to strike at Washington at any unguarded moment. Commanding these graybacks was General Pierre G. T. Beauregard whose fame had soared prodigiously since his capture of vulnerable Fort Sumter. For all his grandiloquence, Beauregard was no indifferent soldier. His position along Bull Run had strategic excellence. It posed a constant threat to Washington. While protecting the railroad running into the invaluable Shenandoah Valley, it also outflanked any direct movement south toward the Confederate capital at Richmond.

Thus, the shadow of the little Créole general lay stern and menacing over the nation's capital and the debates on Capitol Hill. He added suspense to the drama unfolding so rapidly.

Infesting Washington and infiltrating every department of the government in the early months of the war were scores of secessionist ladies, amateur secret service agents of the Confederacy. Flirtatious and bold, they risked everything to help the cause of the South.

Many of these "rebels in crinoline" were ladies of wealth or fashion or both, who, blinded by the Southern fantasy of empire, engaged in this treasonable business. They watched and waited outside doors until they bagged secret papers; they made off with vital maps passed out by government clerks with Southern leanings and smuggled them through the lines hidden in the intricacies of petticoats, false bosoms, bustles, and other feminine accoutrements. "These fascinating female secessionists," said the New York *Herald,* "held the government and the destinies of the country in their delicate little hands."

Most adroit, dangerous and persuasive of these ladies was the delectable widow, Rose O'Neal Greenhow, whose talents ran to politics, espionage, and romance. Rose Greenhow, however, was no amateur—in boudoir or drawing room. Passionately sympathetic with the South, she vowed to use "every capacity with which God had endowed me" in its service.

Her picture, taken during her later incarceration in the Old Capitol Prison, reveals no ravishing temptress, yet too many witnesses have testified to her beauty to doubt it. Fortyish, brunette, curvaceous, she must still have been an appetizing piece of femininity. The handsome face in the picture taken several years before, when she was the toast of the town, the lovely "Wild Rose" to her ardent admirers —and wooers—in the highest brackets of the government, lays at rest all doubt of her fascinating powers. To the enticing parlors of her home at 398 Sixteenth Street, a short "piece" from the White House, came statesmen, diplomats, and Union officers. For a few there were warm embraces; for others feasts of wit lit by her brilliant conversation.

Rose Greenhow was most intriguing. Her social graces were many, winning for her admittance to the charmed prewar White House circle. President Buchanan and his niece,

Harriet Lane, often supped at her table. Senator Seward, now Secretary of State, found her exhilarating. She knew many important personages on Capitol Hill, but her most frequent, intimate guest was Senator Henry Wilson, helmsman for Lincoln's war measures in the Senate. He slid into her charming little home oft and late.

Even after the outbreak of hostilities, Rose Greenhow continued to enjoy the confidences of Union officers and high Republican leaders. Allan Pinkerton, chief of Federal Secret Service, paid high tribute to "her almost irresistible seductive powers" which she used on "persons holding places of honor and profit under the government" to extract military intelligence which she passed on to the Confederacy. Said he: "This very remarkable woman possessed an almost super-human power."

If, as Brady's crude photograph would indicate, she was past the peak of her physical allure, she still had something men wanted badly. Whatever it was, she obtained for it a high price—Northern military secrets. Her sources of information were high up and infallible. She tapped the innermost Northern war councils. To her home on Sixteenth Street came, also, lowly government assistants and obscure clerks with tidbits of information which she passed South through the network she had devised.

It cannot be said, much less proven, that Senator Wilson went from the Senate on July 10th, 1861 to a rendezvous with Rose Greenhow. Only surmise is possible. Yet it is a fact that, on the night of July 10th, 1861, Bettie Duvall, a luscious, seductive Washington girl, a fellow-worker in Mrs. Greenhow's espionage web, disguised herself as a farm girl and crossed Chain Bridge into Virginia. Here she donned a riding habit and galloped off to Fairfax Court House where she entered the Confederate advanced lines.

Conducted at once to General Bonham, Bettie Duvall took out her tucking comb, let down her lustrous black hair and produced a small package "not larger than a silver half-dollar sewed up in black silk." This silken packet contained a cipher message for General Beauregard. It decoded into "Look for an attack by the middle of July." It further revealed that the Federals would advance by way of Fairfax Court House and Centreville. This was precisely what General Beauregard wanted to know. It answered two pressing questions—When would the Federals start? Where would they strike? Beauregard immediately ordered his outposts to fall back to prepared positions.

The atmosphere of Washington was stern and feverish when on July 4th the Thirty-seventh Congress assembled in special session at President Lincoln's proclamation. Events had moved swiftly since the bombardment of Fort Sumter. Washington was an armed camp; soon sixty-four forts would engirdle the city.

Regiments of raw militia and volunteers poured in. Vacant spaces around the nation's capital mushroomed into vast spreads of tents, guns, and canvas-covered wagons. Day and night the streets resounded to the tramp of marching feet and the creak of cannon. The four-year funeral cortège was starting; soon the Dead March from Saul would be familiar music. Encamped in a wide protecting arc from Alexandria to Chain Bridge, thousands of men were drilling feverishly, fighting make-believe battles in training for the realities ahead.

Yet, already Northern headlines were screaming "On To Richmond!" as if it were just a pleasant day's outing. Fed by newspaper clamor, public impatience for battle was rising. Editors and politicians were talking about a six-weeks' war.

On June 26th President Lincoln called a Cabinet meeting to discuss immediate battle. Invited to this meeting was General Irving McDowell, a painstaking soldier who commanded the growing army around Washington. McDowell frankly said that his men were not yet ready; he needed more time. General-in-Chief Winfield Scott, also present, agreed with McDowell, but Lincoln insisted, "You are green, it is true, but they are green also."

There were other urgent considerations. The time of thousands of ninety-day enlistees was running out. Soon these men would be going home. More important was the impending arrival of the Thirty-seventh Congress. Something must be done to dazzle the statesmen. Drills and parades, colorful enough, were hardly sufficient. An actual battle would shoot their voting enthusiasm sky-high. Awaiting the Congress was President Lincoln's request for appropriations and levies of men of such magnitude—four hundred million dollars and four hundred thousand men—as never dreamed of before in the history of the Republic. Invasion of Virginia would send tingles up the lawmakers' spines.

President Lincoln ordered McDowell to attack the Confederate position at Manassas at once. Reluctantly, McDowell made his plans. For security he threw out a five-mile cavalry screen which shut off Confederate underground communication with Washington. He set July 10th as the date for departure. This date was known only to President Lincoln, his Cabinet, and McDowell's most trusted officers. One man on Capitol Hill, presumably, knew the date. This was Senator Henry Wilson, who made almost daily reports to the President on the progress of his huge war program.

Bogged down by incompetency, red tape, and slipshod organization, McDowell was forced to change the marching date to July 16. Again, undated orders were issued.

Now a word as to Mrs. Greenhow's cipher code. Amateurish and later easily unraveled by Federal experts, it was deadly enough in July, 1861. It was hastily devised by Captain Thomas Jordan of the United States Army, an admirer of Mrs. Greenhow, who apparently enjoyed physical intimacy with her. To Mrs. Greenhow Jordan confided his decision to renounce his allegiance to the government and to

join General Beauregard as Colonel and Adjutant General
of the Confederate Army at Manassas. It was arranged that
she would send secret, vital information to him as "Captain
Thomas John Rayford" at Beauregard's headquarters.

Since receiving Mrs. Greenhow's message that the Federal advance would start on July 10th, Beauregard had
heard nothing. July 10th came, but his scouts reported no
Federal movement. In his uncertainty Beauregard decided
to investigate. One George Donellan, a former Interior Department clerk, volunteered for the hazardous task of entering Washington and contacting Mrs. Greenhow. On the
night of July 15th Donellan crossed the Potomac below
Alexandria. On the Maryland side a Southern sympathizer
provided him with a horse. Near the unfinished Washington
Monument he supposedly got off his horse and walked to
Mrs. Greenhow's Sixteenth Street home. Near dawn he
tapped out on her door the signal used by her agents.

Stepping into the dimly lit hall, he met a handsome
woman, clad in a dressing gown tightly girdled about her
shapely waist. She was used to these nocturnal callers, but
she waited for his credentials. "What can I do for you?" she
asked. Donellan gave her a scrap of paper bearing two
words, "Trust Bearer," written in Captain Jordan's code.
They were sufficient. Wasting no time, Mrs. Greenhow
wrote, on a bit of paper, nine fateful code words, "Order
issued for McDowell to march upon Manassas tonight."
Donellan had come in the nick of time. Mrs. Greenhow had
"received a copy of the order to McDowell." She had need
of a messenger at once.

To Donellan she possibly entrusted something else, the
red-dotted map showing the exact route McDowell's army
would take to Manassas, by way of Fairfax and Centreville.
It had vanished after being left at the White House. How
she got it no one has ever known. The map, she said, must
be destroyed, if he was trailed or in danger. The code message must go through. She had, she told Donellan, arranged

a relay of horses to take him back to a boat which would land him near Dumfries, Virginia. Wishing him a safe return, she let him out into the early light. "God save the Confederacy!" she breathed as he left.

On the Virginia side cavalry couriers picked up Rose Greenhow's message and sped it on. By nightfall of July 16th, Rose Greenhow's nine momentous words had reached Beauregard's headquarters near Manassas. Telegraphing at once to Richmond, Beauregard asked to be reinforced by General Johnston's army of ten thousand men stationed near Winchester. Richmond complied immediately by ordering Johnston to withdraw quietly, without suspicion, from the front held by Federal General Patterson and to hurry his men, by the Manassas Gap Railroad, to Beauregard's aid. It was the timely arrival of Johnston's men on the afternoon of the battle which turned the tide and sent McDowell's army reeling back on Washington, defeated and demoralized.

Amazing as it may seem, Donellan knocked again on Mrs. Greenhow's door on the night of July 17th, coming this time by a different route. He brought this message from Colonel Jordan: "Yours was received at eight o'clock tonight. Let them come; we are ready for them. We rely on you for precise information. Be particular as to description and destination of forces, quantity of artillery, etc."

The lady was ready with fresh information and more details. The Union army intended to cut the Manassas Gap Railroad and prevent General Johnston from reinforcing General Beauregard. What more did Beauregard need to know?

There is no record of any meeting between Mrs. Greenhow and Senator Wilson in those days of suspense between July 10th and July 16th. Again, one can only surmise. It cannot be said with any certainty from whom she extracted, by ways best known to herself, the new top-secret date, July 16th. Nor can it be concluded, although the circumstantial trail points that way, that she obtained it from Henry Wilson, who was enamored of her. At this time she moved freely about Washington, visiting the Capitol almost daily. But it is known that Wilson visited her home frequently after hostilities between North and South had actually begun. He even visited her, later, in her cell in the Old Capitol Prison.

On July 16th, shortly after noon, General McDowell's army of 35,000 men marched off for Manassas and the first big show of the Civil War. It was the largest and probably the worst-disciplined and poorest-organized army ever assembled in America. The drive for Richmond was on. The nation was thrilled. Speeding on ahead of McDowell's army were Mrs. Greenhow's nine words of disastrous import.

At this very hour, this hot, sultry July afternoon, an extraordinary scene was being enacted in the Senate. Senator John Breckinridge held the floor, one man pitted against the body of his colleagues, and he would be heard. His state still dangled perilously between Union and secession. He spoke, or thought he spoke, the sentiments of his Kentucky constituents.

For two hours that afternoon he played with treason, but, at best, he could only impede Lincoln's war program. The grandeur of his manner was impressive. With finish and flourish he boldly denounced the Joint Resolution legalizing President Lincoln's extra-legal and dictatorial acts forced by the sudden emergency:

"Mr. President: It may be well to inquire, has not the President of the United States assumed powers not delegated by the Constitution or by the laws? I think the Chief Magistrate of the country—and I have a right in my place to say it—should be rebuked by the vote of both Houses of Congress.

"In approving what the President has done you invite him to do the like in the future; and the whole country will lie prostrate at the feet of the executive power . . ."

Assailing the President for making war and raising armies

on his own authority in violation of the Constitution, Breckinridge said:

"What is the excuse; what is the justification; what is the plea?
Necessity. I deny this doctrine of necessity. I deny that the President
of the United States may violate the Constitution upon the ground
of necessity. In my judgment, sir, if we pass this resolution, we are
upon the eve of putting, so far as we can, in the hands of the President of the United States the power of a dictator."

Sunday, July 21st, 1861. The Confederates were ready,
thanks to Rose Greenhow. Johnston was rushing from the
valley to reinforce Beauregard. McDowell's army had strag-
gled finally to Centreville. In the distance they could see
fresh Confederate entrenchments.

News of impending battle drew Senators, Congressmen,
social leaders, politicians, and riffraff to the scene. Livery
stables in Washington did a flourishing business. Senators
Wade and Sumner drove out in an open barouche to see the
fun. Wade carried his sawed-off shotgun in case of need.
Sightseeing parties, laden with box lunches and champagne,
jogged merrily off to Centreville. It was to be a fine Confederate fox chase which might even wind up at Richmond
before the end of the week.

That night tragic news stunned Washington. The back-
wash of defeat began rolling into the city. Congress prepared to vacate and the city quaked with rumors of a quick
Confederate investment.

On August 1st the Senate met in a chastened mood. The
fate of the Union still hung in the balance, but there was
no despairing of the Republic. Any moment Confederate
columns might come swinging over the Arlington hills.
Today the galleries were filled with spectators anxious to
know what steps were being taken to save the nation.

At this darkened hour Senator Breckinridge rose again
to attack President Lincoln and his war measures. Now
shunned and distrusted, he was treated with "the most for-

mal and freezing courtesy." Daily his carriage brought him
to the Capitol, always alone. Still he kept up his fight. Had
he been speaking in the Confederate Congress he could have
uttered no more pleasing words. But, at least, he played his
game open-handed, without subtlety.

Today his brilliant tongue framed dangerous, almost exultant words. He painted frightening pictures of what was to
come.

"Sir, this drama is beginning to open before us, and we begin to
catch some idea of its magnitude. We are on the wrong tack; we have
been from the beginning. The people begin to see it. Here we are
hurling gallant fellows to death, and the blood of Americans has been
shed—for what? It has been to carry out principles that three-fourths
of them abhor. . . .

"Nothing but ruin, utter ruin, to the North, to the South, to the
East, to the West, will follow the prosecution of this contest. You
may look forward to innumerable armies; you may look forward to
countless treasures—all spent for the purpose of desolating and ravag-
ing this continent.

"Let the war go on, however, and soon, in addition to the moans of
widows and orphans all over this land, you will hear the cry of distress from those who want food and the comforts of life.

"The Pacific slope now, doubtless, is devoted to the Union of
States. Let this war go on till they find the burdens of taxation greater
than the burdens of separate condition and they will assert it. Fight
twelve months longer, and the already opening differences that you
see between New England and the great Northwest will develop
themselves. You have two confederacies now. Fight twelve months
longer, and you will have three; twelve months longer, and you will
have four."

Swept along by the intensity of his feelings, Breckinridge
did not see a tall, breathless figure in a blue uniform enter
the chamber and walk quietly to his desk. It was Senator
Edward Dickinson Baker. Silver eagles gleamed on his
shoulders.

A thrill ran through the galleries as the Senator from
Oregon entered. On this August day, as the hour neared for
Senator Breckinridge to take the floor, the Republican Sena-

tors had met hastily to decide who should reply to the brilliant, persuasive Senator from Kentucky. The choice fell on Baker. As one Senator put it, "the antidote must go with the poison," for Breckinridge's words would go winging across the nation.

But where was Baker? How soon could he reach the Senate floor? Messengers, Senators themselves, went scurrying through Washington. Baker was found drilling his regiment at the foot of Meridian Hill, over a mile from the Capitol. Told he was urgently needed, that Breckinridge was about to move to attack, Baker leaped into the saddle and hotspurred for the Capitol. There was no time to change to the more sombre habiliments of a statesman, and he thus became the first and only member of the Senate ever to address that distinguished body while wearing the uniform of a soldier.

Chafing under Breckinridge's slashing words, the Gray Eagle waited quietly until the Kentuckian had finished and then rose swiftly to his task. Unbuckling his sword, Baker laid it on his desk. It was fine drama. This was his hour, he was almost at his zenith. Even today Baker's crackling words ring out like words uttered in an old Richmond church at an earlier crucial moment in the nation's history. Fixing his gaze on Breckinridge, Baker began:

"Mr. President, the honorable Senator says there is a state of war. What then? There is a state of public war; none the less war because urged from the other side; not the less war because it is unjust; not the less war because it is a war of insurrection and rebellion.

"It is still war, and I am willing to say it is public war. What then? Shall we carry that war on? Is it his duty as a Senator to carry it on? If so, how? Will the honorable Senator tell me it is our duty to stay here, within fifteen miles of the enemy seeking to advance upon us every hour, and talk about nice questions of constitutional construction as to whether it is war or merely insurrection?

"No, sir. It is our duty to advance, if we can; to suppress insurrection; to put down rebellion; to dissipate the rising; to scatter the enemy; and when we have done so, to preserve the liberty, lives and property of the people of the country."

Dramatically Baker leveled his finger at Breckinridge, trumpeting his words as if he sought to speed them across the nation:

"The Senator from Kentucky stands up here in a manly way in opposition to what he sees is the overwhelming sentiment of the Senate, and utters reproof, malediction and prediction combined. Well, sir, it is not every prediction that is prophecy.

"I would ask him what you would have us do now—a Confederate army within twenty miles of us, advancing or threatening to advance, to overwhelm your government; to shake the pillars of the Union; to bring it down around your head, if you stay here, in ruins? Are we to stop and talk about an uprising sentiment in the North against the war? Are we to predict evil, and retire from what we predict?

"Is it not the manly part to go on as we have begun, to raise money and levy armies, to organize them, to prepare to advance . . . Can we do anything more? To talk to us about stopping, is idle; we will never stop!

"Will the Senator yield to rebellion? Will he shrink from armed insurrection? Will his State justify it? Will its better opinion allow it? Shall we send a flag of truce? What would he have? Or would he conduct this war so feebly, that the whole world would smile at us in derision? What would he have?

"These speeches of his, sown broadcast over the land, what clear distinct meaning have they? Are they not intended for disorganization in our very midst? Are they not intended to dull our weapons? Are they not intended to destroy our zeal? Are they not intended to animate our enemies?

"Sir, are they not words of brilliant, polished treason, even in the very Capitol of the republic?"

Baker paused. Deathly silence gripped the Senate at the thought of treason!

"What would have been thought if, in another Capitol, in another Republic, in a yet more martial age, a Senator as grave, not more eloquent or dignified than the Senator from Kentucky, yet with the Roman purple flowing over his shoulders, had risen in his place, surrounded by all the illustrations of Roman glory, and declared that advancing Hannibal was just, that Carthage ought to be dealt with in terms of peace?

"What would have been thought if, after the battle of Cannae, a

Senator had risen there in his place and denounced every levy of the Roman people, every expenditure from its treasure, and every appeal to the old recollections and the old glories?"

Clearly came the answer, given by Senator Fessenden of Maine, in a stern undertone that reached every ear, "He would have been hurled from the Tarpeian Rock!"

The galleries exploded in cheers. "Order! Order!" shouted the presiding officer while Baker readily picked up the allusion:

"Mr. President, a Senator, himself learnéd far more than myself in such lore, tells me, in a voice that I am glad is audible, that he would have been hurled from the Tarpeian Rock. It is a grand commentary upon the American Constitution that we permit these words to be uttered. I ask the Senator from Kentucky to recollect, too, what, save to send aid and comfort to the enemy, do these predictions of his amount to.

"Every word thus uttered falls as a note of inspiration upon every Confederate ear. Every sound thus uttered is a word (and falling from his lips, a mighty word) of kindling and triumph to a foe that determines to advance. For me I have no such words as a Senator to utter. For me, amid temporary defeat, disaster, distraction, it seems that my duty calls me to utter another word, and that word is, bold, sudden, forward, determined war, by armies, by military commanders, clothed with full power, advancing with all the past glories of the Republic urging them on to conquer. . . .

"What of past glories? What of future hopes? Shall we sink into the insignificance of the grave—a degraded, defeated, emasculated people, frightened by the result of one battle, and scared at the visions raised by the imagination of the Senator from Kentucky on this floor? No, sir; a thousand times, no, sir!

"We will rally, we will rally the people, the loyal people, of the whole country. They will pour forth their treasure, their money, their men, without stint, without measure. The most peaceable man in this body may stamp his foot upon this Senate Chamber floor, as of old a warrior and a Senator did, and from that single tramp will spring forth armed legions.

"Shall one battle determine the fate of empire, or a dozen? The loss of one thousand men or twenty thousand, or $100,000,000 or $500,000,000? In a year's peace, in ten years, at most, of peaceful progress, we can restore them all. There will be some graves reeking with blood, watered by the tears of affection. There will be some privation; there will be some loss of luxury; there will be somewhat more need for labor to procure the necessities of life. When that is said, all is said.

"If we have the country, the whole country, the Union, the Constitution, free government—with these there will return all the blessings of well-ordered civilization; the path of the country will be a career of greatness and glory such as, in the olden time, our fathers saw in the dim visions of years yet to come, and such as would have been ours now, today, if it had not been for the treason for which the Senator too often seeks to apologize!"

John Breckinridge was at bay. He still had last, burning, biting words. He was no coward. This was his last counterattack.

"The Senator from Oregon says that these opinions which I have expressed are but brilliant treason; and that is a tribute to the character of our institutions that I am allowed to utter them upon the Senate floor. Mr. President, if I am speaking treason, I am not aware of it. I am speaking what I believe to be for the good of my country.

"If I am speaking treason, I am speaking it in my place in the Senate. By whose indulgence am I speaking? Not by any man's indulgence. I am speaking by the guarantees of that Constitution which seems here now so little respected.

"And, sir, when he asked what would have been done with a Roman Senator who had uttered such words, a certain Senator on this floor, whose courage has risen much of late, replies in audible tones 'He would have been hurled from the Tarpeian rock.'

"Sir, if we ever find an American Tarpeian rock, and a suitable victim is to be selected, the people will turn, not to me, but to that Senator, who, according to the measure of his intellect and his heart, has been the chief author of public misfortunes. He, and men like him, have brought the country to its present condition. Let him remember, too, sir, that while in ancient Rome the defenders of the public liberty were sometimes torn to pieces by the people, yet their memories were cherished in grateful remembrance; while to be hurled from the Tarpeian rock was ever the fate of usurpers and tyrants.

"My opinions are my own. They are honestly entertained. I am not a man to cling to forms of office and to the emoluments of public life against my convictions and my principles; and I repeat, that if indeed the Commonwealth of Kentucky, instead of attempting to mediate in this unfortunate struggle, shall throw her energies into the strife, and approve and sustain the policy of the Federal Administration in what I believe to be a war of subjugation and annihilation, she may take her course.

"I am her son, and will share her destiny, but she will be represented by some other man on the floor of this Senate."

Two months later, at Frankfort, Kentucky, John Breckinridge announced his allegiance to the Confederacy: "I exchange with proud satisfaction a term of six years in the Senate of the United States for the musket of a soldier." On December 2, 1861 the Senate approved this Resolution: "Whereas John C. Breckinridge, a member of this body has joined the enemies of his country, and is now in arms against the government he had sworn to support; therefore, Resolved that the traitor Breckinridge be expelled." It sounded like an afterthought, a futile gesture.

On October 20th, 1861 President Lincoln staggered, heartsick and tearful, out of the War Department telegraph office. It was a bright and sunny afternoon. The wires had just clicked off news of the disaster at Ball's Bluff up the Potomac. Dead on the field of battle was trumpet-voiced Senator Ned Baker. No more would his fervid oratory soar through the Senate Chamber.

As for the lady: Who told Rose Greenhow that McDowell had issued marching orders for July 16th? Who gave her the red-dotted map? Was this vital information passed to her by a man so swept away by her voluptuous embraces as to forget duty, honor, country?

When she was taken into custody a month after the Bull Run débacle, Federal agents seized a packet of love letters. She had destroyed all else. These letters, in a masculine hand, were signed with the single initial H. Could this H have stood for Henry? One of these letters was dated January 30th, 1861. It was written on government stationery bearing the imprint "Thirty-sixth Congress, United States of America" and the seal of the United States Senate. It indicates an intimacy had existed between Rose Greenhow and H even before hostilities began.

Handwriting experts have claimed these letters were not written by Senator Wilson, although they speak of bills before the Senate in which he was interested. No known charges were brought against him, but his share in this business has never been cleared up. Whatever suspicion may have rested on him, he must have explained to the satisfaction of Federal authorities who made no record of it. General Beauregard later said his information at Bull Run had come, through a private source, from "politicians high in council."

Throughout the war Henry Wilson was a pillar of strength to the administration, and, in 1872 he was elected Vice-President of the United States. .

What of his companion, Rose Greenhow? Over her grave at Wilmington, North Carolina, there is a marble cross, erected by sympathetic ladies. On it are carved the words, "Mrs. Rose O'Neal Greenhow—A Bearer of Despatches to the Confederate Government."

But that is another story, far away from Capitol Hill.

24

FETTERS FOR THE SOUTH, IMPEACHMENT FOR A PRESIDENT

It was exactly four years to the day since President Lincoln called for volunteers to invade the South and now on April 15th, 1865, he lay dead in a cheap rooming house on Tenth Street, Washington, cut down by a mad assassin's bullet.

While the embalmers bent to their somber task over the remains of the martyred President, Vice-President Andrew Johnson, in his room at the nearby Kirkwood Hotel, took the oath as Chief Executive. Standing before Chief Justice Salmon P. Chase, Johnson kissed the open Bible at the twenty-first verse of the eleventh chapter of the prophet Ezekiel. As Johnson looked up from the holy book, Chase said, "You are now President. May God support, guide and bless you in your arduous duties."

Andrew Johnson began life as a humble "poor white" from the Tennessee mountains, an indentured tailor's apprentice at the age of ten. He never went to school in his life. He was twenty-one before he learned to write, taught by his wife. Up to then he had to make his mark instead of signing his name. By force and courage he rose above his lowly origin, scaling the political ladder of his own state so fast that he reached the United States Senate in 1857. Democrat but staunch Unionist, Johnson was picked as Lincoln's running mate for the latter's second term in 1864. It was a concession to the War Democrats in the National Union Party which had nominated Lincoln to succeed himself.

Johnson got off to a bad start. Three stiff drinks of whiskey before entering the overheated Senate Chamber to make his brief inaugural address and take the oath as Vice-President proved his undoing. Befuddled or, more accurately, drunk, he launched into a maudlin, undignified, confused harangue that so mortified President Lincoln he reached out and tried to yank Johnson back to his chair by his coattails. Bending over to kiss the Bible, Johnson babbled raucously, "I kiss this book in the face of my nation of the United States." Johnson never really lived it down. That scene was to haunt him the rest of his official days.

The Radical Republicans in Congress welcomed Johnson's accession to the presidency as a "godsend to the country." In the first wave of shock and daze after Lincoln's assassination, Johnson had vowed to hang Jefferson Davis and his "diabolical" clique. Treason was a crime, he said, and he intended to punish the Southern leaders guilty of it. This was music to the ears of the Radicals, who immediately sat down to a temporary political love-feast with the new President. "Johnson," said Senator Ben Wade, arch-Radical, "we have faith in you. By the gods there will be no trouble now in running the government." Wade was head of the cantankerous Committee on the Conduct of the War that had harassed Lincoln throughout the war.

Lincoln, even before his death, had collided with the Radicals, who were led by two iron-willed, imperious men, Thaddeus Stevens of Pennsylvania in the House and Charles Sumner of Massachusetts in the Senate. These two were virtual dictators on Capitol Hill.

The South itself was prostrate, exhausted, bled white, bankrupt, its money worthless, its credit gone. Two million men had trampled it with fire and sword, leaving desolation and wreckage. Wide areas were blackened. Northern victory was absolute. Fighting to the bitter end, Southern defeat was utter. Graves dotted Southern landscapes. Death had reached into thousands of homes. Six hundred thousand men in gray and blue had perished in the holocaust of war. Factories were destroyed, railroads torn up, bridges blown up. Dreams of independence had vanished and Southern leaders were in flight or prison.

The South's defeated soldiers returned to stark chimneys of burned-out homes, hungry wives and children. Three billion dollars in slaves had vanished. The Negroes themselves presented a tremendous political and social problem that would take years to settle. A dispirited people faced a seemingly hopeless future. The task of building up the stricken cotton empire appalled even the strongest of heart.

In 1863 President Lincoln had proposed humane, lenient reconstruction of the Southern states once the war was over. He called it his "ten percent plan." He would pardon all but a few of the higher officers of the Confederacy on taking the oath of loyalty to the Union. As soon as one-tenth of a state's voters in 1860 had completed this method of re-enfranchisement, the state might reform its government and apply for re-entry into the Union.

"I hope," said Lincoln, "there will be no persecution, no bloody work after the war is over. No one need expect me to take part in hanging or killing those men, even the worst of them. We must extinguish resentment if we expect harmony and union."

Wondrous words those, like the others that preceded them in his Second Inaugural: "With malice towards none, with charity for all, with firmness in the right as God gives us to see the right, let us finish the work we are in, to bind up the nation's wounds, to care for him who shall have borne the battle, and for his widow and his orphans, to do all which may achieve and cherish a just and a lasting peace among ourselves and with all nations."

But now Lincoln was gone and his fine words were stifled

by hate. The Radicals on Capitol Hill set about to undo his every official act save the Thirteenth Amendment. With indecent haste after his death, they even stripped the mourning draperies from the public buildings in Washington. Desiring vengeance on the South, this radical group proceeded to scrap Lincoln's plan for milder, saner reconstruction of the South. "White supremacy" must go, they declared. The South must pay for its long misdeeds of slavery.

President Johnson had cooled off since his threat to hang Jefferson Davis and other Confederate leaders. In July, 1865, he issued a general amnesty proclamation pardoning the Confederate rank and file which had fought against the Union but requiring the leaders, those who had led the South's bid for independence, to make personal applications for pardons. He made it clear that he would follow the reconstruction policies of the dead Lincoln. In this he collided squarely with the most bitter clique of politicians ever assembled on Capitol Hill.

In a slashing speech at Lancaster, Pennsylvania, Radical leader Thaddeus Stevens offered his program for "restoring" the Southern states to the Union. Said Stevens, Lincoln had pretended the Confederate states had never even left the Union. Now Johnson was making the same pretensions. But it was only a deception, said Stevens. The Confederacy had been a hostile nation bent on destroying the American Union. Now that it was conquered territory, it would be treated as such. Slavocracy—70,000 former slaveowners— must be wiped out. Every plantation of two hundred or more acres, worth $10,000 or more, would be carved into smaller pieces. Forty acres would be given to every adult former slave. The rest would be sold at $10 an acre and the proceeds used to pay off the national debt. Thus would slavocracy perish and a new democratic South rise from the ashes and confiscation of the old. If Southerners did not like this, they could leave the country. Stevens never used mincing words.

In the election of 1866 Radical control of Congress became absolute. Led by Stevens and Sumner, Congress now began passing the Radical reconstruction acts, but first they wiped from the slate all that Lincoln and Johnson had put there. These acts fastened military government on the South, which was divided into five military districts of which Virginia was number one. Ruling each district was a Union major general. The reconstructed state governments set up by Johnson were swept aside. Old state constitutions were abolished. Before a state could be readmitted to the Union, it must adopt a new constitution which permitted former slaves to vote. To the military governors of the five districts was given power to supplant Southern civil officials as they saw fit. To make sure the provisions of the Reconstruction Acts were carried out, Federal bayonets would be distributed throughout the South.

Thus began the tug of war between President Johnson, armed with vetoes which were over-ridden at will, and the Radicals who held absolute control of Congress.

25

THADDEUS STEVENS IMPEACHES
ANDREW JOHNSON

I.

It was the perfect day for impeachment of the President of the United States. If the Radical conspirators, or to be more exact, if Thaddeus Stevens of Pennsylvania, failed to whiplash the impeachment resolution through the House of Representatives today, Saturday, February 22nd, 1868, he would set the clock back (as was actually done) so that, on the record, even though it was Monday, February 24th, President Andrew Johnson would stand humiliated before the American people, "impeached of high crimes and misdemeanors," on Washington's Birthday.

Thad Stevens had an uncanny, satanic flair for political fitness. Today the "ungrateful, despicable, besotted, traitorous" Andrew Johnson would be stripped, scourged, and made ready for crucifixion on the nation's Golgotha. Within a fortnight "honest, old" Ben Wade of Ohio, President of the Senate, would move into the White House. "President" Wade would gladly carry out the harsh, vengeful plans Stevens & Co. had cooked up for shackling the prostrate South.

Today Thad Stevens was Robespierre, Danton, and Marat all rolled into one. He needed only a guillotine on Capitol Hill and a tumbril to send to the White House to fetch President Johnson for official decapitation.

311

The "high crimes and disdemeanors" charged to President Johnson might be summed up in a word, veto. His major offense, as seen from this perspective, was his attempt to frustrate the schemes of Stevens and his Vindictives for reducing the South to utter poverty and desolation.

The South must be treated as a conquered province, declared Stevens, as he forged a military yoke to weld about its neck so tightly that it would remain for a generation. Johnson had other ideas. He preferred Lincoln's milder reconstruction policies. This brought on the clash between Johnson and Congress, which is another way of saying Thad Stevens, in the year of grace 1868.

No man ever hated another so blackly as Stevens hated President Johnson. First indictment against the Tennessean was his Southern blood. In 1864, when Johnson was offered as running mate for Lincoln's second term, Stevens asked acidly: "Can't you find a candidate for Vice-President without going down into those damned rebel provinces to pick one up?" Three years later he was to spew out: "Johnson is a moral leper whom you should not touch. He should be socially ostracized as unfit for decent society." His pet quotation was an editorial in the New York *World* depicting Johnson as "an insolent drunken brute, in comparison with whom even Caligula's horse was respectful."

In 1867 Congress was ruled by Radical Republican majorities which bowed under the whip of the most arrogant, unforgiving taskmaster ever seen on Capitol Hill. The Democrats in the House were just so many doormats for Stevens to wipe his feet on. Audaciously, Stevens and his henchmen announced that reconstruction of the South was the business of Congress. The President must keep his hands off. Determined to make a figurehead of the Chief Executive, the Radicals strong-armed their Reconstruction measures through Congress. Boldly Johnson hurled them back with vetoes based on unconstitutionality. His vetoes were over-ridden with coarse jokes.

In January 1867 Stevens and his Radicals conceived and enacted the Tenure of Office Act crippling the President's power of removal and appointment and reducing him to a virtual vassal of the Senate. It provided that all civil officers whose appointment had required the Senate's approval could be removed only by permission of the upper body. To this measure was attached a proviso, "That the Secretaries of State, of the Treasury, of War, of the Navy, and of the Interior, the Postmaster General and the Attorney General shall hold their offices respectively for and during the term of the President by whom they may have been appointed and for one month thereafter, subject to removal by and with advice and consent of the Senate."

This was the impeachment trap set by Stevens and his gang. Into it walked President Johnson with his eyes wide open.

Among President Johnson's holdovers from Lincoln's Cabinet was Edwin M. Stanton, Secretary of War, who, like Stevens, was a domineering, insolent man. His Civil War record was excellent. He had rooted staggering graft out of war contracts, but he secretly ran with the Radicals, even while Lincoln was still alive. He could not make friends; rather, he made the wrong friends. It was arrant treachery. Like a stool pigeon, Stanton would slink off from Cabinet meetings to Capitol Hill to report to Stevens what had occurred.

In August of 1867 Johnson, aware at last of Stanton's double-dealing, demanded his resignation. Stanton refused and took refuge behind the Tenure of Office Act. Johnson thereupon suspended him and appointed General Grant *ad interim* Secretary of War until the Senate returned in the fall.

Impeachment was in the air when the Fortieth Congress assembled in December of 1867. Brusquely the Senate denied President Johnson permission to suspend Stanton, to whom Grant meekly surrendered the office. Losing patience,

Johnson now committed the deed which Stevens & Co. had long hoped he would. He fired Stanton, thus springing the impeachment trap and committing the "great transgression." The day was February 21, 1868. Johnson had crossed his Rubicon!

The stage director and chief impeacher in the bitter melodrama on which the curtain had just risen was Thad Stevens, who carried Congress around in his vest pocket. The Great Commoner, he would, if he could, visit such degradation and suffering on the South that it would linger for a generation. His reconstruction formula was confiscation, "stripping a proud nobility of their bloated estates"; ruin; retribution, "punishments longer remembered than death"; to set black over white; to give every freedman forty acres and a mule; to pay off the national debt by "selling off" the South.

It is safe to say that, had there been no Stevens, there would have been no impeachment. For the House of Representatives in 1868 was Thad Stevens. Now seventy-six years old, haggard, a wrinkled apparition and literally dying on his feet, he was the Simon Legree of his party. He hoped to fend off the Grim Reaper just long enough to drag Johnson to the bar of the Senate. That done, Death could take over at will.

Hated and feared, he was yet obeyed. He obtained his majorities by "sarcasm, taunts, dragooning, and cracking the party whip," as well as by absolute dictation of party patronage. Cadaverous and sardonic, his brown wig awry, he sat always on the center aisle halfway back from the rostrum where he could crack his cat-o-nine-tails over his party "slaves" or catch the Speaker's eye and transmit not his desires, but his decrees, to "Smiler" Colfax in the Chair.

Stevens' tongue-lashings were awe-inspiring, volcanic. Few colleagues dared question the wisdom of his pronouncements. He was not eloquent, but his raking, unparalleled abuse shriveled those at whom he aimed it. On his adversaries he showered coarsest invectives without mercy. His words were always calculated carefully to cut to the quick. His scorn of an opponent was a thing incarnate. His verbal knout hurt deep. Absolute boss of Congress, he disdained praise and censure alike. Yet, he was a fascinating, picturesque figure to watch in action as he vented scorn, acid, contempt, and biting words on all who opposed him.

The salient feature of his face was a big, protruding upper lip which drooped at the corners. Nature had marked him for cruelty and, for good measure, had crippled him with a hideous clubfoot. His deformity had embittered him. Dickens could not have invented a more malevolent character. In politics he was relentless and ruthless. To a party member who complained that his conscience would not permit him to vote as Stevens had demanded, he sneered: "Conscience, indeed! Throw conscience to the devil and stand by your party!"

In 1868 two passions ruled him: love of power and hatred of Andrew Johnson. To one who asked what grounds he proposed to use in impeaching Johnson, Stevens shot back: "I'll take that man's record, his speeches, and his acts before any impartial jury you can get together and I'll make them pronounce him either a knave or a fool without the least trouble. My own impression is that we had better put it on the ground of insanity or whiskey or something of that kind. I don't want to hurt the man's feelings by telling him he is a rascal. I'd rather put it mildly and just say he hasn't got off that inauguration drunk yet, and just let him retire to get sobered up."

Stevens had come into his own during the Civil War. As chairman of the House Ways and Means Committee, he rendered valiant service to the nation, but thereby his individual power became such as none had ever wielded on Capitol Hill before him.

Stevens was a bachelor. He had a negro mistress, Lydia Smith, whom he euphemistically called his housekeeper.

For years she presided over his domestic ménage in a small house on B Street near the Capitol. An inveterate gambler, he was well-known in the dens of chance along Pennsylvania Avenue near the Capitol. When Congress closed for the day he would shuffle from one to another, a welcome guest always. He could sit all night at a faro table and appear in the House next morning, drawn with lack of sleep, but ready to cut down any opponent who crossed him.

He was no hypocrite; he played his games in the open. And he was charitable. Obsessed by absolute equality of black and white, he was buried, by his own request, in a negro cemetery in his home town, Lancaster, Pennsylvania.

The news of Stanton's dismissal reached Capitol Hill at two-thirty, sweeping through the House and Senate like wildfire. On the House floor pandemonium broke loose. Routine business—an appropriation for "guns, gun carriages, shot and shell"—all went by the board. Radicals hovered about Stevens, baying like wolves for permission to rush in for the kill.

Stevens was ready. He was the man of the hour. Tomorrow was Washington's birthday. Johnson himself could not have timed it better. Stevens had waited four years for this opportunity to destroy Johnson, who now lay trapped at his feet. The jubilee had come, in the nick of time. His iron will had kept him alive for this great moment.

Stevens swayed to his feet. A grim smile raised the corner of his lips. Excited members drew back to see what he would do. His lamp was burning low, but here was something to inject new elixir into his faltering veins.

Towering malevolently over the conflagration on the House floor, clinging to the arm of ultra-Radical John Bingham of Ohio, Stevens, like a pale, sadistic Mephistopheles, moved from group to group, belching out: "Didn't I tell you so? If you don't kill the beast, it will kill you!"

Now he barked out his orders. The House Reconstruction

Committee would meet in the morning to frame an impeachment resolution. The House would convene at noon. His minions must be in their seats. He rapped the floor with his cane to emphasize his words. Then he flashed a signal to the Speaker that the business of the House was over for the day and the gavel fell.

That night Stevens relaxed in his B Street home. Lydia Smith, his housekeeper, gave him a supper of eggs and Virginia bacon. It was the only thing about the South he liked.

Morning dawned dismally. Snow whirled through Washington. By breakfast time masses of people were tramping through the slush toward Capitol Hill; by ten, excited hundreds were clamoring for admission to the House galleries. The corridors soon seethed with immovable, suffocating crowds. Women in fine clothes and furbelows pleaded for seats, bubbling with gayety, as if it were a busman's holiday instead of the attempted damnation of a President.

House pages sliced through the packed corridors, holding aloft bundles of telegrams which poured in for the members. Newspaper correspondents fought their way to the press section to find it usurped by members of the fair sex who refused to budge. Long before noon, Capitol police locked arms before the doors of the House chamber to hold back the crowds threatening to spill onto the floor.

Conspicuous among the ladies in the gallery was beautiful Kate Chase Sprague, daughter of the Chief Justice of the United States, who would preside over the High Court of the Senate when it tried the President on the indictment of Stevens & Co.

At noon Speaker Schuyler Colfax rapped for order. Colfax was radiant. How many, or how few, suspected that already Credit Mobilier gold was jingling in his pockets? Now the curtain was up, but where was the great tragedian? His seat was empty. The noise and buzzing in the gallery went on at a high pitch.

Wedging themselves onto the House floor came members of the Senate, which had met and adjourned hastily so that the sedate Conscript Fathers could witness impeachment of the "great criminal" on whose guilt they would pronounce judgment. Impeccable Senator Sumner was there, looking "dignified and calm," and inwardly rejoicing. He was Stevens' *alter ego* in the Senate. "Zach" Chandler appeared "bold as a lion." On the rostrum beside the Speaker sat "bluff" Ben Wade, now heir apparent, surveying the scene which he anticipated would make him President within a fortnight.

Prayer must come first. The Senate chaplain had already and significantly intoned: "Thou settest up one and puttest down another. Thy hand is at the helm of the nation. Thou raisest up kingdoms and overturnest thrones and powers and dominions." He might have added something about impeaching Presidents. He left little for the House chaplain who, caught by the excitement, stumbled over his words as he approached the throne of grace.

Thus began this momentous day in the House. A Democrat from Wisconsin, Charles Eldridge, aroused mirth by proposing that Washington's Farewell Address be read to the assemblage. The Chair bluntly denied the request. A wag in the gallery chirped, "How about Johnson's Farewell Address?" Those around him whooped in glee.

Minutes dragged by. One o'clock. Where was Stevens? The galleries were getting restless; the House was merely going through motions. Nobody came, nobody went, nobody cared but for one thing. Startling rumors floated by. Men in Confederate gray were supposedly marching in from Maryland to protect the President and drive Stevens and his Radicals from the Capitol. They listened and scoffed. All knew that behind closed doors nearby Thad Stevens and his Reconstruction Committee were dressing up the Resolution which would send Andrew Johnson, "drunken sot," reeling out of the White House and perhaps into a penitentiary.

At two-twenty a bustling outside the door near the rostrum told the chamber that the great actor was making his entrance. The galleries hushed abruptly. Chatter on the floor ceased. All eyes turned to the door as Thad Stevens, leaning heavily on his cane, hobbled into the chamber. At his heels filed his committee. His baggy, unkempt clothes hung loosely about his emaciated frame. Out of his ghastly face his eyes burned like fire as he slowly crawled to his seat.

Spectators in the galleries swayed forward, craning their necks to see what manner of man was about to indict the Chief Executive of the nation and rush him to trial before the Senate for "bloodcurdling crimes." "There he is! There he is!" A stir ran through the galleries. Stevens felt the drama around him. He was master of the stage, at the high zenith of his power, and he knew it. He looked tired and broken, "as one from the very brink of the grave." Dead silence prevailed as he rose, "haggard and trembling," to offer the pronouncement that has no parallel in the nation's history. The galleries held their breath. It was history-making.

Slowly, enunciating every word, the clerk of the House read the preamble and then: "Resolved, that Andrew Johnson, President of the United States, be impeached of high crimes and misdemeanors." The impact of the resolution seemed to stun those who heard it. Simple in its wording, but devastating. Stevens' leering gaze swept the floor as he rose again. Feeble in body, but still aflame with arrogance, he bluntly demanded: why debate the Resolution? Put it to a vote at once. Johnson had committed a crime. His guilt was as clear as light:

"Mr. Speaker, it is not my intention in the first instance to discuss this question; if there be no desire on the other side to discuss it, we are willing that the question should be taken upon the knowledge which the House already has.

"But I will not discuss this question unless the gentlemen on the other side desire to discuss it. If they do, I will for the present give way to them and say what I have to say in conclusion."

He would have the last word! Yet the Democrats, "the other side," to which Stevens contemptuously referred, did wish to speak. Outnumbered and browbeaten, they could only delay and protest. The better to direct the impending saturnalia of vilification, Stevens dragged himself to the rostrum to sit between the Speaker and "good, old" Ben Wade.

Representative James Brooks, Democrat from New York, sprang to his feet "to resist this untoward, this unholy, this unconstitutional proceedings!" Leveling his finger and his gaze at the bitter old man on the rostrum, Brooks shouted:

"Supppose you should succeed in passing your resolution of impeachment; suppose you achieve a majority in this House and obtain all you want in the Senate—what then? You can impeach the President of the United States for the hat he wears or the color of his coat, if you choose . . .

"Suppose you succeed, suppose you make the President of the Senate President of the United States, you settle that hereafter a party with a sufficient majority in the House and the Senate can depose the President of the United States.

"I tell you in behalf of thousands and tens of thousands and hundreds of thousands and millions of the people of this country we will never, never, so help me God! submit, never."

It was fine, but futile. Stevens only grinned while the Radicals "roared with derisive laughter." Now Stevens gave the nod that let loose his character assassins already straining at the leash to blacken and besmirch. It was an all-out debauch of partisan venom, this so-called debate on the impeachment resolution. The *Congressional Globe* bears eloquent witness to the depths to which men can stoop when driven by party lash to demean and degrade a fellow being who, after all, in this case was the President of the United

States. There were those "who would as readily have voted that the President should be hung in front of the White House, as that he should be impeached in the Capitol, had their leaders presented papers for that purpose."

Up rose Representative John Farnsworth of Illinois to hurl maledictions at "this ungrateful, despicable, besotted traitorous" President of the United States. This man, anxious to do Stevens' bidding, had this to say:

"Sir, this nation has been too long disgraced by this man, this accidental President, made so by the assassin's pistol, this man, who, in an evil hour, was thrust upon the country. Too long has he been an incubus and a disgrace to this great and glorious nation.

"Let him be removed. I would say, if it were the last day but one before the termination of his term, and my vote would remove him, remove him. If it would cut short his term one hour I would cut it short and send him down to the future incapable hereafter of holding any office of honor, trust or profit, thus proving his own words, that there is power enough in a Republic to punish a traitor."

But "Pig Iron" Kelly of Pennsylvania was not to be outdone as he rose to vent his malice:

"Mr. Speaker, we are about to bring to trial the great criminal of our age and country, a man who for two years has been plotting with deliberate and bloody purpose to overthrow the institutions of our country.

"Possessed by the thought of the Presidency and the possible perpetuation of his power, there stood between him, Vice-President elect, and the position in which it would take but his own selfish interest to persuade him that the perpetuation of his power was essential to the life of the nation, but one life, that of Abraham Lincoln, and that life, a few days after Mr. Johnson was inaugurated as the President's constitutional successor, violence removed . . .

"Lincoln was murdered and other distinguished patriots may be. It is known that men ascend to power over bloody steps . . ."

Here came handsome John Logan of Illinois, still basking in the fame of his fine Civil War record, to fire this merciless, double-shotted tirade:

"He has not only insulted the nation by his conduct as President of the Senate, but he has disgraced that high office in which he was placed by the death of his illustrious predecessor; he has dragged, as a demagogue, the robes of his high official position in the purlieus and filth of treason;

"Mr. Speaker, I believe before my God this bad man's intention is and has been to reinaugurate revolution in this country. He sees he is a disgraced man. He sees that the last revolution has failed, and he can only look for the perpetuation of his power to the inauguration of another.

A brilliant, unterrified young Democrat, William Holman of Indiana, now ventured to ask the reading of George Washington's Farewell Address. It was the second time it had been requested. Wham! The Speaker's gavel hit the desk. The Farewell Address was out of order!

"I suppose, Mr. Speaker," said Holman, "the Constitution of the United States would scarcely be in order. I will not ask to have it read."

But the Radicals, that is, Stevens, had quick misgivings. The public would resent such indignity to the great patriot on his natal day. The Address would be read—much to the dismay of the galleries, which were not interested in the first President's fine political legacy.

Afternoon glided into night. Up through the darkness like a massive beacon surged the brilliantly lighted dome of the Capitol. Far below it the tide of hate and slime rolled on as Stevens' minions, like jackals tearing at a dead lion, sunk their forensic fangs into the "apostate," the "tyrant," the "criminal," the "usurper," even charging Johnson with complicity in Lincoln's assassination.

Ebon Ingersoll of Illinois rose, his mouth frothing with hate, to invoke the shade of Nero and his degradations:

"I shall, for one, be grievously disappointed if, within ten days from this time, honest old Ben Wade is not the President of the United States.

"When that monster of Roman history, Nero, poisoned his brother his party declared that he had saved Rome. When he procured the assassination of his wife, they praised him for his justice. And when he had assassinated his mother they kissed his bloody hand and returned thanks to the gods. No matter, then, what the President may do, he will have a party so long as he retains power and patronage. But let us not falter in our plain duty. To forgive the President would be to betray the Republic."

At ten that evening the House adjourned to convene at ten on Monday morning, which would still be February 22 by the House clock. It was agreed that a vote on the Impeachment Resolution would be taken at five on Monday. This would give Stevens *et al* more time to finish painting the President as the blackest criminal of the age.

Sunday was a day of excitement in Washington. Politicians and lawmakers jammed hotel lobbies. Telegraph wires were overloaded. Barrooms, gambling halls, and prostitution palaces did a flourishing business. Monday brought more snow and an even greater trek to the Capitol. Masses of spectators struggled to get within even hearing distance of the House chamber.

When Speaker Colfax asked Stevens if he wanted to continue the "debate," Stevens said, "Let it go on." Go on it did, for another seven hours. Slumped in a chair beside the Speaker sat Stevens, a grim, imperious Caesar, waiting for the last word, the final knife thrust. It was a repetition of Saturday's orgy at an even higher pitch.

Incredible things, some almost without parallel in the history of Congress, were said this day. Out of the raging mouth of Elihu Washburne of Indiana came this flaming calumny:

"His whole official career as President has been marked by a wicked disregard of all the obligations of public duty and by a degree of perfidy and treachery and turpitude unheard of in the history of the rulers of a free people; his personal and official character has made him the opprobrium of both hemispheres and brought ineffable disgrace on the American name.

"Surrounded by redhanded rebels, advised and counseled by the worst men that ever crawled, like filthy reptiles, at the footstool of power, the President has used all the vast authority of the government to prevent a reunion of the States, the restoration of harmony and peace and happiness to the country.

"Sustained and supported by the administration, murder, rapine, incendiarism, robbery, and all the crimes stalk through the whole land with a bloody step; and every day he remains in office adds to the long list of victims of rebel vengeance, cruelty and hate."

Reader Clarke of Ohio leaped in to charge President Johnson with complicity in the assassination of President Lincoln:

"The lawless and defiant spirit of President Johnson, indicate the animus that has for two years borne him onward in his career of crime. If Washington had been Paris this morning would have found Andrew Johnson a fugitive, fleeing from an infuriated populace, or hanging upon a lamppost in front of his mansion. For offenses no greater than his the slow but determined English seized upon their sovereign and cut off his head.

"For much less offense than is charged against President Johnson the French people dragged a Bourbon king from his throne to the guillotine without waiting for the slow process of law."

Charles Newcomb of Missouri could not resist comparing the President with Nero and others of his bloody ilk:

"He has from the hour, when, in a state of inebriation, in the Capitol of the nation, in the presence of the people and in the presence of the representatives of all the nations on the earth, he took oath of office, down to this day, been a perpetual reproach to his high position and a disgrace to the American nation.

"For these and other reasons that will be faithfully preserved by this sleepless chronicler, history will justify this proceeding, and assigning to Andrew Johnson a place with Nero, Torquemada, George Jeffreys and other names that stand out in history as warnings to those who come after."

"Beast" Ben Butler of Massachusetts opened his wide mouth to let out:

"For a tithe of these acts of usurpation, lawlessness and tyranny our fathers dissolved their connection with the government of King

George, for less than this King James lost his throne and King Charles lost his head."

William Loughbridge of Iowa whipped himself into a fury as he charged the President with planning to put himself "at the head of the army" and to "take possession of this Capitol, disperse this illegal Congress and consign the people's Representatives here who have advocated impeachment to the dungeon and the scaffold."

Hiram Price of Iowa said, "every vile traitor and bloody-handed rebel of the South is now uncoiling themselves under the warmth of Johnson's smiles."

William Stokes, Republican from Tennessee, Johnson's own State, rose to apologize for having supported Johnson in the election and to heap indignity on his compatriot:

"Sir, I did help to put him in, and as God is my judge, I intend to help put him out; believing that God will forgive me for the commission of one wrong by coming forward and doing a righteous act— an act that will relieve the country of the worst tyrant and usurper that history was ever called on to record."

Orange Ferriss of New York wildly predicted that the people would cut off the head of Andrew Johnson:

"An apostate Executive, who has used the power of his high office to thwart the will of the people has completed the full measure of his infamy. . . .

"His defenders remind us of incidents in English history. It was Charles the First who quarreled with his Parliament because they opposed his unlawful measures. The end of Charles was speedy. He died upon the scaffold.

"Perhaps the President will attempt the role of the English King. If he attempts it, history will repeat itself."

These are but samples of the rancor and venom which issued from the throats of Stevens' satellites on February 24th, 1868. Andrew Johnson, however, had his defenders. They were hooted and howled down, but they would have their say.

Up rose a distinguished, respected, and fearless Democrat from Stevens' own state, former Chief Justice of Pennsylvania, George Woodward. With clear, penetrating logic he cut into the rottenness of the charges against Johnson and denied the right of the House to impeach the President and the Senate's right to try him:

"Ten States are absent and their Representatives excluded from these Halls. Twenty Senators are absent from the Senate that would try such an impeachment.

"What criminal was ever arraigned before a court from which twenty of his legal triers had been excluded?"

The sharpest indictment of Stevens & Co. came from the lashing tongue of Democrat Jacob Golladay of Kentucky:

"Surely this man must be a great moral monster! He must have brought down upon us war, famine or pestilence, or surely this grand menagerie of howling patriots would not call him traitor, culprit, criminal. Alas! no; nothing of this sort. What has he done then? Speak it, in God's name!

"In my judgment this whole impeachment movement is a trump card.

"Mr. Speaker, there are two prominent ideas and insinuations with which to beslime the fair name of Andrew Johnson . . . one that Johnson had complicity with Mr. Lincoln's murder, the other that he might procure the death of other distinguished patriots. Can political malice or personal malignity go further? Truly we have fallen upon evil times when our rulers can thus be arraigned for such crimes as murder unsupported by the least shadow of a shade of foundation."

The House clock ticked off four-thirty. Stevens was now to have the last word. The flood of venom on the floor subsided. Outside the wind moaned. Speaker Colfax rapped a warning, but it was needless. Unbelievable quiet prevailed.

Pallid and corpse-like, Stevens stood up and shuffled forward feebly, "his sunken eyes gleaming with a half-smile of triumph." Leaving their seats, his Radicals huddled around the rostrum. "A beautiful, touching and solemn picture," said a Radical newspaper.

His palsied hand held a paper on which he had scrawled what he wished to say "in conclusion." He began speaking in a weak whisper, but he was the Stevens of old, implacable, full of poison, determined to destroy Andrew Johnson, although arm in arm with death itself, for so it seemed at the moment. Soon his lips were moving but uttering no sound. His voice deserted him. Handing the paper to a clerk to finish reading, he sank into his chair, spent and wan.

Out of the wretched two-day vilification of the President now emerged, in Stevens' closing words, the motive behind his all-out hatred of Johnson: the President had tried to block his reconstruction schemes:

"In my judgment his conduct in regard to that transaction was a high-handed usurpation of power which ought long ago to have brought him to impeachment and trial and to have removed him from his position of great mischief. He has been lucky in thus far escaping through false logic and false law. But his then acts, which will on trial be shown to be atrocious, are open evidence of his wicked determination to subvert the laws of his country.

"If Andrew Johnson escapes with bare removal from office, if he be not fined and incarcerated in the penitentiary afterward under criminal proceedings, he may thank the weakness or the clemency of Congress and not his own innocence."

He finished with a fine, Parthian flourish:

"As we deal with the first great political malefactor, so will be the result of our efforts to perpetuate the happiness and good government of the human race. This is not to be the temporary triumph of a political party, but is to endure in its consequences until this whole continent shall be filled with a free and untrammeled people or shall be a nest of shrinking, cowardly slaves."

There were scattered Radical handclaps, but the galleries emitted not a sound. The moment was too tense. The heart of every onlooker stepped up its beat. It was five o'clock, fated hour for the vote on the "great transgression." The Speaker ordered the impeachment resolution read. In a late upsurge of strength Stevens, without rising, demanded the yeas and nays.

It began with a vigorous nay from Representative George Adams of Kentucky. Faster and faster, as the clerk intoned the roster, the yeas accumulated. The galleries quivered. Awe-struck spectators were murmuring "The President is impeached!" Near the end of the roll call, Speaker Colfax whispered something to Stevens who smiled wanly.

The roll call ended in dead silence. The chamber breathed noiselessly. What next? Speaker Colfax was not to be denied his pound of flesh, too; he must help doom Andrew Johnson. Sententiously he spoke:

"The occupant of the Chair cannot consent that his constituents should be silent on so grave a question, and therefore, as a member of the House, he votes Yea. On agreeing to the Resolution there are 126 Yeas, Nays 47."

It was done! There was no outburst. Thad Stevens had impeached the President of the United States! Those who witnessed the scene were stunned and subdued. House members sat transfixed for moments, appalled by the magnitude of the deed. It was the first time such an indignity had ever been inflicted on the Chief Magistrate of the nation.

Enthroned on the rostrum, a triumphant Stevens held court. Around him crowded his Radicals bubbling with homage. Now he was king! He lacked only a sceptre. But, too weak to walk, he was supported to a carriage by two of his faithful. Slowly he drove to his B Street home and the kindly ministrations of Lydia Smith.

He had done a great day's work. There was nothing like it in the history of the nation. New life was surging through his debilitated body. Andrew Johnson was impeached of high crimes and misdemeanors. He, Thaddeus Stevens, had brought it about!

26

IMPEACHMENT INTERLUDE

II

They were a motley crew, these House impeachment managers! Speaker "Smiler" Colfax had appointed them with, of course, "help" from Thad Stevens. Among them were to be found:

John Bingham of Ohio, "a shrewd, sinuous, tricky lawyer" whose sidewhiskers gave him the aspect of a church deacon. John Logan of Illinois, handsome, dark-skinned, straight as an Indian and worthy of better associates. George Boutwell of Massachusetts, whose hate of Johnson was matched by his love of notoriety. Thomas Williams of Pittsburgh, an unscrupulous man whose disregard of truth was notorious. James Wilson of Iowa, who came late but welcome into the Radical fold. Ben Butler, who was to take active leadership of the prosecution of Johnson. Thickset, bald, droop-eyed, he was as cunning and tricky as an unscrupulous lawyer could be. Lincoln once said that Butler was "as full of poison as a dead dog." And, of course, poison-fanged Thad Stevens.

Feverishly Stevens and his impeachment managers fell to their task of devising articles of impeachment which, on March 2nd, they presented to a much-alarmed House. Two days before, Speaker Colfax had tremblingly announced receiving a letter from the Chief of Police of New York revealing that a large quantity of nitro-glycerin (then a new and awesome explosive) had mysteriously disappeared. It might have been taken to Washington!

Consternation momentarily struck the ranks of the Radicals. Any moment the Capitol might go skyward and the huge new dome come tumbling down. A Democrat ventured to suggest it was an augury of God's wrath at the infamy the chamber had witnessed, but the Old Commoner merely growled "humbug." Thad Stevens did not "scare" easily.

There were eleven articles of impeachment. The first nine, based on Johnson's presumed violation of the Tenure of Office Act, embodied little legal conviction. The Tenth, "Beast" Butler's handiwork and the only one of the eleven which told the bald truth, charged Johnson with speeches in which he had heaped "disgrace, ridicule, hate and contempt" on Congress. Johnson had indeed shot his harpoon deep into the flanks of Stevens & Co. Butler's hide was tough, but he smarted under the President's barbs.

The eleventh article was Stevens' very own. Disgusted at the mildness of the first ten, he sneered openly at them. Even the Senate, stacked as it was for a verdict of guilty, would laugh. He would show them how to put claws and fangs into an article which would tear the very heart out of Andrew Johnson.

This historic eleventh article, the so-called omnibus article, was an *omnium gatherum,* combining all the charges in one—" a trick to catch wavering Senators," "a testimonial to the undiminished shrewdness and intellectual strength of the veteran whose physical forces were close to their ends." In this article, which became the gist and vital portion of the trial of Andrew Johnson, Stevens crystallized the accumulated malice of his diseased mind.

Audaciously, contemptuously, and defiantly, he proceeded to rowel his Radicals behind his creation. Taking the floor of the House he went at it hammer and tongs:

"Never was a great malefactor so gently treated as Andrew Johnson. The people have been unwilling to blot the records of their country by mingling his crimes with their shame—shame for endurance for so long a time of his great crimes and misdemeanors.

"If there be shrewd lawyers, as I know there will be, and cavilling judges, and, without this article, they do not acquit him, they are greener than I was in any case I ever undertook before the court of quarter sessions. If it be inserted his own letters show both the removal and the attempt to defeat reinstatement of the Secretary of War. How, then, can he or his counsel hope to escape, even if there were no other charge—it is worth all of them put together—from conviction unless it be upon what I know they will rely on, the unconstitutionality of the tenure of civil office act. I may say that the Senate have four times voted upon the constitutionality of that very bill. Every Republican voted in its favor.

"What chance, then, would Andrew Johnson have had we not left out the article I desire, in order to give him a loophole of escape? Gentlemen can see how fair we are. If my article be inserted what chance has Andrew Jackson to escape, even if all the rest of the articles should fail?

"Unfortunate man! Thus surrounded, hampered, tangled in the mesh of his own wickedness—unfortunate, unhappy man, behold your doom!"

He whiplashed it through a frightened House and then went home satisfied that all was well.

That same evening Senator Ben Wade and his cronies sat before an open fire picking his Cabinet. "Ben Wade will be President in a fortnight from today. The trial once begun will be speedily ended." So hopefully prophesied the correspondent of a radical newspaper. Wade believed it. He and Mrs. Wade were already making plans for moving into the White House.

27

SPECTACLE, SOUND, AND FURY

III

"Hear Ye! Hear Ye! All persons are commanded to keep silence on penalty of imprisonment while the Senate of the United States is sitting for the trial of the Articles of Impeachment against Andrew Johnson, President of the United States."

So chanted the Sergeant-at-Arms of the Senate on Friday, March 13th, 1868. It was exactly one o'clock.

Next came the good chaplain of the Senate, who besought divine blessing "that the proceedings of the High Court which is about to meet may be sanctioned by the High Court of Heaven." Thad Stevens & Co. were not interested in celestial approval; their chief concern was a verdict of guilty by the High Court of the Senate.

The state trial of President Andrew Johnson, *in absentia,* before the High Court of the Senate was the greatest spectacle ever staged by the American Congress. It was the dramatic pinnacle of seventy-nine years of lawmaking, the finest, most awesome showpiece in the legislative history of the Republic. Yet, after all, it was only a solemn, hollow farce.

Tickets for Broadway's most spectacular attraction were never more avidly sought than the badly printed pasteboards which admitted the bearer to the Senate chamber this historic Friday. The impeachers intended it to be a mighty drama. At least, Andrew Johnson could not afterwards say that they had not given him an impressive, breathtaking send-off. Indeed, they sent him ten tickets, as if he or his family desired to witness his own political lynching.

Washington was now a "seething caldron." Hysteria had seized the city. Place-seekers arrived in droves. Political vultures, smelling carrion afar, roosted in every nook and cranny of the Capitol. The spoils of Andrew Johnson's dethronement would be staggering. Hotel lobbies surged with crowds. Saloons and brothels were overrun. Important personages and curiosity-seekers arrived by every train.

Over this transcendent spectacle hovered a brilliance and a splendor which far outshone the dreams of her planners. They had studied the impeachment of Warren Hastings and sought to clothe their extravaganza in rainbow pageantry which would rival, or at least be a worthy imitation of, the setting so vividly painted by the pen of Macaulay. Like the historic English legal drama, the trial of Andrew Johnson had grandeur, theatricalism, and gripping moments, but there were no dukes and duchesses, no queen in a royal box draped with silks and satins, surrounded by the "fair-haired daughters of the House of Brunswick"; no Prince of Wales "conspicuous by his fine person and noble bearing"; no peers "robed in gold and ermine."

Nor was there a "Siddons, in the prime of her majestic beauty" looking "with emotion on a scene surpassing all the limitations of the stage." Nor were there gathered from all parts of the republic "grace and female loveliness, wit and learning, the representatives of every science and art." On the contrary every cheap, place-hungry politician who could wangle a ticket in return for promised votes was on hand hoping to partake of the spoils and crowding into the Senate chamber.

Nor were its walls "hung with scarlet," as were the gray walls of the great hall of William Rufus where Hastings was given his day or, rather, his years in court. Yet the Senate chamber was emblazoned with enough pomp and circumstance to make the onlookers gasp with admiration. It was something new to America.

Butler and his minions had read closely Macaulay's celebrated description of the fabulous scene in the English House of Lords in 1788. They observed how Edmund Burke had prepared himself for Hastings' prosecution by storing his mind with all the dazzling, enchanting, mysterious story of India—"the burning sun, the strange vegetation of the palm and cocoa tree, the rich tracery of the mosque where the immaun prays with his face to Mecca, the drums and banners and gaudy idols . . . the turbans and the flowing robes, the spears and the silver maces, the elephants with their canopies of state, the gorgeous palanquin of prince and the closed litter of the noble lady." With Macaulay, pop-eyed shyster lawyer Butler sauntered through the "spacious provinces of Aurungabad and Bejapoor"; peeked into the bazaars where he saw "the muslins of Bengal and sabres of Oude" mingling "with the jewels of Golconda and the shawls of Cashmere."

Imagining themselves latter-day Edmund Burkes, Butler, Stevens & Co. stored their minds with just two things: how to dragoon the Senate into a verdict of guilty and, if votes were needed for conviction, how to buy them with coin of the realm.

One feature of Warren Hastings' trial they sought to avoid. Hastings' trial had dragged on for seven years to end in acquittal. They planned to try the President of the United States as if he were a common horse thief and to kick him out of the White House as fast as an apparently willing and prejudiced Senate could wangle a verdict of guilty past the watchful eye of the Chief Justice of the United States.

One thing was certain: there was not the remotest possibility that a future historian, gazing on the trial of Andrew Johnson, would ever be reminded—as was Macaulay—of "the days when Cicero pleaded the cause of Sicily against Verres" or when "before a Senate which still retained some show of freedom Tacitus thundered against the oppressor of Africa."

Dethroning the ruler of a mighty nation was drama in itself. Charles I and Louis XVI had faced their accusers, appearing in the flesh to plead their cases. Warren Hastings, of lofty mien, had confronted his judges. Andrew Johnson never set foot in the Senate chamber where he was tried. It was this which gave the trial a sense of unreality. There was no defendant, no culprit at the bar, no President of the United States fighting in dead earnest, at the last ditch, for his political life. Still, it was a setting and an audience such as a king might have asked for.

Charles I and Louis XVI had battled for their lives and lost. The High Court of the Senate could not behead Andrew Johnson, but it could consign him to everlasting disgrace, strip him of office, then pass him on to a jury to be fined ten thousand dollars and imprisoned for five years.

The gallery was "resplendent with bright and beautiful women in the most gorgeous apparel," aflutter with ribbons, gay dresses, feathers of myriad hues, corsages of flowers, smiles and a thousand sparkling feminine baubles. Huge diamonds blazed on hundreds of delicate fingers. Necklaces of precious stones hung in gleaming strands about shapely throats. Gowns, elegance, extravagance, fashion, jewels, beauty were all splashed together in fabulous prodigality. It was a social event par excellence. Then, as now, pulchritude had ways of getting what it wanted, such as, in this instance, tickets of admission to the Senate chamber.

Queen of the gala audience was radiant Kate Chase Sprague, who flashed "the most fetching eyes on earth" down on her husband, Senator Sprague, whose vote for Johnson's guilt was already dangling over the Radical bag.

Plumped down in the middle of all this grandeur was the woman who expected soon to be the next First Lady of the Land, Mrs. Benjamin Franklin Wade.

The diplomatic gallery was a picturesque, glittering tableau of gold lace, colorful uniforms, bejewelled women, and foreign ministers dripping with the insignia of European honors. Through the eyes of these "ambassadors," Italy, Turkey, Prussia, Greece, Great Britain, Sweden, China, Spain and lesser lands had come to witness "the peaceful deposition of a sovereign ruler." The scene might well have been transported out of the Elizabethan court to the Senate chamber to grace the spectacle of a President arraigned like a common criminal before the country's highest tribunal.

Correspondents from every important paper in the country jammed the press section, writing ceaselessly. Cartoonists, then in their infancy, made on-the-spot caricatures of the great and not-so-great. Page boys, adorned with red ribbons, infiltrated the sacred purlieus of the Senate floor, bearing an unending stream of missives from one august gentleman to another.

Dominating this stupendous farce was not the impressive, dignified Chief Justice of the United States, Salmon Portland Chase, "the incarnation of dignity, self-possession and repose," resembling a solemn Buddha sitting high on the rostrum clad in the traditional robes of his exalted office?

Nor was the limelight held by bald, squint-eyed, pompous, paunchy "Beast" Butler, who seated himself in one of the red leather chairs provided for the impeachment managers to the front and right of the rostrum. "Insolent, intolerant, audacious" as Stevens himself, Butler felt this was his chance for immortality. He was now steering the impeachment. The outcome would give him over to history not as the man of evil, silver-spoon memory, but as the crusader who drove the iniquitous Andrew Johnson out of the White House.

Nor yet was Thad Stevens the main show. Now he was so feeble and ghastly, so near death, he had to be borne to the Senate daily in a chair by two husky negro boys. Of these youths Stevens had asked:: "Boys, I wonder who will carry me when you are dead and buried." It was his lone sally at humor. His spirit was flickering, but he still brandished a cleaver. Beneath his dried-parchment cheeks glowed a slight flush of excitement. Supernatural-looking, he was still the evil genius of the show. Verging on collapse, he sat sipping brandy to keep him alive for the last scene, Johnson's political demise. Old Thad would see it through. He bore out Johnson's jest that Stevens was like a human Vesuvius. Apparently dead and extinct, he would burst suddenly into a "living flow of passion."

Master of the shuttling scenes of the trial, dominating every move, every moment, was the silent, unseen actor-defendant, Andrew Johnson, whose presence was as real, as vocal as though he stood at the bar of the Senate pleading his own case. Unheard, invisible, waiting calmly in the White House a mile away, he ran off with the show, much to the dismay and surprise of the impeachers.

Now take a look at the fifty-four Senators, the "impartial judges," who were to listen to Stevens, Butler & Co. and then pass sentence on Johnson. Forty-two of them belonged to the party which had dragooned impeachment through the House. At least twenty-eight of these had condemned the prisoner in advance of trial. The Radicals were already counting votes. Wade, Sumner, and Chandler were as busy as bees. Through their checkered, prejudiced minds were running many "ifs." To a majority, the oath "to do impartial justice to Andrew Johnson" meant nothing, but they realized that among the forty-two Republicans were a few with a finer sense of honor. What if seven Republicans refused to cower beneath the Stevens lash? What if even bribery failed to move the "immovables?" The Senate never looked so dignified, so impressive, as it did this day when Johnson's trial opened. Sumner was at his sartorial best; the hairdresser had toiled long and artistically on his wavy brown locks. Ben Wade resembled an executioner in his Sunday best;

one could almost see his invisible axe. Banked behind the Senators was a solid wall of Representatives, one hundred and ninety of them come over from the lower House.

Where were the other ten states? There should have been twenty other Senators, but ten Southern states were excluded from Johnson's jury.

Such, briefly, was the setting when the Sergeant-at-Arms made his second appearance to chant: "Andrew Johnson, President of the United States! Andrew Johnson, President of the United States! Appear and answer the Articles of Impeachment exhibited against you by the House of Representatives!" A thrill ran through the throng and heads were turned as if expecting to see the President suddenly materialize. But Andrew Johnson came not, though his five-man counsel moved out from the Senate lobby to a table to the left of the rostrum.

By May 4th the evidence was all in, the sound and fury over. The great American travesty had reached its crisis and the case against Andrew Johnson ws closed. Came for Stevens & Co. twenty-five witnesses rehearsing the malice and slander which had deluged the House floor on Washington's Birthday. For Johnson came sixteen witnesses. His entire defense rested on his conviction that the Tenure of Office Act was unconstitutional. He had violated it to make a test case which the Supreme Court could adjudicate. As for the dismissal of Secretary of War Stanton, Johnson felt that the act did not protect that weasley gentleman because he was appointed by President Lincoln.

Every spectator from page boy to the Chief Justice knew in his heart that what he had seen and heard was no more than the gorgeously staged, attempted massacre of a too formidable opponent.

But Thad Stevens could not let the prosecution close without using his knife. Dragging himself from the edge of the yawning grave he offered a nineteen-page summary of abuse and malignity. It was not extemporaneous. He had prepared it with infinite care.

Sustained by the intensity of his hate, he rose and began reading. It was his last chance to besmirch Andrew Johnson. Snarling and bitter, he whipped the Senate as he had so often the House. He would have welcomed Johnson's decapitation there on the Senate floor:

"And now this offspring of assassination turns upon the Senate and bids them defiance. How can he escape the just vengeance of the law? Wretched man, standing at bay, surrounded by a cordon of living men each with the axe of an executioner uplifted for his just punishment!"

Save for the Democratic Senators, every Senator now trying Johnson, ranted Stevens in a faded whisper, had already pronounced his "solemn doom." Exhausted by his own passion, his frame shook, his voice dwindled. He sank into a chair and handed his paper to the clownish Butler to finish reading:

"Will anyone of them"—asked Stevens through Butler—"vote for his acquittal on the ground of its unconstitutionality? I know that Senators will venture to do any necessary act if endorsed by an honest conscience or an enlightened public opinion; but never for the sake of the President nor anyone else would one of them suffer himself to be tortured on the gibbet of everlasting obloquy.

"How long and dark will be the track of infamy which marks his name and that of his posterity! It requires no gift of prophecy to predict the fate of this unhappy victim!"

His two Negro boys sidled up to Stevens and carried the drooling old man out of the Senate chamber to his B Street home and Lydia Smith.

Loud-voiced and confident, John Bingham closed the case against the President with a jabbing stump speech flowing with fine rhetoric and patriotic invocation:

"May God forbid that the future historian shall record of this day's proceedings, that by reason of the failure of the legislative power of the people to triumph over the usurpations of an apostate President through the defection of the Senate of the United States, the just and great fabric of American empire fell and perished from the earth.

Now the durbar closed in a fantastic demonstration in the galleries by Stevens' well-rehearsed claque. Like a scene out of the French Revolution, frantic, wild-eyed men and women rose to their feet, shouting, raging, clamoring for a verdict of guilty. In a flash it swelled to a tumult.

"Order! Order!" shouted the astounded Chief Justice, only to be drowned by a torrent of hisses and derision and cries of "Guilty! Guilty!" Toughs crashed through the galleries, knocking spectators down, hurling out threats and curses.

Up dashed the Senate Sergeant-at-Arms and Capitol Police to quell the disorder, but Senator Cameron of Pennsylvania shouted, "I hope the galleries will not be cleared." Little wonder; this scene had been carefully prearranged. It would impress weak-kneed and doubting Senators that the people were demanding Johnson's official execution. Order was at last restored and the Chief Justice solemnly announced that the case was closed.

Telegrams flowed out of Washington that night. "The recreant will be out of the White House before the end of the week." "Beast" Butler regaled a New Hampshire Republican Convention with: "The removal of the great obstruction is certain. Wade and prosperity are sure to come with the apple blossoms."

This was May 4th. Apple blossoms were about to burst. So, unsuspected by the impeachers, were their hopes.

28

THE MOVING FINGER WRITES . . . NOT GUILTY!

IV

Saturday, May 16th, 1868 was Andrew Johnson's judgment day. On that day the Senate voted on the high crimes and misdemeanors charged against him by Thad Stevens & Co. The hour was high noon.

Mathematically, the impeachers had it all figured out, but it did not add up as securely as they had wished. There were fifty-four Senators. Nine Democrats and three Conservative Republicans, who had trailed with Johnson, would certainly vote for acquittal. To eject Johnson from the White House the Radicals must muster thirty-six votes—two thirds—as required by the Constitution.

Subtracting these twelve acquittal Senators there remained forty-two Republican Senators. For a verdict of guilty thirty-six of these must be whipped into line. Into the ranks of these thirty-six the impeachers sent their spies, threateners, whippers-in, and bribers. "Beast" Butler was prepared to "buy Senators as he would swine." Of a doubtful Senator he said, "Tell the damn scoundrel that if he wants money there is a bushel of it to be had."

From bribery the impeachers turned to something else that had moved men in all times and ages: sex. Why not use it to stain a President with indelible infamy? And use it they did. Luscious ladies with inviting curves went swishing out to corral votes. It was a strange sort of prostitution. For a vote against Andrew Johnson, a Senator could have anything he wanted. How many traded? That will never be known.

Riding herd on the thirty-six, the impeachers dragooned the wavering ones down to eleven on whom was poured the hottest fire in American political history: Fessenden of Maine, Fowler of Tennessee, Grimes of Iowa, Henderson of Missouri, Ross of Kansas, Trumbull of Illinois, Van Winkle of West Virginia, Sprague and Anthony of Rhode Island, Morrill of Maine, and Edmunds of Vermont.

These eleven men were bullied, cajoled, and intimidated. Spies invaded their homes, their private lives were ransacked, and the party lash laid unsparingly on their backs. Letters, telegrams, and resolutions of mass meetings back home deluged them, all bearing the same specious demand: Drive the great criminal and impostor from the White House. It was the biggest mass plot in the history of Congress. The conspirators even enlisted the good, or evil, offices of the Grand Army of the Republic and the General Conference of the Methodist Church in their nefarious plot to obstruct justice.

Four Senators crumpled under Radical pressure: Morrill, Edmunds, Anthony, and Sprague, the last the husband of glamorous Kate Chase and son-in-law of the Chief Justice, who presided over the trial. Young Sprague wanted a second term in the Senate and he believed voting with the Radicals was the way to achieve it. Not that he believed Johnson guilty; he did not.

This left seven holdouts, but these could wreck the whole fabric of impeachment. How Thad Stevens reviled the very names of these seven! Dogs they were, ungrateful dogs at that! When it was over he intended to make outcasts of them, just as he expected to make Andrew Johnson one this very day, May 16th, 1868.

Six of the seven were regarded as hopeless, impervious to bribery, threats, and terrorizing. They were tried by every fire the Radicals could devise. They turned down enough money to fill Butler's bushel basket several times over. In one way or another each had committed himself to a belief in Johnson's innocence and a determination to give the President an impartial trial. Now, if only the impeachers could cut one out of this pack, they could save their case against Johnson. Not that they believed at this moment that it needed saving. They had endless confidence; it was as great as their lack of scruples. But they wanted to be extra sure, to take no chance.

The more they studied the seven wavering ones, the more evident it became that the verdict would pivot on the vote of one man—Senator Edmund Ross of Kansas, who was uncommitted, at least as far as they knew. On him they concentrated, even persecuting him with threats of assassination. He was badgered at his meals, at his lodgings. Terrorists dogged him night and day They would extort from him a vote for Johnson's guilt no matter what it took. Intimidation was visited on this man such as has no parallel in the history of Congress. The impeachers intended to give him no rest, to run him to earth, wear him down, so frighten him that he dare not vote other than with them.

From Kansas, they arranged to have a telegram sent him: "Kansas has heard the evidence and demands the conviction of the *President. (Signed) D. R. Anthony and 1000 others." To Ross' everlasting credit he had backbone enough to shoot back, "I do not recognize your right to demand that I shall vote either for or against conviction. I have taken an oath to do impartial justice and I trust I shall have the courage and honesty to vote according to the dictates of my judgment and for the good of my country."

Political and physical death stared this man in the face. Brazenly, he was told that if he voted to acquit Johnson a charge of bribery would be pressed against him.

The impeachers overlooked nothing in their drive on Ross. They reckoned with every factor that could influence him,

even on a young and charming woman whose role in the
sinister drama is still very much in the dark. Her name was
Vinnie Ream.

In the catacombs of the Capitol, in a room near the crypt
once intended for George Washington, a young sculptress
was putting the finishing touches to her model of a statue
of Abraham Lincoln. Her blue smock was streaked and her
hands dirty. Her plaster model was all but completed.

Far above her on the Senate floor the sombre impeachment drama heaved towards its climax. It was the day before
the vote. Vinnie Ream was not today one of the hundreds
who pushed and milled in the corridors and lobbies, but she
was caught by the hysteria that had seized Washington as
the day of reckoning approached.

A radiant young woman, she shed a glow about her dank
"studio." Twenty-one, petite, a bit on the rolypoly side, she
had overbright eyes, a wealth of dark curls, and a God-given
talent for sculpture. In 1866 Congress had commissioned
her to execute a life-sized statue of President Lincoln. In a
generous mood Congress had at the same time provided her
with this "studio" in the depths of the Capitol. One day in
the future her genius would flower in the fine bronze figure
of Admiral Farragut that today gives its name to Farragut
Square in Washington.

Often, between debates, lawmakers dropped down to her
sunless cubbyhole to chat and watch her working. Her ready
wit and flair for making friends drew also fashionable ladies
and artists by twos and threes to mirate. Old Thad Stevens
occasionally hobbled down to take a look and grumble his
satisfaction. To her marble bust of him Vinnie had imparted
a statesmanlike quality which pleased the grim septugenar-
ian considerably.

To her "studio" came also, in these hectic days before the
voting, the Conservative Senators seeking a quiet place to
confer and solidify their thinning ranks. The Radicals had

learned of this. They had also suspected the girl of seeking
to influence Senator Ross' vote in favor of acquittal.

Today, May 15th, Vinnie Ream was worried. She could
not work; she had not slept all night. She had suddenly been
sucked deep into the impeachment drama. Nervous and exhausted, apprehensive over what might happen, she removed her smock and was washing her hands when there
was a step outside her door. It was Senator Ross of Kansas,
a small, spare man of considerable conscience and now the
quarry of the Radical bush-beaters.

Vinnie bowed graciously. "Welcome, Senator."

"Ah, Vinnie, what a pleasure to get away from it all, if
only for a moment or two."

He walked around the platform in the center of the room,
studying the plaster figure of the careworn, martyred President. Then he stood for some moments absorbed in thought.

"A great man. Would that he had lived." He paused. "I'm
worried, Vinnie, hounded to death. I can't believe Andrew
Johnson is as despicable as he's made out. I'd have dismissed
Stanton myself had I been President. I can't damn this man
on what I've heard."

"The President has promised to come and see my plaster
model," said the girl.

"Let's hope he's still President so that he can come as he
promised. You knew President Lincoln, Vinnie?"

"He was very kind to me," said Vinnie. "I thought I told
you about it."

"So you did, but tell me again so I won't forget it."

Vinnie smiled. "When I came to Washington four years
ago Senator Browning of Illinois asked the President to sit
for me. I had no training, no background, just a country
girl. I wanted to make a marble bust of the President, but
first I had to make a model. Senator Browning told the
President I was young and poor. That seemed to appeal to
him. He said, 'So she's young and poor, is she? Well, that's
nothing against her. Tell her she can come.' That's how I

got in. The President gave me half-hour sittings for months. I took a tub of plaster to the White House and watched him while he worked and modeled him in the meantime. I got to know him well."

"That's a wonderful memory."

"Yes, it is," said the girl. "I hope my statue will show him as I remember him."

"It will, Vinnie. It will make you famous."

There was silence. "Senator, I want to confide in you. I had a visitor yesterday. Representative George Julian."

"A man of much cunning," smiled Ross.

"He came to warn me. He threatened to take my studio away and have my model rejected by the government unless I spoke to you about. . . ."

The Senator nodded. "I think I know. About my vote. Butler and Stevens must have sent him. That's the way they do things."

The girl shook her head. "I haven't slept all night."

"Don't worry, Vinnie. Stick it out."

"I told Mr. Julian I had nothing to do with the way you voted. That I knew you would vote the way you saw it."

"Right you are, Vinnie. Just as my conscience tells me."

"And I'll help you do it," said the girl resolutely.

It was the morning of the great day, if great it could be called. Senator Ross' vote still dangled, that is, he was still actually and openly uncommitted as far as the impeachers knew. Onto the stage this morning strode a new and powerful persuader, General Daniel Sickles, to make the final assault on Ross' integrity.

A great ladies' man was Sickles, overpowering to the fair sex. The glamor of slaying a man who had stolen his wife's affections still clung to him. Nor was it lessened by the loss of a leg at Gettysburg, where he commanded a corps of the Union Army. Sickles was handsome, no question about that.

All night he and other Radical spies had trailed Ross. This

morning, as the Senate assembled for the final scene, Sickles took his stand in the Senate lobby where he could waylay Ross and drive home a last threat—vote guilty or else.

"Good morning, General Sickles!" It was Vinnie Ream.

The soldier turned and bowed low. "Good morning, Vinnie."

The sculptress had volunteered the night before to fend Sickles away from Ross. Now she was about that business.

"I have been wanting to see you, General," said Vinnie, flashing her winning smile on him. "You promised to come and see my model of the Lincoln statue."

"So I did, but Vinnie . . ." The General was not interested in statues at this moment, yet he prided himself on his gallantry to the ladies.

"You can't go back on your promise, General."

"I'm so busy, Vinnie, so busy. So much to do. I'll come tomorrow."

"Not today, General?" pleaded the girl.

Old Thad Stevens passed by, high on his chair carried by his Negro boys. His burning eyes flashed at the girl.

"Hardly, Vinnie," said Sickles. "You'll have to excuse me today."

The girl held on, making small talk for dear life.

"How about tomorrow?"

"Well, all right."

"Is that a promise, General?"

"A promise."

"Cross your heart."

Through the lobby at this moment walked an erect, slender figure, Senator Ross of Kansas. The general was crossing his heart and trying to shake off the determined girl as Ross passed almost like a shadow and entered the Senate chamber. It was Sickles' last chance to sway his vote. He turned quickly but Ross had vanished.

The spectacle was vivid, impressive. With a rustling of

his stiff, black robes the Chief Justice took his seat on the rostrum and the crier intoned the command of silence. The galleries were "glowing embankments ascending from edge to summit under a burden of beauty." Celebrities overflowed the place, yet "indescribable anxiety was written on every face." The diplomatic gallery was never so full. The press section was writing ,writing ceaselessly.

The actors and witnesses of the drama took their places quietly. The usual hum in the gallery was missing. The House managers came in two abreast. Bringing up the rear was Thad Stevens, borne on a chair by his two Negro boys. His wig was askew, but he was smiling, a sardonic sort of smile. He had come to gloat. The President's counsel moved to their places. They had riddled the prosecution, but the ways of Stevens & Co. were too dark and devious for their abilities. Anything could happen.

Outside the day was cloudy, dark and foreboding; the Senate gas jets shed a rich glow over the gloom in the chamber. Tension was heartbreaking, but things moved fast toward the grand dénouement. The Radicals pressed through a quick motion to vote, first, not on the first article of impeachment, but on the eleventh, Thad Stevens' catchall, the trick article which supposedly left no loophole for Johnson's escape. It was done fast. Thad Stevens had ordered it.

Now more drama. It was piling up. A bustle at the door and in came Senator Grimes of Iowa, faint and feeble, supported by four men. It was a heroic thing to do, but he had a vote to cast for Andrew Johnson, and cast it he would. Why should a stroke of paralysis three days ago stand in the way of his duty as he saw it? It did not. Pale and twisted with pain, he took his seat. The galleries wanted to cheer, but dared not.

Next an admonishment from the Chief Justice to the "citizens and strangers in the galleries that absolute silence and perfect order are required." It was needless injunction. Stillness, like death, gripped the chamber. "Some members of the House near me," wrote a Representative, "grew pale and sick under the burden of suspense."

In the galleries hundreds of pencils hovered over tally papers. The clerk read the eleventh impeachment article. Thad Stevens never looked so confident. It was his article; he was proud of it. It was like a knife reaching into Andrew Johnson's heart. He had, so it seemed, now only to twist the knife about a bit. His cavernous eyes shone.

"Call the roll!" ordered the Chief Justice.

These three words brought this stupendous drama to its mathematical crisis—how many Not guiltys and how many Guiltys. His voice seemed to echo ominously through the chamber. It rolled like a thunderclap, though he spoke in low tones in framing the fateful words. Yes, call the roll and get it over!

The clerk began droning. It was alphabetical. First on the roll was Anthony of Rhode Island.

"Senator Anthony!"

The Senator rose in his place. There was no hesitation.

"Mr. Senator Anthony, how say you? Is the respondent Andrew Johnson, President of the United States, guilty or not guilty of high misdemeanors as charged in this Article?"

Gazing intently into the Chief Justice's eyes, Anthony replied firmly, "Guilty." Touché. Stevens & Co. had drawn first blood. The galleries expired audibly in mass. But the Radicals needed thirty-five more votes.

Next Bayard of Maryland and Buckalew of Pennsylvania, both Democrats, with "Not Guilty." Simon Cameron of Pennsylvania brought a titter through the chamber. So great was his anxiety to doom Andrew Johnson that, before the clerk had half-completed the question, he shouted "Guilty."

It went on. Now there were seven votes for conviction. Smiles began curling the lips of the impeachment managers; even Thad Stevens was smiling. The pieces were slipping into their right places.

"Mr. Senator Fessenden! How say you?"

He was the first of the seven doubtful Republican Senators and the galleries strained forward as his name was called. Up stood Fessenden, calm and erect. He had weathered the storm of Radical abuse, insult, and browbeating like a rock on the coast of Maine, whence he came.

"Not guilty!" It was electrifying for the Senate, for the spectators. Johnson's friends in the gallery sighed with relief. The nervous strain was growing unbearable.

Now came three more doubtful Republican Senators. Stevens' eyes fairly consumed them as he waited for them to vote.

"Fowler! Grimes! Henderson!" The stricken Grimes tried to rise but the Chief Justice told him, "Mr. Grimes, you need not rise." Yet the Senator from Iowa would stand. Paralysis could wait. Rising he threw all his remaining energy into a strong "Not guilty!"

Fowler, Grimes, and Henderson in a row. Three not guiltys. Four all told now. These doubtful Republicans were voting as they saw fit, not as Thad Stevens had willed it.

The drama carried on and the tension was like a taut wire threatening to snap. Spectators shivered with excitement. Now for Edmund Ross of Kansas. The chamber held its breath. So did Vinnie Ream, now sitting in the front row of the gallery. She knew all along just how he would vote. Only she had known it.

Up to now twenty-four had voted guilty, fourteen not guilty. Waiting his turn, Ross had sat quietly, though nervously, tearing up little slips of paper which littered his lap.

"Mr. Senator Ross!"

His moment had come, and there was no hesitation. He rose with ease and a wan smile. Clearly in a voice no one could mistake—not even Thad Stevens—he answered "Not guilty." Later he was to say: "When I voted not guilty I felt that I was looking into my open grave." His was the fifteenth vote for acquittal.

With showmanship and a toss of his fine head the great

Charles Sumner rose to vote guilty. He was an actor to the last. What a villainous role he had played in all this!

Fifteen for Andrew Johnson. Four more and Thad Stevens' great conspiracy would come tumbling down like a house of stacked cards. Came Saulsbury, Democrat from Delaware with a not guilty. And Vickers of Maryland likewise. Then the two remaining doubtful Republican Senators Trumbull and Van Winkle voting, strong-voiced, for acquittal. Nineteen. That was enough.

Last came Ben Wade, who saw the Presidential prize slipping from his grasp. He need not have done what he did. The case was lost, but he voted guilty. It was as dishonorable as was the vote of Speaker Schuyler Colfax for the impeachment resolution in the House.

Stunned and speechless, the impeachment managers sat riveted to their seats. It was unbelievable. Solemnly the Chief Justice proclaimed:

"Upon this Article, thirty-five Senators vote guilty and nineteen Senators vote not guilty. Two thirds, not having pronounced guilty, the President is, therefore, acquitted upon this Article."

Andrew Johnson was exonerated by a single vote!

In a blinding flash it was over. Above the crowds Thad Stevens was borne away by his Negro boys. His face was black with rage and disappointment. "The country is going to the devil," he mouthed.

As the last vote was cast a young man, William Crook, President Johnson's bodyguard, scrambled out of the gallery, dashed down Capitol Hill, and ran all the way to the White House. Hustling up to the President's study he blurted out the news to a man who listened, composed yet with tears running down his cheeks—to a man who was still President of the United States.

But Crook did not pause here. He hurried up to a bedroom where, in a rocking chair, sat a frail little lady old before her time. It was Eliza McCardle Johnson, who had stood beside Andrew through the thick and thin of it all.

"He is acquitted! The President is acquitted!" cried out Crook.

She took the young man's hand, but long moments passed before she could find her voice. Her eyes shone with tears as she said, "I knew he would be acquitted. I knew it."

Yet the conspirators must have their victory and their victim. Little Vinnie Ream was evicted from her "studio," though she protested that removal of her model of the Lincoln statue would ruin it. What did the conspirators care! The devil take her and the statue, too! Lincoln was dead— just like their case against Andrew Johnson.

But—strangely, and to his credit—Thad Stevens gagged at persecuting this young woman. Ordering her studio restored to her, he took the floor and whiplashed his unwilling minions into accepting his dictum. It was almost his last act on the floor of the House. Chivalry was not all dead in Stevens, though his body was soon afterwards. On August 11th, 1868 he went to whatever reward awaited him.

If only Vinnie Ream's statue of Lincoln could speak! What tales it could tell from its place in the Rotunda of the Capitol.